Education and Inequality

The Roots and Results of
Stratification in America's
Schools

Caroline Hodges Persell

THE FREE PRESS
A Division of Macmillan Publishing Co., Inc.
NEW YORK

Collier Macmillan Publishers
LONDON

The Free Press
A Division of Macmillan Publishing Co., Inc.
866 Third Avenue, New York, N.Y. 10022

Collier Macmillan Canada, Ltd.

First Free Press Paperback Edition 1979

Library of Congress Catalog Card Number: 76 – 46707

Printed in the United States of America

Casebound printing number

2 3 4 5 6 7 8 9 10

Paperbound printing number

1 2 3 4 5 6 7 8 9 10

Library of Congress Cataloging in Publication Data

Persell, Caroline Hodges.
    Education and inequality.

    Bibliography: p.
    Includes index.
    1. Educational equalization--United States.
2. Minorities--Education--United States. I. Title.
LC213.2.P47   370.19'0973   76-46707
ISBN 0-02-925140-0
ISBN 0-02-925130-3 pbk.

To Patricia and Stephen,

with love and appreciation

Contents

List of Tables and Figures

Preface

I BEGAN PONDERING the question of education and inequality in the 1960s, as the civil-rights movement was getting underway. As I worked for the National Scholarship Service and Fund for Negro Students, from 1962 to 1966, I wondered why ethnic minorities and students from lower social classes did not always do as well in school or continue their education as far as their white middle-class counterparts. During this time, I was meeting many "disadvantaged" youngsters and adults who impressed me with their acuity, verbal facility, and drive. Hence, I was not particularly convinced by either the genetic or the cultural-inferiority explanations of educational differences. Moreover, I was struck by the dramatically disparate life chances between majority and minority members of our society. I reflected on how limited my own life would have been if my family were black. My parents probably would not have gone to school where they did (Deerfield, Hamilton, and Cornell), my father undoubtedly would not have had the job he did (as a patent attorney for a large corporation), and we would not have had the income and style of life that we did (living comfortably in a wealthy suburb). My family would have begun life with the same genetic potential, but how different the course of our lives would have been had we been born black or lower class. These realizations left me with several interrelated questions.

First, how is social origin related to educational results? Second, why do so many people apparently accept the vast racial and economic inequalities in society? Third, how does education relate to this process? I did not immediately realize how tightly related these questions were. Only after more than ten years of observing, reading, and thinking did I begin to formulate some answers. This book presents the theoretical explanation that gradually suggested itself to me, and reports the evidence of others that bears on this interpretation.

Acknowledgments

THIS BOOK WAS GREATLY HELPED by the energetic research assistance of: Ken Boyer, James Castagna, Alison Davis, Stephen DiCarmine, Joan Donnellan, Karen Helsing, Debra Lombardo, Paul Mendelson, Carol Morrow, and Gail Seneca. I very much appreciate their work.

I am deeply grateful to a number of people for their comments on parts or all of an earlier draft of this book, including: Judith Alpert, Floyd Hammack, Dorothy Jessop, Carol Morrow, Gail Seneca, Gladys Topkis, Dennis Wrong, and Gilda Zwerman. Needless to say, they cannot be held responsible for the way I have utilized their remarks.

The speedy typing of Charlotte Fisher, Meredith Gould, and Geraldine Novasic enabled me to finish the manuscript in time for a most welcome vacation. I heartily thank them. I sincerely thank Stephen DiCarmine, Debra Lombardo, and Pat Read for their devoted help in proofreading this book.

Parts of this book were supported by grants from the National Institute of Education of the U.S. Department of Health, Education and Welfare, the National Science Foundation, and the Institute on Pluralism and Group Identity. Contractors under government sponsorship are encouraged to express freely their professional judgment in the conduct of the project. Points of view or opinions stated do not, therefore, necessarily represent official National Institute of Education or National Science Foundation position or policy.

1
The Problem

THE WIDELY-DOCUMENTED FINDING that social standing is related to educational achievement has elicited consternation, concern, and explanatory efforts. The three most prevalent explanations suggest a deficit in the principal participants in the situation: the children, the parents, or the teachers. While widely publicized, these theories are technical enough to lose many concerned with the issues they touch, which is unfortunate since each theory presents explanatory and evidentiary problems. Their inadequacies, considered below, call for an alternative theoretical approach to the problem. But, lest we mistakenly assume the initial existence of the phenomena being explained, consider first the evidence suggesting that social and economic standing is related to educational achievement. Major research in the United States (Coleman et al., 1966), in Great Britain (Plowden Report, 1967), in France (Boudon, 1973), and in other industrial nations (Husen, 1972) reveal this finding. Many smaller studies yield comparable results. In an annotated bibliography of 80 American studies spanning 1938–1965, Goldstein (1967) concludes that children of low-income families do not do as well in school as children from more affluent homes, by every conceivable measure. Proponents of equal opportunity have been concerned with this recurrent finding, because they hope to reduce social inequalities by equalizing educational achievement. Hence considerable effort has been directed at trying to explain exactly why background factors are so strongly related to school achievement.

One of the three major explanations, the IQ-deficit theory, suggests that the genetic deficiencies of blacks (Jensen, 1969) or of lower-class individuals (Eysenck, 1971; Herrnstein, 1973) explain why they do more poorly in school and in life. The cultural-deficit theory holds that the cultural, family, linguistic, cognitive, and attitudinal backgrounds of certain children are so different or lacking that they cannot learn in school. The third explanation

1

suggests that teachers hold lower expectations for lower-status or minority children, and that is why these children learn less.

Each of these explanations is considered in some detail below. Here, suffice it to say that they fail to explain a number of apparently anomalous findings. First, the genetic-racial explanation is undermined by the analysis of Mayeske (1972), who found that the relationship between ethnicity and achievement disappeared when certain economic and social factors were controlled. If the effect of ethnicity can be explained by social and cultural factors, achievement differences cannot be due to genes.

Second, the genetic interpretation cannot explain the finding that socio-economic status is more important for academic attainment than is IQ (Bowles and Gintis, 1976: 31).[1]

Third, the achievement gap between high- and low-status students appears to increase over time (e.g., Coleman et al., 1966; Douglas, 1968; Harlem Youth Opportunities Unlimited, 1964; Hobson v. Hansen, 1967). If the differences between social groups are due to cultural or genetic attributes groups bring with them to school, the gap would be greatest when they first enter school and then gradually narrow over time. Instead the differences increase with each passing school year. Both genetic- and cultural-deficit interpretations have attempted to handle this by saying that there is an *interaction* between what children bring to school and their educational experiences, but this interpretation has not yet specified the forms such interaction takes.

Fourth, some lower-status children do show substantial cognitive gains when they are taught intensively (Bereiter, 1967; Hawkridge, Chalupsky and Roberts, 1968; Heber, 1972). Moreover, contrary to Jensen's (1969) global assertion that "compensatory education has been tried and it apparently has failed [p. 2]," a number of well-designed compensatory-education programs demonstrate remarkable achievement gains (e.g., Hawkridge et al., 1968; Kiesling, 1971). If genetic or cultural deficits impair the learning capacity of lower-status children, such children would never be able to learn success-fully. But this is patently false.

Fifth, it is curious that the powerful relationship between social background and school achievement, which is observed in industrial nations, does not appear in less industrialized societies such as Uganda (Heyneman, 1976), Chile (Farrell, 1973), and similar developing countries included in the International Educational Achievement (IEA) study (cited in Anderson, 1974; Platt, 1974). If there are genetic or cultural deficiencies associated with being of a lower status, we would expect them to be reflected in less-industrialized countries as well, but they are not. This very interesting exception to the pattern observed in industrial nations requires explanation.

[1]Alexander and Eckland (1975: 464), however, found that "aptitude" and "aspirations" were more importantly related to attainment than parental social status. But, in their sample, urban and large schools and low-aptitude students were underrepresented, which may account for the apparent discrepancy between their findings and those of Bowles and Gintis (1976).

Sixth, if teachers' expectations play a part in the lesser achievement of lower-status students, as Clark (1965), Rosenthal and Jacobson (1968b), and Silberman (1970) suggest, we are left with the problem of explaining why teachers hold lower expectations for certain children, and how those expectations influence educational results. In short, at this point a teachers'-expectations explanation raises more questions than it answers.

A final difficulty with these deficit explanations rests on their unstated premise that educational inequality is the cause of economic inequality. This instrumental–meritocratic assumption is not supported by available evidence. If the assumption that education is related to life achievements were correct, we should find a reduction or elimination of occupational and economic inequality in situations where educational inequalities have disappeared. Has this happened? The absolute amount of inequality in educational attainment has declined in the last 50 years, as the compulsory education age has risen and as educational opportunities have expanded, both in the United States and in Western Europe. But this reduction of educational inequality has not resulted in less economic inequality in the United States (according to Chiswick and Mincer, 1972, cited in Bowles and Gintis, 1976: 34), in England (Kelsall et al., 1972), or in Western Europe (according to Boudon, 1973). Where equalization of schooling has occurred, it has not been accompanied by economic equality.

General trends, then, indicate little or no reduction of economic inequality in the face of increasing educational equality, and special educational programs in the "war on poverty" have had an equally low impact. In his systematic survey of such programs, Ribich (1968) found that the economic benefits of compensatory education were generally low, with a few exceptions (cited in Bowles and Gintis, 1976: 35). Both Ribich (1968) and Averch et al. (1974) conclude that giving money directly to the poor would have accomplished more income equalization than the educational programs themselves have achieved.

Bowles and Gintis also consider the question of whether reduction of the education gap between white and black males has equalized incomes. Citing U.S. Census Bureau figures, they note that by 1972 the education gap between white and black males 25–34 years old had shrunk to 4 percent (compared to the 38-percent gap between whites and blacks of all age groups in 1940). Nevertheless, the income gap between black and white young men was 30 percent. Bowles and Gintis (1976: 35) conclude that while blacks certainly suffer from educational inequality, the real source of their inequality lies in their unequal economic power. In a related vein, they note that economic inequality between the sexes persists, despite comparable levels of schooling for men and women (Bowles and Gintis, 1976: 35).

In brief, the above data reported by Averch et al., Bowles and Gintis, Boudon, Kelsall, Ribich, and the U.S. Census Bureau suggest that education does not operate as the great equalizer the instrumental–meritocratic ideology claims it to be. Why, then, is the belief in an instrumental meritocracy so widely held? This is an anachronism that must be dealt with in an inclusive theory of education and inequality.

In view of these problems with the IQ, cultural, and/or teacher-deficit theories of educational achievement, it is necessary to approach the problem from an alternative perspective. In asking why social status is related to educational achievement, these popular explanations take too much of the problem for granted (cf. Young, 1971). Specifically:

1. These formulations assume that the causal locus can be found in individuals and their strengths or deficiencies instead of examining the social contexts that impinge on individuals.
2. They suggest that cognitive achievement is the only important educational outcome. But there are other results of schooling. Why are they emphasized less than cognitive outcomes?
3. Even if we agree that cognitive learning is one important educational objective, current formulations do not examine what kind of academic achievement is deemed important, and how it is measured.

These important questions cannot be raised without recasting the problem as it is currently formulated in American sociology. To do this we need a comprehensive theory of educational outcomes and their relation to society. Such a theory should explain *how* observed relationships between race, class, and educational outcomes occur and *why* education is related to societal inequalities. The first task, therefore, is to develop such a theoretical framework.

2

A Theoretical Synthesis

THE THREE MAJOR EXPLANATIONS of differential school achievement, which look to deficiencies in the child, the parents, or the teachers, have divorced themselves from the historical foundations of sociology, in particular from the influences of Marx and Weber. These thinkers viewed education as inevitably bound up with—indeed, dependent upon—other institutions of society, such as the economy and the polity. I concur with this broader emphasis and think that any theory of educational outcomes must begin with an examination of education in its wider social context. An inclusive theoretical explanation cannot stop there, however; it must indicate how the social context of education is related to educational practices and forms, how those educational features influence the participants in the situation, and with what consequences. In short, to understand the relationship between education and inequality, we need a theory that integrates variables from four levels of analysis:

 I. Societal Level
  A. Structure of dominance
  B. Legitimating ideologies
 II. Institutional Level
  A. Educational structures
  B. Educational ideologies and concepts
 III. Interpersonal Level
 IV. Intrapsychic Level (consciousness)

At the societal level, Marx and Weber suggest the importance of stratification for education. American sociology has studied stratification in relation to unequal educational opportunities and has examined the correlation between education and social mobility. Rather than focus primarily on mobility,

5

however, I think it is extremely important to understand how stratification systems reproduce and legitimate themselves. Focusing on reproduction directs attention to the unequal power and resources of different groups and asks how they manage to maintain themselves. One means of control is through shared belief systems, control being maintained far more effectively when power is legitimated by such means. Identifying legitimating ideologies in society, and analyzing how they exercise their hegemony, is crucial to an understanding of our educational system. I surmise that the structural basis of stratification in a society and the legitimating ideologies used by that society are critical determinants of the degree to which the society relies upon the educational system as a mechanism for legitimating social inequality. There are grounds for proposing that the United States, which is the principal focus here, relies heavily upon the educational system to recreate and legitimate structures of dominance in society. In this book I suggest how and why this occurs. My perspective suggests that the structure of dominance in society is related to educational structures and ideologies. Weber (1946: 426) was the first to use the term, "structure of domination" in his comparative analysis of educational systems. I am using the term as he did, to indicate that people in positions of greater power and privilege do not retain these positions by accident, but use their superior resources to maintain themselves. The privileged must dominate those subordinate to them in order to maintain their superordinate position. The forms this dominance takes—whether military, political, ideological, or symbolic—vary widely, but the fact of dominance remains. The concept, "structure of dominance," is used because it conveys the notion of inherent conflict much more vividly than does the related concept of "stratification." Moreover, the term "structure of dominance" permits comparisons with societies in which different structures of dominance prevail.

Seen within this perspective, organizational forms within our educational system are postulated as being influenced by structures of dominance, and major educational ideas are assumed to be congruent with the interests of dominant groups in society. Postulating the importance of educational structures and ideologies does not explain how they affect educational outcomes. To do this, we need a theory of process, including a theory of how consciousness is socialized. Such an explanation requires a theory of socialization —a theory indicating how educational structures and concepts impinge upon the participants in a situation, how they shape the interactions that occur in schools, and how these processes influence the consciousness that emerges. This interpersonal level of analysis is largely undeveloped in Marx, Weber, and their more recent followers' works (except for Collins, 1975). More helpful here is that body of sociological writing, loosely termed "symbolic interactionism," which suggests how structures and ideologies may influence the attitudes and behaviors of individuals.

Societal Level

As already noted, we cannot view education without also considering its societal context. This societal, or macro, level of analysis is enriched by the contributions of Marx and Weber. Each highlights specific societal features and provides orienting ideas that help to recast the problem of education and inequality.

A Marxian orientation is materialist, historical, concerned with the totality of phenomena, and dialectical (Cohen, 1975; Lefebvre, 1968; Levitas, 1974; Williams, 1973). The materialist perspective stresses the social *conditions* of life. In Marx's words, "It is not the consciousness of men that determines their existence, but, on the contrary, their social existence that determines their consciousness [1904: 11]." In Marx's view, there are very specific conditions of life that are central; specifically the ownership and control of productive resources. Ownership or nonownership forms a critical axis for Marx, dividing the world into social classes with opposing interests. A major concern of this work is to analyze how concentrated wealth ownership is related to educational practices. Production may be analyzed into the forces of production (levels of technology, land, labor, capital, available energies, etc.) and the social relations of production, which consist of how human effort is organized for productive activity. The forces and the social relations of production are sometimes described as comprising the *base* of society. But, as Williams (1973: 5) so helpfully emphasizes, this base must be conceived of as a process, not as a static entity. Thus, Marx's concept of materialism places material conditions and specifically economic conditions at the center of human activity. Other activities and beliefs, including education, are in some sense *determined* by economic conditions.

The word "determine" has several quite different meanings. There is the "notion of an external cause which totally predicts or prefigures, indeed totally controls a subsequent activity (Williams, 1973: 4)." There is, in addition, a "notion of determination as setting limits, exerting pressures." In what sense might inequalities in economic forces and relations of production set parameters for or exert pressures on education? Those pressures or parameters may not always prevail, nor may they always be the only factors operating in a situation. (In any given situation, religious, ethnic, or other factors may also be operating.)

The historical nature of Marxism suggests that events cannot be understood apart from their history, and that the history of noneconomic institutions cannot be understood independently of the history of the forces and relations of production. Hence educational structures must be examined historically, and in relation to economic changes.

Another key feature of Marxist thought is the assumption that history unfolds dialectically. The dialectic operates in many spheres, including the creative role individuals can play. According to Ollman (1973), the law of development through contradictions is the most important of the laws of the dialectic. Since complex totalities are comprised of a number of elements and tendencies, these processes may change at different speeds or in incompatible ways, leading to contradictions within the system and ultimately, perhaps, to the transformation of the system. The notion of contradiction suggests that education does not merely reproduce the social relations of production in an orderly fashion, but also contains potential for change (cf. Bowles and Gintis, 1976).

Weber differs from Marx in that he sees more than economic bases for domination. This might be explained by the fact that Weber was trying to explain stratification in different types of societies, not only industrial ones. In his comparative work, Weber (1946: 426–434) suggests a theory of how the content and ends of education correspond to the type of authority that prevails in a society (see Table 2.1).

TABLE 2.1. Weber's three types of domination and educational ends, processes, content, and evaluation

| | TYPE OF DOMINATION | | |
	Charismatic	Traditional	Rational-legal
Educational Ends	To awaken heroic qualities or magical gifts.	To prepare students for a particular style of life.	To impart specialized expert training.
Educational Processes	Magical rites. Cannot be taught or trained for, only awakened. One acquires a new soul through rebirth.	Cultivation for a conduct of life.	Training for practical usefulness in business, science, the military.
Educational Content	Heroic/magical forms.	Culture	Specialized expert training.
Evaluation	Hero trials testing whether one possesses magical powers.	Exploration of whether a person's mind conforms to the ways of thought required of a cultivated man.	Examination of mastery of a specific body of knowledge.

Synthesized from Weber, 1946: 426–434.

Weber's (1946: 426–434) analysis suggests that the structure of dominance and authority in a society is intimately bound up with educational goals, processes, content, and evaluation. Thus we see that in societies where traditional authority prevails, as in Confucian China, the goal of education is preparation for a particular (traditional) style of life. This goal is reflected in educational processes, content, and the tests deemed appropriate measures of goal attainment. In contrast, societies based upon rational–legal authority are concerned with training specialists who have mastered specific skills and knowledge. While no society illustrates an undiluted version of only one type, societies do approximate one type more closely than the others. Hence, Weber suggests that educational forms, beliefs, and practices vary in systematic ways in different societies. What may seem to us to be "natural" conceptions of educational structures or pupil ability may be linked with prevailing forms of dominance and authority. Furthermore, educational ideas and structures may serve ideological functions, maintaining and legitimating the existing structure of dominance.

The concept of ideology, as advanced by Marx and Engels and developed by Althusser (1971), Gramsci (1971), Habermas (1970), and Williams (1973) is very helpful for understanding how dominant groups maintain control. One can preserve control through physical or economic coercion, but naked power is far more effective cloaked in beliefs that make it appear legitimate. For Marx, "ideology" refers to a belief system that justifies the position of dominant groups, at the same time that it portrays social existence in an illusory or mystifying form. Thus ideology serves to portray the position of dominant groups in such a way that it seems "natural," inevitable, and the best way for things to be for everyone.

The relationship between economic relations and ideology appears in at least two distinct versions. In one view, there is a direct, one-to-one relationship between economic relations, prevailing ideologies, and concepts in society. This view draws on Marx and Engels' (1947) ideas in *The German Ideology:*

> The ideas of the ruling class are in every epoch the ruling ideas, i.e., the class which is the ruling *material* force of society is at the same time its ruling intellectual force. The class which has the means of material production at its disposal has control at the same time over the means of mental production. . . . The ruling ideas are nothing more than the ideal expression of dominant material relationships [1947: 39].

By virtue of its economic dominance, the ruling class controls the world of ideas as well. This model suggests a direct correspondence between material and mental production and allows little room for ideas or ideologies to have independent consequences. As Lichtman (1975) notes, this early position of Marx tends to suggest that material production alone is real, while other dimensions of social life (such as ideas, theories, ideologies) are mere products or reflections of this underlying activity and, thus, essentially "illusory and epiphenomenal." Althusser (1971) agrees that this view denigrates ideologies and other so-called superstructural elements. Althusser (1971: 267) argues that ideology has a material existence, meaning that ideology is represented in the actions of individuals and institutions. Ideologies exist in observable human practices.

A second modification of the early position of Marx is based on the realization that while ideologies may originate historically in the relations of economic dominance, over time ideas and ideologies become established in practice and may have independent, even contradictory, effects. This view of ideology is more consistent with Marx's dialectical approach.

In addition to denying the independent existence of ideologies, the early base-superstructure model appears to suggest that a dominant class at any given time has complete control over all ideologies, ideas, and institutional practices. As such, it fails to explain the endurance of institutional patterns, ideologies, and practices initiated under previous modes of production even if unrelated to the requirements of a changed economy (cf. Williams, 1973; 1961). Williams suggests the helpful concept of "residuals" to refer to experiences, meanings, and values from a previous social formation which cannot be expressed in terms of the dominant class culture, and yet which have persisted.

In recognition of the difficulties involved in the base-superstructure proposition, an alternative formulation was developed by Lukacs (1971). This development emphasizes social *totality* rather than the architectual metaphor of base and superstructure. The concept of totality is useful for understanding how social being determines consciousness (Williams, 1973: 7) but it loses a great deal if the many social practices which form a concrete social whole are seen only as complexly interacting, without direction. Williams reminds us that "certain kinds of institutions, laws, . . . theories, ideologies, which are claimed as natural, or as having universal validity or significance, simply have to be seen as expressing and ratifying the domination of a particular class [1973: 7]."

For this reason, Williams thinks that the notion of totality can be used only when it is combined with the crucial concept of hegemony. For Williams (1973), hegemony suggests

> . . . the existence of something which is truly total, which is not merely secondary or superstructural, like the weak sense of ideology, but which is lived at such a depth, which saturates the society to such an extent, and which, as Gramsci put it, even constitutes the limit of common sense for most people under its sway. . . . For if ideology were merely some abstract imposed notion, if our social and political and cultural ideas and assumptions and habits were merely the result of specific manipulation, of a kind of overt training which might be simply ended or withdrawn, then the society would be very much easier to move and to change than in practice it has ever been or is. This notion of hegemony as deeply saturating the consciousness of a society seems to be fundamental. And hegemony has the advantage over general notions of totality, that it at the same time emphasizes the facts of domination [p. 8].

Thus the development by Gramsci and Williams of the concept of ideology suggests a phenomenon much more pervasive, subtle, and influential than earlier formulations.[1] Ideology is no longer a single idea or set of ideas that we can identify and carve out like removing mineral crystals from their matrix, but one that goes to the heart of commonsense assumptions about our world. Therefore it is difficult to become aware of ideology, and more difficult still to change it. This conception of ideological hegemony differs sharply from "ethos" or "cultural values" in that the ideology which saturates society benefits certain classes or groups in society considerably more than others. Certain ideologies are not equally in the interests of all members of society.

Habermas (1970) provides an example of the totally saturating nature of ideology when he describes technology and science as "ideology." Rationality, science, and technology have become for many Westerners the only way of dealing with both reality and other people. And, as Habermas (1970) notes, "By virtue of its structure, purposive-rational action is the exercise of control [p. 82]." While rationality may offer a valuable approach to many problems, it should not be forgotten that rationality is a relative concept, that it may support the interests of certain groups (manufacturing and mercantile groups) more than others (tribal societies, landed aristocracy, or unemployed ghetto residents), and that it may not be the best approach to all situations (relations with the environment, relations between people).

While ideologies serve the interests of dominant groups, they also have some grounding in reality (according to Lefebvre, 1968; Marx; Mephum, 1972). They are not only illusion and lies. Ideologies both render social reality intelligible and guide practice within it (Mephum, 1972). This helps to explain how they can become taken for granted, how they can so completely saturate a society.

In the following analysis, the concept of ideology is used to look at pervasive, taken-for-granted assumptions in education, to examine the relation between educational concepts and reality, and to consider whether systematic relations exist between those depictions and the interests of dominant groups in society.

While these ideologies are assumed to have emerged historically from the economic and social relations in society, they are recognized as containing dialectical possibilities in their own right. They may have independent consequences not always representing the interests of dominant groups.

Institutional Level

It seems likely that material and social conditions influence the institutional level. This premise directs our attention to the structural features of educa-

[1] I am deeply indebted to Zvia Naphtali (work in progress) for her ideas about the concept of ideology in Marx. I have drawn heavily upon her work in the foregoing discussion.

tional institutions. I suggest that these are influenced by the structure of dominance in society, particularly economic dominance, and have important influences upon educational outcomes.

A central focus of sociology is the issue of power and control. Schools generally diminish the power and control of all children who attend them, but there are systematic differences among children in the power and control they experience in educational structures. These differences may be economic (the resources they receive), political (the influence their parents have on the educational process), ecological (where they go to school, and with whom), interpersonal (the expectations teachers hold), or bureaucratic (the failure rate). Children may experience different authority relations or different social relations in the schools they attend. In short, a guiding question here is: which dominant (and subordinate) groups attend what kinds of educational structures with what consequences? I am postulating that structural differences exist in the educational institutions attended by children from different groups, resulting in varied consequences.

I suggested above that societal ideologies are related to the structures of dominance. I would suggest further that societal structures of dominance and ideologies are related to prevailing educational ideologies and ideas. As Berger and Luckmann (1967) remind us, all social reality is socially constructed. That is, the meaning of educational ideologies and concepts can not be taken for granted but must be considered as problematic. Such ideologies as "merit" and "equal opportunity," the concept and practice of IQ testing, the concept of "cultural deprivation," and definitions of knowledge, curriculum and achievement need to be seen as socially constructed. Alternatives to these concepts and assumptions presumably share the same weakness. Therefore, the validity of such concepts needs to be rigorously examined in light of available scientific evidence, a standard shared by competing perspectives. At the same time, we need to avoid the pitfall, noted by Whitty (1974: 125), that overemphasizing the socially constructed nature of reality leads to neglect of the question of why reality is constructed in particular ways.

Berger and Luckmann further maintain that social institutions are legitimated by symbolic universes, just as Marx maintains that dominant groups attempt to sustain their dominance by means of ideologies. Thus prevailing ideas and practices are supported by the claim that they are based on "objective reality." One form this "objectivity" takes is citing supporting "evidence" from scientific research. We examine this "objective" evidence adduced to support certain concepts.

It is critical to stress that different institutions and social structures can be and are legitimized by different symbolic universes. Berger and Luckmann also argue that those in positions of power can influence the socialization processes that transmit one rather than another symbolic universe and thus legitimize some, rather than other, dominant groups and institutions. Therefore, not only ideologies, concepts, and theories are examined for their legitimating roles, but also educational structures and practices such as classification and tracking, segregation, and evaluation practices.

Finally, Berger and Luckmann assert that definitions of reality have self-fulfilling potency. Or, as Thomas (1931) noted, "The things that men believe to be real are real in their consequences [p. 189]." Thus Berger and Luckmann suggest that social definitions of reality may change the behaviors and attitudes of individuals holding or encountering those definitions. Therefore, the social and educational ideologies and concepts held by teachers, administrators, and researchers may have important consequences for the way a child is perceived, the expectations held for the child, how the child is taught, and what is learned.

Given these considerations, educational ideologies and concepts are examined here in terms of: (1) factors influencing the construction of some rather than other definitions; (2) the possibility that certain definitions legitimize some, rather than other, institutions and dominant groups; (3) the role of the school as an agent of socialization in creating or transmitting some, rather than other, legitimating symbolic universes; and (4) the consequences of some, rather than other, definitions for the personal and educational development and life chances of individuals.

While Berger and Luckmann (1967) do not examine the implications of their views for education, a similar orientation is brought to bear on education by Young (1971) in his edited collection, *Knowledge and Control*. Young sees existing educational categories that "distinguish home from school, learning from play, academic from non-academic, and 'able' or 'bright' from 'dull' or 'stupid,' as socially constructed, with some in a position to impose their constructions or meanings on others [1971: 2]." He assumes, with Dawe (1970), that the "notion of control involves the 'imposition of meaning' " (quoted in Young, 1971: 4). In this assertion we can see the world divided into *creators* and *receivers* of definitions, or as a continuum in which people have a greater or lesser role in creating the definitions of their situations. Young (1971) sees school interaction as "in part a product of the dominant defining categories which are taken for granted by the teacher," and he sees as a major problem the exploration of "how and why certain dominant categories persist and the nature of the possible links to sets of interests or activities such as occupational groupings [p. 6]." In his paper, "Curricula as Socially Organized Knowledge," he considers the dialectical relationship between access to power and the opportunity to legitimize certain dominant categories, and the processes by which the availability of such categories to some groups enables them to assert power and control over others [1971: 8]." Thus, Young is calling for greater specification of the differential power which influences the construction of dominant categories.

While Young suggests the exciting potential of a social-construction orientation, he raises but does not answer a number of important questions. We need a much clearer specification of who are the *definers* of reality and what their interests are. We also need to know more about who the *receivers* of those definitions are. Do definitions confront all children equally? That is, is it just the status of being a child or other attributes as well that determine the degree to which one is a receiver rather than a creator of definitions?

Young (1971) raises the very important problem of how some rather than other categories gain institutional legitimacy. In addition, we need to know more about why some definitions are legitimized while others are not. Young points to the possible links between dominant categories and sets of interests or activities, but clearly we need both conceptual and empirical specification of those connections and interests. Finally, we need to understand many more details about the processes through which subjective definitions are brought closer to relevant objective definitions, and what consequences these processes have for stratification systems. This problem is addressed most usefully from a symbolic-interactionist perspective.

Interpersonal Level

The symbolic-interactionist approach is derived from the ideas of Mead (1934) and focuses on what Blumer (1969) terms the "situated action." This view raises questions about the processes of interaction in a given situation and about the situational significance of beliefs and values. One of the major tenets of symbolic interactionism, as articulated by Blumer (1969), is the view that "human beings act toward things (or people) on the basis of the meanings that the things have for them [p. 2]." This suggests that the way teachers and other school personnel behave toward children with different social attributes will depend upon the meaning those attributes have for teachers. Thus class or race might indicate low learning ability to some teachers. This orientation shifts our focus from the defined attribute of the pupil to the meanings imputed to a particular characteristic by teachers or others in important positions, and the consequences of those meanings for school–personnel behaviors. Furthermore, symbolic interactionism suggests that participants modify their own behavior based on their interpretations of others' actions.

Richer (1975) calls for essentially this approach to the study of how schools affect children. He comments that the work of Coleman et al. (1966) and Jencks et al. (1972) lacks theoretical structure. Richer (1975) favors Glaser and Strauss' (1967) grounded-theory approach, to get at the relevant conceptual system by utilizing the sensitizing notions of the world view of the principal actors—teachers and students—and hence develop a set of appropriate observational categories.

While I think this theoretical approach sensitizes us to features we might overlook, there are limitations if it is relied upon exclusively. As Huber (1973) has noted, there is the possibility that "in the absence of theory, the social givens of the researcher and the participants serve as a theoretical framework, giving the research a bias which reflects the unstated assumptions of the researcher, the climate of opinion in the discipline and the distribution of power in the interactive setting [p. 282]." If the entire definition of the situation is taken from the participants, as perceived by the researcher, some elements beyond the view of participants will be completely ignored. Carried to its extreme, the perspective recommended by Richer runs the risk of ignoring what Blumer (1969) has termed "the obduracy of the world." In a like vein, Lichtman (1970–71) remarks, "Concrete physical and social reality is neither identical to nor exhausted by beliefs or judgments about that reality [p. 92]." Merton (1973) has paraphrased Thomas (1931) to say, "The things that men do not believe to be real can also be real in their consequences." In short, a critical limitation of symbolic interactionism (and phenomenology) is the possibility that all of "reality" may not be captured in the definitions held by participants.

Finally, the symbolic-interactionist perspective runs the risk of remaining at the intrapsychic and interpersonal level of analysis. If we concentrate exclusively upon learning what definitions of the situation teachers or pupils hold, we overlook the question of why certain definitions are more relevant for teachers or pupils than others. Single-minded concern with the participants' definitions of situations excludes the possibility that parameters are set upon social interaction and definitions by the economic, political, and social contexts in which they occur. Richer appears to have moved independently toward the position of the British phenomenologists, such as Davies (1971), Esland (1971), Gorbutt (1972), Keddie (1971), and Young (1971), who have begun raising many interesting questions about education. But he runs the same risks they do, of neglecting the problem of how and why reality is constructed and maintained in certain ways (cf. Whitty, 1974: 125).

Intrapsychic Level

For all its limitations, the unique contribution of the symbolic-interactionist perspective should not be lost. It helpfully distinguishes between subjective perceptions of principal actors and "objective" interests, which may not always overlap completely. Moreover, this perspective provides us with a theoretical view of how social structure is related to personality, attitudes, and behaviors. This link is provided by Mead (1934), who perceives the origins of "self" as influenced by the social context in which one lives. Mead suggests that one's human qualities are created and reinforced in interaction with others. The emergence of self is influenced, for Mead, by the meanings imputed by others to one's self and one's actions. While I cannot agree with the extreme formulation of a "looking-glass self" (Cooley,

1902/1922), that denies resistance from temperament, personality, natural drives (cf. Wrong, 1961), still the idea that one's sense of self is influenced by social interactions is helpful for explaining how and why social interactions may affect the people experiencing them.

Drawing upon this perspective, it is plausible that the definitions of situations operating in educational situations may influence what is taught and how; and may affect the sense of self[2] which participants in the situation develop (cf. Rist, 1976).

An Integrated Theoretical Framework

As stated at the outset, an adequate theory of the relation between education and inequality needs to integrate four levels of analysis, the societal, institutional, interpersonal, and intrapsychic. Moreover, it needs to do this in a coherent way that explains observable phenomena at all levels.

I begin with the premise that the structure(s) of dominance in a society is intimately bound up with the ideologies employed to legitimate that dominance. Four characteristics of the societal-stratification system appear to be related to the legitimating ideologies in a society: (1) the structural basis of dominance (wealth, occupational position, caste); (2) the amount of stratification in society (including the range and amount of key resources controlled by various groups); (3) the degree to which position is inheritable; and (4) historical changes in the basis of stratification. A central premise of this book is that the structure of dominance in society is related to educational outcomes. For this premise to be plausible, however, it is necessary to understand how and why societal inequalities affect educational outcomes. Hence the ultimate value of the interpretation offered here depends upon its capacity to integrate and explain available evidence at all four levels of analysis.

To begin the analysis, we must explicate the societal-level inequalities and their legitimating ideologies, as well as educational structures and ideologies. Then we can explore the hypothesized causal linkages between structure of dominance and educational ideologies, structures, interactions, and outcomes (see Figure 2.1).

In my view there are multiple axes of stratification in the United States, but they are not equal in influence and prominence. The primary basis for inequality is the difference in the ownership and control of productive resources. In addition, there is a hierarchy of occupational statuses and a caste system based upon race and sex.

The wealth, occupational, and racial structures of dominance are legitimated largely by a societal ideology of merit, competition, and social mobility

[2]Here the term "self" is being used to include character, psyche, and personality, hence including much that does not originate solely in interaction.

FIGURE 2.1. Theoretical model of relevant variables and their interrelationships

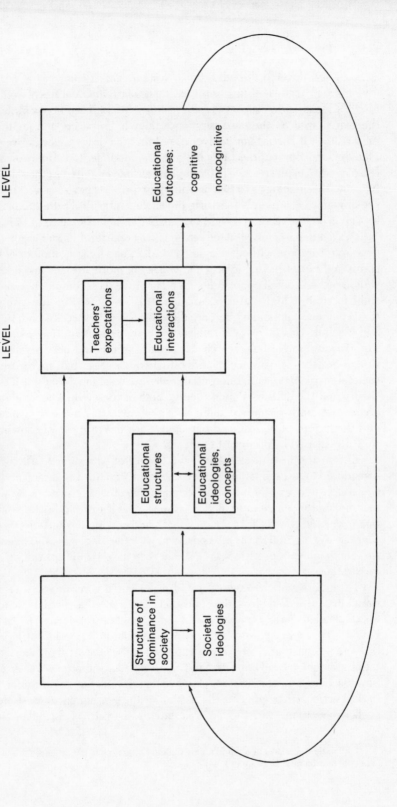

as mediated through the educational system. This ideology is so pervasive that it obscures and legitimates the existence of vast inequalities of wealth and justifies racial and occupational inequalities. While I am here emphasizing the part played by the meritocratic ideology in obscuring and legitimating inequalities, it should not be overlooked that the discrepancy between that ideology and the realities of its imperfect embodiment in American society has played an explosive role in fueling protest movements.[3] At the same time, by using this ideology as a touchstone, these protests have been restricted to seeking more completely to realize the meritocratic ideal rather than change it. The protests have not sought to change the range or shape of the stratification system in society, but only to equalize opportunities for members of all groups to compete without prejudice for the same limited number of higher status and better paying jobs. The ideology of merit stresses that education should provide equal opportunity for all to prove their competence and their right to attain a high-status occupation. It is predicated on the assumption that a person's talent and effort are directly related to success, both in school and beyond. This ideology is reflected in commonsense notions as well as in sophisticated scientific research. Its persuasiveness and pervasiveness help to explain the prevalence of individualistic, rather than institutional or societal, explanations of differential school success, including the IQ-deficit theory and the cultural-deficit theory. Both of these educational ideologies are subsequently examined, along with general testing and sorting practices, and definitions of educational outcomes with the purpose of showing how they are shaped by dominant groups in society.

Also at the institutional level, the history of educational structures are considered to ascertain influence by emergent structures of dominance. Then the consequences of educational ecology, meaning segregation by wealth, income, and race, are examined. Organizational features reflecting differential power and control are examined for their development and effects. I posit that these structural forms are consistent with the ideologies and interests of the dominant groups in society and that they have significant consequences for students.

To understand the cognitive and experiential consequences of educational structures and ideas, the educational processes that mediate them need to be specified. Teachers' expectations are one likely candidate. To avoid the limited explanatory power and evidentiary limitations of prior formulations, however, I consider closely the part played in the genesis of teachers' expectations by societal and educational structures and assumptions. I then analyze how teachers' expectations are related to their interactions with students, and to the curriculum taught. Finally, I examine the consequences for students of such expectations and their manifestations. In brief, I formulate several

---

[3]I am indebted to my colleague, Dennis Wrong, for refusing to let me ignore this important aspect of meritocratic ideology in American society.

micro-theories about the genesis and transmission of teachers' expectations, so as to develop the interpersonal level of this explanatory framework.

All of the above factors—societal structures of dominance, ideologies, educational concepts, structures, and practices—are seen as influencing the academic achievement of different groups of students and their emergent self-concepts. These socialization experiences shape educational and occupational aspirations, leading to the socialization of consciousness, the internalization of the meritocratic ideology, and the legitimation of inequality at a personal level.

Underlying this theoretical formulation, the relation of educational outcomes to life outcomes is quite different from that postulated by the instrumental-meritocratic ideology. The functional relation of the cognitive content of education to one's position in the stratification system is much less than the instrumental-meritocratic ideology assumes, while noncognitive outcomes of various kinds, including self-concept and world view, may be much more important. In short, I stress that American education creates and legitimates inequalities, both in school and beyond. At the same time, these processes may be generating the basis for challenging those inequalities.

A Definitional Note

The broad theoretical position advanced here is that a less favored position in the structure of dominance—whether dominance is based upon wealth, market position, or caste—will be related to lesser educational achievements and attainments in all societies where the educational system is called upon to legitimate social inequalities. This is why I use the general terms "social standing" and "socioeconomic status" in Chapter 1.

In the more specific case of capitalist industrial societies such as the United States, position in the class structure is the most important correlate of educational results, although caste position may also be independently related. By class I mean objective position in the system of economic ownership and control, whether or not consciousness of class exists in the participants. Under capitalism, groups variously placed in the economic system possess differential control over productive processes and unequal access to profits. The structural potential for common awareness is there, but may not be realized. Class consciousness arises when groups sharing an objective position feel a solidarity based upon awareness of their common interests in opposition to those of another class. In the United States, I postulate that ownership position, market position, and caste position (defined in Chapter 3) are related to educational results, not because of the individual limitations of members of less powerful groups, but through the operation of structural and ideological processes that subtly and overtly shape the content and form of education. These educational contents, forms, and interactions, in turn, influence the educational results we observe.

To assess the plausibility of these theoretical assertions, however, it is necessary to draw upon empirical research that does not measure class in these terms. In the literature surveyed here, parental class is usually defined and measured by occupational prestige or educational level. In this usage, class refers to the categorization by researchers of individuals, sharing one or more common attributes, into what are designated "social classes," e.g., upper class, upper-middle class, working class, and so forth. When the term social class appears in subsequent summaries of research findings, it should be understood that it refers to this abbreviated meaning of the concept.

3

Structures of Dominance and Societal Ideologies

INDIVIDUALS AND GROUPS IN SOCIETY strive to maintain and advance their positions relative to others. What are the primary resources in this contest? Marx stresses the preeminence of ownership of the means of production, while Weber has been interpreted as emphasizing status-group membership and life style. Which view more closely describes the situation in American society and why?

As I see it, there are three major bases for inequality in America: the ownership of wealth, market capacity, and caste. These three forms are similar in that within each of them there are some individuals and groups with more power and provilege than others. Those with more actively work to maintain or increase their relative advantages; hence the term "structure of *dominance.*" They may try to support their dominance by influencing legislation, thus gaining the institutionalized force of the state or they may advocate compatible ideologies, thus buttressing their positions with persuasion and a sense of legitimacy.

The three bases for inequality in the United States differ in their initial grounds for distinguishing people (ownership, market position, caste), but they are similar in that they all result in differentiating people economically. Economic resources have great potential for securing power and influence. While other means can sometimes gain power and influence, over generations, economic resources are likely to prevail in industrial societies. Therefore the range of economic inequalities within the three structures of dominance warrants careful examination. By assessing the magnitude of differences within spheres, we can ascertain their relative importance. Does the United States have a multidimensional stratification system, as some social scientists (e.g., Dahl, 1961) have suggested, or are the three forms of inequality hierarchically related?

21

Ownership of wealth constitutes the single largest source of inequality in the United States, and this wealth is heavily concentrated in the hands of very few people. The discrepancies between rich and poor are mind boggling. The top 20 percent of all families own at least 76 percent of all privately held wealth (see Figure 3.1), while the bottom 20 percent of all families own virtually none (1962 Federal Reserve Board Study, cited by Thurow, 1976). Moreover, wealth is more concentrated than even these very unequal distributions suggest. Those with wealth totaling more than $5 million (the top .008 percent of the population) have as many assets as the bottom *half* of all families (1969 Internal Revenue Service report, cited by Thurow, 1976). In 1968 *Fortune* magazine was able to locate 166 individuals worth at least $100 million, and admitted to missing quite a few more (Parker, 1972: 131). An estimated 512,000 individuals have a net worth of more than $500,000, and an additional 12.3 million individuals have estates worth more than $60,000 (U.S. Internal Revenue Service, 1972). In stark contrast, at least 15 million families have a net worth of zero or owe money. In 1967, the last time such figures were published, the wealth of the richest 2 percent of Americans was greater than the total annual U.S. Gross National Product (Parker, 1972: 123).

Wealth alone, however, tells us little about its potential for power and control. While paintings, jewelry, and large estates may command social esteem from some, wealth is more meaningful when we consider its source. It is the ownership and control of productive wealth (for example, corporate stock and bond holdings) that is significant in American society. In 1953 the richest 1 percent of adults held 76 percent of corporate stock and 77.5 percent of bonds (Lampman, 1962). These findings are consistent with those of three

FIGURE 3.1.   Income[a] and wealth[b] by quintile

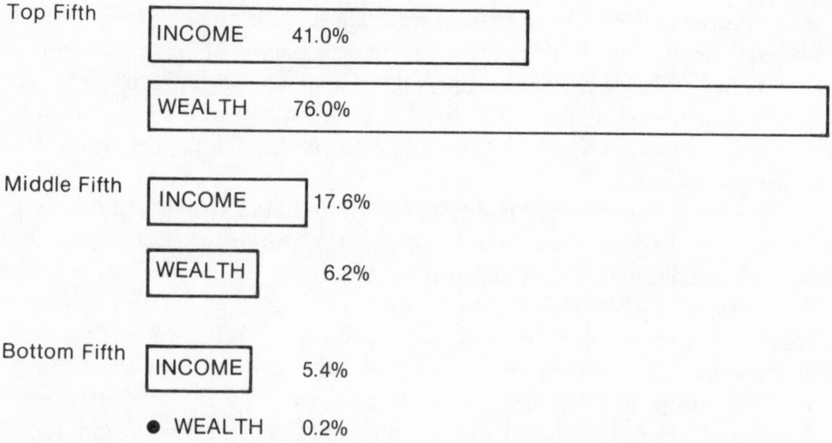

Top Fifth

| INCOME | 41.0% |

| WEALTH | 76.0% |

Middle Fifth

| INCOME | 17.6% |

| WEALTH | 6.2% |

Bottom Fifth

| INCOME | 5.4% |

● WEALTH   0.2%

[a]U.S. Bureau of the Census, 1975, p. 392.
[b]Thurow, *The New York Times Magazine*, April 11, 1976, p. 33. ©1976 by The New York Times Company. Reprinted by permission.

Harvard economists (cited by Heilbroner, 1961), a senate-committee estimate (cited by Heilbroner, 1961), and Lundberg's (1968) research.

The concentration of wealth in the hands of so few people has enormous potential for power and influence, especially when we consider that this productive wealth is centered in relatively few corporations. In 1973, the 500 largest corporations in the United States (one-tenth of 1 percent of all manufacturing establishments) employed three-fourths of all workers in manufacturing (Bowles and Gintis, 1976: 60), and in 1962 the 500 largest companies owned nearly 70 percent of manufacturing assets (Giddens, 1975: 159).

Not only have these patterns of concentration persisted over time (cf. Berle and Means, 1932: 27), but there seems to be considerable historical continuity with respect to the major owners. The very rich of 1925 were generally the lineal descendents of the very rich of 1900, and the very rich of 1950 are very much the progeny of the very rich of 1925 (Mills, 1956). Indeed, with each passing generation, the fraction among them who are "self-made" men—those who pushed their way out of a "lower class into the highest circles"—declines (Mills, cited in Aptheker, 1968: 136).

How were these fortunes made? Economists posit a nonmeritocratic origin. Most of these large fortunes are "instant wealth," as Thurow (1976) suggests, made in a short time. Thurow sees this as true of recent millionaires as well as of the old fortunes made by Rockefellers, Mellons, Fords, Whitneys, Posts, and so on. Great wealth is made by "operating in financial markets to take advantage of 'disequilibrium' in rates of return on capital investment [Thurow, 1976: 32]. . . ." Furthermore, individuals who make such fortunes are not especially gifted financial or industrial wizards. Instead, Thurow argues, the economic theory of the "random walk" explains why some individuals acquire fortunes and others do not. At any given moment, this theory suggests, many investment opportunities look equally inviting, but some eventually fail, some earn the market rate of return, and a very few make big winners (Thurow, 1976: 33). In brief, to be very wealthy in America today means to have inherited wealth or to have won a financial lottery. Neither of these means is consistent with the meritocratic ideology.

Thus, wealth (and all its attendant life chances) is far more unequally distributed than income (see Figure 3.1), the differences between rich and poor are immense, and the only special talent required to obtain wealth seems to be good luck. Why do such inequalities survive, indeed, frequently escape notice? One key to answering this question lies in the existence of other, more observable bases of inequality in society.

Many social scientists argue that the occupational order forms the backbone of the class structure (e.g., Blau and Duncan, 1967; Parkin, 1971). While exclusive or even primary emphasis on the occupational order diverts attention from inequalities of wealth, the existence of differential market positions does form a significant basis for differentiation and contains the potential for certain forms of dominance as well.

Wealth eliminates the need to sell one's labor in the market, and caste characteristics severely restrict participation in the market. What other factors influence bargaining power or scarcity value in the market? Value is determined to a considerable degree by the disequilibrium between supply and demand. The supply of people in a given occupation is influenced by the skill level required (including knowledge, specialized language, tools, and ability to perform certain tasks), by the number of people who enter the occupation (through long training, certification, testing, and so forth), and by the successful exclusion of competitors. Restraints on competition may be established politically and legally by means of licensing, certification, or other procedures handled through the state, as well as informally through discrimination. The demand for a particular occupation may be affected by factors beyond its control, unless the occupation is successful in manipulating the perceived need for it or can secure political-legal sanctions, which, for example, legislate certain functions (e.g., the requirement for external evaluation of federally funded social programs or compulsory vaccination programs). To the degree that an occupation monopolizes a given sphere of knowledge and its application, it may be increasingly able to define what is needed. When other members of society regard a particular occupation as essential to their well-being, the demand for it will increase. In short, market advantage is determined by differential skills and the perceived need for services, both of which are influenced by the past and present social and political power an occupation controls.

Differential market advantages result in different rewards. The most obvious disparity is in income, that is, average annual earnings. Other economic rewards include such perquisites as stock options, expense accounts, paid travel, opportunities for additional income, sick pay, pensions, health insurance, and other benefits. Market situation has important social consequences as well. Working conditions, types of co-workers, and type of authority relations are important concomitants of one's market position, as Collins (1975) and Dahrendorf (1959) have indicated. Finally, the amount of control or autonomy over both content and conduct of work is an important consequence of the market situation.

In short, I have advanced a conflict rather than a functional view of occupational advantage in the market situation. The functionalist view explains differential rewards in terms of the social value and importance of various occupational positions. This position is dubious if we examine the claim that foremen make more money than workers because they contribute more to the productive system. As Parkin (1971: 19) notes, this claim offers more of a value judgment than an explanation. His critique is supported by observations from worker-managed coal mines in West Virginia. Those mines eliminated foremen, while increasing productivity and cutting costs.

Differential market situations are reflected in the distribution of earnings. In 1968, the top fifth of full-time earners averaged $19,300 annually, while the bottom fifth earned $2650 on the average (Jencks et al., 1972: 211). In relative terms, this means that in 1974 the top fifth earned 41 percent of total earned income, the middle fifth 18 percent, and the bottom fifth 5 percent (U.S. Bureau of the Census, 1975: 392). As great a discrepancy as these figures show, they conceal the large range within the top category. Samuelson (1967) has vividly illustrated the current income distribution: "If we made an income pyramid out of a child's blocks, with each layer portraying $1000 of income, the peak would be far higher than the Eiffel Tower, but almost all of us would be within a yard of the ground [p. 112]."

Thus large differences in income, work situations, social contacts, and life chances are associated with different market situations. Despite considerable disparities in income, however, the resultant inequalities are considerably less than those attached to the ownership of wealth.

We need to distinguish between occupational position and social honor. Weber (1947: 424–429) importantly separated class, referring to market situation, from status, referring to social honor. Many sociologists regard class and status as separate dimensions of stratification, but the distinction is more useful for analyzing inequalities in traditional societies than in industrial societies (Parkin, 1971). American sociologists in particular have overemphasized the autonomy of status, usually by failing to indicate its sources (Parkin, 1971: 29). Examples of apparent inconsistencies between class and status, such as electricians and railroad conductors ranking higher economically but lower in prestige than schoolteachers and clergy (noted by Gouldner and Gouldner, 1963) do not, in Parkin's view, reveal discrepancies between class and status position at all but merely between income and status. Income is only one of the factors associated with class position, while working conditions, autonomy, and type of work are all related to status. Over time, I would argue, economic position can accrue social status. Tainted money, such as that of the "robber barons" or of underworld kingpins, needs several generations of "good works" and public relations to acquire social honor, but if status is the goal, the history of industrial societies shows that wealth can eventually procure it.

Related to the problems of status are those revealed in studies of occupational prestige, ascertained by asking a sample of the population to rank order various occupations in terms of their prestige. This procedure assumes that the prestige given different occupations stems from the sum total of individual assessments, thus leading to the view that the distribution of social honor is legitimate because it rests upon popular evaluations of common worth (Parkin, 1971). As Riessman puts it, "Status . . . can derive only from the respect and honor that others are willing to give. Therefore status has a highly personal quality [cited in Parkin, 1971: 41]." It is not always clear from empirical studies whether it is the individual's personal evaluation of the social worth of various positions that is being measured or the assessment of what seems to be the factual social standing of these positions. "Thus, the fact that so many ranking studies report a high level of 'general agreement' should not necessarily be taken as an index of popular feeling regarding matters of status; what is often being measured is the perception of an existing status hierarchy, and not our own private evaluations of the way positions ought to be socially ranked [Parkin, 1971: 41]."

This sociological preoccupation with the status of occupations obscures how occupations secured market advantages historically and how they currently maintain them. In short, it makes status appear to be *due to* esteem rather than *derived from* ownership or market advantages.

The third form of differential power in American society is caste, or racial stratification. Caste, according to Berreman (1972), refers to the "invidious distinctions imposed unalterably at birth upon whole categories of people to justify the unequal social distribution of power, livelihood, security, privilege, esteem, freedom—in short, life chances [p. 410]."[1] Caste position is reflected in the public esteem accorded members of various groups, the power they wield, the rewards available to them, and the nature and form of their interactions with others (Berreman, 1972).

Systems of racial stratification differ from caste systems in that the birth-ascribed status of different racial groups is associated with "alleged physical differences among social categories, which are culturally defined as present and important [Berreman, 1972: 390]." But Berreman, the anthropologist, reminds us that " . . . no society in the world ranks people purely on the basis of biological race, i.e., on any basis that a competent geneticist would call 'race,' which means on the basis of distinctive shared genetic makeup derived from a common gene pool. Race, as a basis for social rank, is always a *socially* defined phenomenon which at most only very imperfectly corresponds to genetically transmitted traits . . . [Berreman, 1972: 390]." Thus, it is socially defined categories and not physical differences that distinguish groups of people and bar some from particular economic and interpersonal transactions.

In America race is related to all aspects of life chances, from health, life expectancy, and medical care, to housing, education, and income.

While wealth ownership among blacks is seldom studied,[2] the income differentials between blacks and whites have been examined extensively. Fully employed white men earned an average of $10,400 in 1970, compared to black men, who earned $6760 on the average, and black women who earned $4680 (Jencks et al., 1972: 216). Thus, black males earned 65 percent

---

[1]Here I am considering only race as an attribute of caste. Sex may also usefully be analyzed as a caste attribute, wherever opportunities, rights, and privileges are systematically allocated on the basis of sex.

[2]Black wealth owners are probably seldom studied because there are relatively few of them and they are not very wealthy compared to wealthy whites. *Ebony* magazine periodically reports on black millionaires and business successes, but their fortunes are small and usually in black-related enterprises such as insurance or magazine publication, rather than in industrial corporations. This may well be due to the historical (and contemporary) impossibility of blacks obtaining large capital support.

and black females 45 percent of the earnings of white males. Moreover, blacks are also more likely than whites to be unemployed or underemployed (Jencks et al., 1972: 217).

The ratio of black to white wages rose during World War II, remained constant for the next 20 years, then rose again somewhat in the late 1960s (Jencks et al., 1972: 216). In the long run, however, the absolute differences between the two races have tended to increase. Like the poor in general, the relative position of blacks has improved somewhat, but not enough to narrow the absolute gap between the races (Jencks et al., 1972: 211).

In short, with respect to income, as well as other life chances, consistent racial discrepancies exist in American life. However, as Jencks et al. have established, the income differences between races are not as great as those between individuals. Thus, if we were to rank the three forms of inequality on economic grounds, the largest inequalities occur with respect to ownership of wealth, followed by those associated with differential market situations and racial differences.

I have thus far identified three forms of differentiation in American society: wealth, occupation, and caste. Many American stratification scholars would conclude that these provide distinct and independent bases for stratification. In so doing, they would be in keeping with numerous portrayals of American society as composed of multiple competing interest groups, but not dominated by any one system of stratification (cf. Dahl, 1961, for an example of this orientation). Adherents to this view emphasize the openness of the recruitment process and the diversity of the interests within and between groups that compete for power in a pluralistic system.

What evidence exists bearing on the question of the relative independence or dependence of these three systems of stratification? Dahrendorf (1959) and Burnham (1941) in Europe, along with Bell (1960), Galbraith (1967), and Keller (1963a), in the United States, have argued that a new class has emerged, whose expertise offers a rational and meritocratic basis for stratification. While this *may* describe cleavages in formal or bureaucratic organizations, it does not fully describe cleavages at the societal level (cf. Parkin, 1971: 45). Moreover, we must ask about the *range* of decision making that lies within the purview of the expert specialists from the "new class." Do they make broad-scale policies, or do they merely provide technical expertise on narrow aspects of issues, which are then decided by boards of directors or chief executives?

We must ask further whether the individuals holding high positions are free to challenge the prevailing assumptions and policies of the organization and its directors. Who decides who will be promoted within major organizations? In other words, what are the *sources* of bureaucratic power, and can those sources be withdrawn? People who advance in organizations generally share the same assumptions and interests as those in positions of higher authority. Moreover, managers often become large stockholders, even if they do not hold a controlling interest, so their interests and those of other large stockholders increasingly overlap.

Finally, the parameters of the market situation (the overall demand for given positions) are set primarily by the economic needs of the largest industrial corporations. While there may be competition for relative advantage within an existing market structure, the overall framework is largely determined independently of the occupations or individuals, except to the degree that they can exercise effective collective action. These parameters undoubtedly shape the content and the organization of the work to be done.

In brief, therefore, I find little basis for believing that the occupational structure or the individuals within it are independent in major ways from the ownership of wealth. To give one example, the decision to hire and fire individuals is central to their market situation. But decisions to hire or fire substantial numbers of individuals are virtually always beyond the control of the people directly involved. These policy matters are determined by top management or by chief executives and directors. Lower-level managers may participate in decisions about how people will be fired, but the decision to cut costs rather than reduce profits is a given.

The political, economic, governmental and international influence of the very rich has been documented by Baltzell (1958, 1964), Domhoff (1967, 1970), Hunter (1965), and Raines (1975). Their work and the arguments above suggest that the biggest source of inequality (whether of income, power, or life chances) in America is the enormously unequal distribution of productive wealth.

I would argue that the racial caste system would be considerably undermined, if not eliminated, if it did not support vast economic inequalities. Racial differences are relatively unimportant in Brazil, where blacks participate more equally than in the U.S. in a highly stratified economic system. Furthermore, it could be argued that some members of the ownership class have been moderately influential in modifying the American caste system. While many were unconcerned, and none were in the forefront of the civil-rights movement, there were at least four foundations representing major wealth-holding families which followed up on the civil-rights movement and provided grants for programs that were considered socially responsible and in keeping with a meritocratic image of society. Thus, the Ford Foundation gave $7 million in 1964 to the National Merit Scholarship Fund to establish the National Achievement Scholarships for black students, as well as money to the United Negro College Fund and to ten black institutions for faculty and staff development and student assistance (Nielsen, 1972: 355). The Mott Foundation, the Rockefeller Brothers Fund, and the Carnegie Corporation also contributed to various "responsible" black educational institutions and other organizations. These efforts may have been designed to create the impression that the meritocracy in the United States is open to members of all races. Giddens (1975) has pointed out that when economic position is coterminous with race, it is more likely to lead to even greater class consciousness than when economic and racial categories are divergent. The most visible of these contributions were preceded by growing racial awareness and militancy, so it is possible that foundations were coming to perceive the situation as Giddens did, and acted accordingly. Thus, it could be argued, inferentially, that when members of the wealth-owning class felt threatened by the racial caste system, they did something to placate those in it.

I have argued that the three structures of dominance in American life are not independent of each other. Instead there is a hierarchy among them. That is, the occupational structure is, with a few notable exceptions, subordinate to the ownership of productive property. The racial caste system has served the interests of wealth owners by insuring large numbers of workers required to work for low hourly rates, and has assisted most whites in the market by excluding blacks from better jobs. Therefore, to the extent that racial minorities lack independent economic resources, to the extent that the economy requires the form of labor a racial caste system provides, and to the extent that caste does not endanger the economic and social order, the racial caste structure of American society served the interests of both wealth owners and whites competing for market advantages. Hence these structures of dominance are themselves hierarchically arranged, with caste subordinate to the market situation, in turn subordinate to the ownership of productive wealth.

If this delineation of the structure of dominance is accepted, the next question to be addressed is: how does this structure maintain, reproduce, and legitimate itself? It does so, I contend, through both structural means and ideological hegemony. The structural means include expansion of the economy and in particular the growth of the white-collar sector during the past 30 years with attendant increases in earnings and consumption; occupational upward mobility for some and the development of institutions that obscure the major differences between groups, set parameters within which debates and conflicts occur, and modify expectations about life and world views.

Except for slight dips in 1946 and 1949, the U.S. Gross National Product has risen steadily since 1945. At the same time, the number of jobs in the white-collar sector has increased from 22 million in 1950 to 38 million in 1970 (Bowles and Gintis, 1976). As a result, many individuals, looking back over their own life history or comparing themselves with their parents, feel better off in an absolute sense. But relative to other groups in society, most people have not changed. The rich have gotten richer at a faster rate than anyone else, and a few professions have increased their income. Otherwise, it is as though everyone has been on an escalator (cf. Milner, 1972). Moreover, the proportion of the poor has not changed, and their degree of absolute improvement has been the smallest (Jencks et al., 1972). At least one economist (Rostow, 1975) suggests that this growth has been fueled by technological innovation and by cheap energy. Both of these conditions seem less likely in the future, particularly the latter. Therefore, growth may diminish if not flatten out; and thus this structural factor may attenuate in the future.

Related to the expansion of the economy, and of the white-collar sector in particular, is the opportunity for upward mobility which these changes have permitted. In a static economic and social system, each instance of upward mobility must be accompanied by comparable downward mobility. Thus, for all those who feel that the system has enabled them to get ahead, there are an equal number (potentially) who feel that the system did them in. If economic growth slows down or the white-collar sector stays level, the number of individuals who experience upward mobility is likely to decrease.

If both of these features which help to maintain, reproduce, and legitimate the system of dominance are substantially weakened, we may predict that a greater burden will fall upon the third mechanism, namely the institutions that serve to reduce awareness of major differences, set the parameters within which debates and conflicts occur, and modify individual capabilities and expectations. In other eras and societies the church probably served this function, while the frontier may have played a similar role earlier in American history. In today's America, the institution of education is called upon to maintain, reproduce, and legitimate the inequalities of society. Structural means, however, go hand in hand with belief systems that support and legitimate them. Therefore, we look briefly at societal belief systems to see whether structures of dominance are related to societal ideologies. (We consider educational structures in Chapter 4 and educational belief systems in Chapter 5 to see if they are related to the structure of dominance in American society.)

To be sustained, societal beliefs must correspond to reality in some way. The American belief system about social inequality consists of a number of interrelated elements. First, there is the belief in upward mobility, based on the premise of equal opportunity and selection by merit rather than ascriptive criteria. As noted above, there has been some upward mobility, at least in absolute terms, for a considerable proportion of the population. Relative mobility has been much smaller. However, we may infer that to those for whom the system has worked, the belief system must seem credible. Such individuals have *experiential validation* of the societal belief.[3] Therefore, these individuals are often ardent champions of the meritocracy (e.g., Bell, 1972). They are, moreover, unlikely to question the criteria of merit that are applied, since these standards reflect favorably on those benefited. If the individuals themselves are not upwardly mobile, their fathers or someone

[3]Who are the people most likely to have experienced such upward mobility? Very often they operate on the boundaries of dominant groups, as supervisors or gatekeepers. Thus, teachers have often experienced upward mobility, as have foremen, army sergeants, social workers, and politicians. Those for whom the system has "worked" are likely to be in the position of socializing new members of society or an organization, or of selecting those who will be advanced within it.

they know may have been. So, despite the relative infrequency of mobility, cases can always be found to support a meritocratic ideology.

Another belief system that prevails in America is one that minimizes differences between people. We are all really middle class, so it says, and any differences that exist are only ones of degree. Parker (1972) dubs this "the myth of the middle class." Mills (1956), Raines (1975), and Thurow (1976) have noted how the inheritance laws seem designed to give this impression. Under existing laws, estates of $20 million and above are supposed to be taxed at the rate of at least 69 percent. Actually, lawyers have helped clients in that bracket pay an average of only 26.8 percent in taxes (Raines, 1975: 48). Or, as Mills (1956) so succinctly put it, for every law, there is a way to avoid it.

A second claim of the "middle-class belief system" is that ownership of stock in industrial corporations is widely dispersed. In 1975, 25.3 million Americans (or 11.8 percent of the population) owned stock (New York Stock Exchange, 1976: i). Many more individuals may also own stock indirectly through pension plans, insurance policies and so on. Therefore, this belief bears some correspondence to reality as well. However, as Giddens (1975) notes, dispersal of ownership actually contributes to the effective control by directors who can exercise control even though they own only a relatively small proportion of the stock. Moreover, of those 25.3 million stock holders, most actually own only a very small amount. In 1975, 50 percent of them owned portfolios worth less than $10,000 and 85 percent of them owned portfolios valued at less than $50,000 (New York Stock Exchange, 1976: 8). These relatively small holdings do nothing to distribute actual economic control.

The minimal-differences belief emphasizes the common humanity of the rich. As Mills (1956) notes, we hear about the disconsolateness of the rich, of their troubles, illnesses, and loneliness, all of which suggests that they are no different from ourselves. Another basis for similarity hinges upon our political system. Since everyone has one vote, the system can be adjusted and improved if people are dissatisfied. While the right to vote is clearly established (although many minorities and women were disenfranchised for a long time), critics argue that the available parties and candidates do not represent any real choice. While Dahl (1961) describes competing interest groups, Domhoff (1967) and Raines (1975) document political influence by the very rich in both political parties.

Furthermore, while everyone has the vote, the acceptable range of political content is quite limited. Hence, Giddens (1975) argues that "the stability of capitalist society depends upon the maintenance of an insulation of economy and polity, such that questions of industrial organization appear as 'non-political' [p. 114]."

Finally, the minimization of differences is sustained by the low visibility of the very rich. Most people are separated from them by distinct residential areas, schools, clubs, places of work, and social activities. Therefore, most people neither see nor know very wealthy individuals at all, much less in their natural setting. (Education contributes to this isolation, as I subsequently demonstrate.)

American sociology has also contributed to how social inequalities are perceived. I have already alluded to the preoccupation with prestige and status rather than social class. Moreover, even when class is identified and studied, it is in terms of distribution rather than control.

In America, the multidimensionality of social status is stressed with no concern for the systemic sources of status differences. Furthermore, there has been intensive study of social mobility, but very little concern with how systems of inequality reproduce themselves. For a long time, the functional theory of stratification prevailed, which explained unequal rewards as due to relative contribution to society. This "explanation" is consonant with the interests of the "new class" of academics and government officials as well as with the interests of property-owning elites.

In keeping with the rational, meritocratic beliefs about how society is run, American sociology excluded power from the study of stratification, and relegated it to political sociology (Huber and Form, 1973). Thus the possibility of coercion was effectively eliminated from the study of social class.

These, then, are some of the prevailing belief systems in American society. Both beliefs and structures may operate to maintain, reproduce, and legitimize the structure of dominance. How else can we explain the fact that of the three forms of inequality, caste and occupational differences arouse some concern, but wealth inequalities seem not to? One explanation for this curious anomaly resides in the educational system. We will look at the historical emergence of educational structures (see Chapter 4), to see whether they have been influenced by the structure of dominance or societal ideologies.

4

Educational Structures

AMERICAN EDUCATION is often discussed as though it were monolithic. With a few exceptions, everyone is assumed to receive a similar education, at least through the ninth grade. But this belief needs to be examined critically.

To begin with, American students are educated in *spatially distinct settings*, including public and private schools, upper-middle-class suburban schools, schools in older suburbs and large cities, and rural or small town schools. These spatial distinctions are highly related to the economic, occupational, and ethnic composition of various schools and classrooms (see Table 4.1).

TABLE 4.1. Structural mechanism and type of segregation

STRUCTURAL MECHANISM	SEGREGATION BY
Residential segregation, Neighborhood schools	Race, parental occupation
Private/public-school division	Wealth, occupation, race, religion
Tracking	Occupation, race

Residential segregation and neighborhood schools result in major racial and economic segregation within the schools. Blacks represent an increasingly large proportion of the nation's largest central cities but a very small, and often decreasing, proportion of the suburban rings around those cities. In 1970, the proportion of blacks in the 10 largest cities ranged from a low of 16 percent in Boston to a high of 71 percent in Washington, but the percentage in the suburban rings around those cities ranged from 1 percent in Boston to 6 percent in Washington (U.S. Bureau of the Census, 1970a and b, cited in Farley, 1975: 171–2). This residential segregation is primarily racial rather

33

than economic, according to Farley (1975: 177). Furthermore, suburban racial composition varies more than these figures suggest, because there are "exclusive" suburbs with few or no blacks and older ones which have most of the suburban blacks. Therefore, few suburban communities and their schools are racially mixed in any significant way.

The economic composition of most schools tends to be relatively homogeneous as well. In older suburbs or cities, children of higher-income families are more likely to attend homogeneous neighborhood schools, selective public schools, or private schools, and to be in higher tracks, while lower-income and ethnic-minority children are most likely to attend school together. The economic homogeneity of both schools and communities in such upper middle-class suburbs as Great Neck, Scarsdale, Greenwich, Palo Alto, and Lake Forest is well known. The average dwelling unit in those communities sells today for more than $75,000, and the median income is at least two or three times the national average.

Private day and boarding schools are also economically homogeneous. A recent study (Baird, 1976) of boarding schools found that the median family income of students was $30,000, and this figure undoubtedly obscures a high upper range. Thus, the mechanisms of residential segregation, public and private education, and tracking result in schools that are relatively homogeneous with respect to race, income, and occupation (cf. Sexton, 1961).

These spatial and social aggregates have other distinctive features as well. They differ with respect to their governance and economics, educational goals, formal structures, openness to change, teaching staffs, and the social relations within them. In order to better understand the structural differences between urban, private schools and upper-middle-class suburban schools (and thereby be in a position to examine their consequences), I consider each type in turn. Since I agree with Katz (1971: xviii) that it is necessary to study the origin and development of education to appreciate the way it interweaves structure and purpose, I devote some attention to critical historical events, particularly with respect to urban public education and private boarding schools.

Urban School Systems

Urban school systems have two overriding features: they are bureaucratic and they are differentiated. Drawing upon the work of Anderson (1973), Katz (1971), and Weber (1946), I see bureaucratic structure as characterized by these features:

1. authority residing in the office, not the person;
2. qualification for office based upon expertise;

3. centralization of control, with authority hierarchically distributed;
4. division of labor based upon differentiated functions;
5. a system of rules and regulations governing the rights, duties, and behavior of participants;
6. standardized and "objective" procedures for dealing with individuals;
7. impersonal relations between individuals.

It is important to note that this bureaucratic form of organization is almost nonexistent in private boarding schools and exists in modified form in upper-middle-class suburban school systems. As Anderson (1971: 19) has shown, bureaucratic structure is related not only to the size of the school or school district but also to the social-class composition of the student body. He found that social class accounted for 46 percent of the variance in behavior control (one indicator of bureaucratization) when school size, school type, and district size were held constant. By behavior control Anderson means the extent to which rules and regulations exist in the school and are enforced. School type refers to the type of program offered (academic, vocational or combined). Hence the social-class composition of the school is strongly related to the amount of behavior control in it, with lower-class schools showing more control. By way of contrast, school type accounted for only 3 percent, size for only 3 percent, and district size for only 1 percent of the variance in behavior control when student social class was held constant.

While urban schools are currently bureaucratic, they have not always been organized along these lines. Alternative organizational forms existed in earlier epochs, but they were transformed or eliminated over time. Katz (1971: Chapter 1) notes that pre-Civil War American education had four organizational alternatives. He terms them "paternalistic voluntarism," "democratic localism," "corporate voluntarism," and "incipient bureaucracy." After discussing the possibilities and limitations of each, Katz describes how the bureaucratic model came to prevail. Katz (1971) feels that ". . . bureaucracy was intended to standardize far more than the conduct of public life," this reaction stemming "from a gut fear of the cultural diversity of American life [p. 39]." Katz (1971) suggests the ". . . racist implication of such a point of view," by which he means the ". . . attitude that considers one group to be different from and inferior to another in some basic and essential fashion [p. 39]."

In this sense, structure, like the classificatory schemes and other concepts to be considered, may be seen as having been socially constructed by certain groups with negative consequences for other groups. We need to know more about how concepts and structures were constructed, what groups played various roles in those processes, and the conditions under which definitions and structures change. Recent historical work by Bowles and Gintis (1976), Cohen (1968), Hammack (1969), Karier, Violas and Spring (1973), Katz (1968), Lazerson (1971), Ravitch (1974), Spring (1972), and Tyack (1974), in conjunction with earlier work by Callahan (1962) and Cremin (1965, 1961), provides a good basis for drawing conclusions about how educational structures emerged and the factors that shaped their development.

Both radical and traditional historians of education concur that American education has undergone three periods of relatively rapid expansion. The "rise of the common school" (from about 1840 to 1860) saw the expansion of universal elementary education—at least through the North and East. The rise of universal secondary education occurred from about 1890 to 1930, and was accompanied by major transformations in the urban public school system. Finally, there has been the rapid expansion of higher education in the United States, beginning before 1960 but accelerating in the decade from 1960 to 1970.

As several observers have noted (Bowles and Gintis, 1976; Karabel, 1972; Trow, 1966), each expansion of educational opportunities has been accompanied by educational differentiation, that is, requiring different educational programs for different students. Furthermore, ideological portrayals of these expansions have often differed from their actualities. For example, while the common-school ideology filled the rhetoric of reformers, Cremin (1965) has noted that the common school was essentially a Northern and Western phenomenon, reaching its apotheosis in rural and small-town America west of the Alleghenies. It flourished where there was already reasonable homogeneity of race, class, and religion. Hence the common-school ideology may have existed more to justify the expenditure of tax monies for compulsory public education than to describe reality.

The educational structures that emerged with the expansion of secondary education in the United States were compulsory, centralized, bureaucratic, and differentiated. As long as the economy could use child labor, education was voluntary (Edwards and Richey, 1947). Not until the middle of the nineteenth century did business leaders begin to support public education. Their support appeared in a period of massive immigration, increasing labor unrest in the face of factory speedups, declining wages, and periodic recessions marked by massive unemployment (Bowles and Gintis, 1976; Corwin, 1965; Curti, 1935/1968; Edwards and Richey, 1947).

Prior to that century, schools had been subordinate to the church. In American colonial society this was reflected in Protestant religious values (Corwin, 1965; Edwards and Richey, 1947). As religious dominance over the schools declined (partly because of conflicts among religious groups themselves),[1] and as the American economy shifted from a mercantile to a manufacturing one, the economy increasingly came to dominate education.

The content of education shifted perceptibly during the nineteenth century. In 1827 prayers and Bible readings were virtually universal in public

[1]See Ravitch (1974) for a vivid description of the religious issues that fanned conflicts in the New York City schools during this period.

schools. Although the notoriously religious character of the *New England Primer* was toned down somewhat in editions appearing after 1800 and it was replaced gradually by new spelling books and readers, the most popular of those also sought to instill religious principles. As late as 1848, Webster's *Elementary Spelling Book*, of which a million copies were being sold annually, was outspoken in its religious character (Curti, 1935/1968: 17). But succeeding editions of the *Spelling Book* increasingly contained economic as well as religious maxims. Webster sought to inculcate respect for property and honest labor, the virtues of poverty, and contentment with one's lot. Children were told that property was acquired by industry and economy, that only a few were rich enough to keep a coach, and that it was "the meanest of all low tricks to creep into a man's inclosure [sic] and take his property." Time was not to be wasted and exact accounts were to be kept (quoted in Curti, 1935: 33–4). As Curti (1935/1968) concludes, "other half-truths, equally fitting to a society in which some had more and others less, were read and reread by American youth who learned their letters from the old 'blue-back' (Webster's *Spelling Book*, pp. 33–34)."

Business not only influenced the content of major books used in schools but also sought to reform the structure of education and change its goals. Tyack (1974) has extensively studied how business and professional elites, in coalition with university people and the new school managers, planned a basic shift in the control of urban education at the beginning of the twentieth century—to put it in the hands of a small committee composed of "successful men." According to Tyack, they wanted to reshape the schools to fit the new social and economic conditions of an urban industrial society. They sought to do this by changing the size and social class of school boards, and by altering decision-making procedures in those boards. Whereas the older ward boards had been decentralized in many smaller communities of the larger cities, the proposed new boards would be citywide and smaller. Decision-making power that had previously been placed in the hands of committees of the board was to rest with "expert managers" within the parameters set by board policies.

These reformers were upper-class industrialists, many of whom had masterminded the corporate expansion and consolidation that occurred so dramatically at the turn of the century. As Tyack (1974: 143) notes, the capitalization of corporations valued at a million dollars or more jumped from a total of $170 million in 1897 to $5 billion in 1900 to more than $20 billion in 1904. Many of the men who supported the centralization of schools had helped to shape that corporate model and to build the trusts.[2]

[2] It is these economic changes that I find lacking in Ravitch's (1974) very interesting account of ethnic and religious cleavages in New York City. Without considering economic changes we cannot explain why immigration and urbanization were encouraged. While there were undoubtedly ethnic and religious overtones to the educational conflicts in many areas, there were also very strong economic concerns, as Hammack (1969) and Tyack (1974) so carefully point out.

The upper-class reformers found ready allies among university presidents and professors of educational administration. As Tyack (1974) notes:

> University presidents and professors of educational administration helped to create a useful consensus of 'experts' on the reorganization of urban schools. Presidents Charles W. Eliot of Harvard, Nicholas Murray Butler of Columbia, William Rainey Harper of Chicago, and Andrew Sloan Draper of the University of Illinois achieved national prominence in the movement, speaking before reform associations, writing in national periodicals, and masterminding political strategy in a number of cities. While he was a professor at Columbia, Butler and elite allies commanded a 'school war' (his term) in 1896 which destroyed the ward school boards in New York. . . . [3]
>
> Essentially, these university presidents regarded the ideal role of large city superintendent as parallel to their own careers. . . . The city superintendent was to be a captain of education, a commander whose scope was limited only by the reach of his statesmanship [pp. 133–34].

These educational entrepreneurs, as Tyack dubs them, felt comfortable with the men of great wealth and power and worked easily with them to change the structure of urban schools so as to permit wide powers for the new managers of urban education.

But before the new experts could fill the jobs, they needed to be trained, and that job fell to the professors of educational administration. As Tyack (1974) notes:

> Although they lacked the power and access to the intimate circle of the business elite enjoyed by university presidents, most of them admired businessmen and were in turn often accepted by corporate leaders as useful allies. By the turn of the century, specialized university training was becoming the hallmark of the "expert" so touted by progressive reformers [p. 135].

The new professors of educational administration gave the stamp of university approval to elitist assumptions about who made good board members and to the corporate model of school organization. Early textbooks on school management expressed the idea that successful men were disinterested. A school board composed of such people would be efficient, respect the expertise of the superintendent, and consider the needs of the city as a whole. This support was not unreciprocated. As school boards became reformed, they increasingly demanded university-trained experts, thereby expanding the market for courses in educational administration (Tyack, 1974: 136–140). At this moment in history, the interests of large businessmen and educational leaders coincided nicely, with the result that they joined forces in many cities to reform the schools (cf. Fisher, 1972).

Only a few school people doubted that businessmen represented the good of society in general. Margaret Haley, a classroom teacher from Chicago,

[3]This "school war" is vividly described in Ravitch (1974).

announced before the National Education Association in 1904 that public-school teachers must recognize that their struggle to improve conditions in the schools was part of the same great struggle which manual laborers had been making for humanity through their efforts to obtain decent living conditions for themselves and their children. She called upon the public school to aid the workers in their struggle to secure a more equitable distribution of the products of their labor (Curti, 1935/1968: 242). Counts (1927), a somewhat more influential dissenter, wrote that the supposed disinterestedness of the elite:

> . . . is a pious fraud. The member of a dominant group, because he is peculiarly tempted to identify the interests of society with the interests of his class, is particularly inclined to regard himself as a spokesman for society at large. We should come to recognize each individual for what he is; namely, an individual who . . . is likely to represent the interests of some particular element or faction in society [p. 96].

But such appeals fell on deaf ears among both educational leaders and the rank and file of teachers (Curti, 1935/1968: 243). The existence of these critical views, however, makes the conservatism of the public-school directors all the more striking. It is not as though intellectual alternatives did not exist. On the contrary, they did but they were ignored.

The prevailing reform movement led to substantial changes in the structure of educational governance. After reform, business and professional men predominated on urban boards. By 1916, more than three-fifths of the members of city committees were merchants, manufacturers, bankers, brokers, real-estate men, doctors, or lawyers. Subsequent studies by Struble (cited in Tyack, 1974: 141) and Counts (1927) confirmed that workingmen and women were grossly underrepresented.

Procedures as well as structures changed in this period. Reformers belonged to a national business elite, and they exchanged ideas about strategy and structure: "St. Louis reformers, for example, borrowed a plan developed by a New York commission, while businessmen from Boston and St. Louis advised merchants in Chicago about how to reorganize their school system [Tyack, 1974: 139]." The growth of national rather than regional businesses facilitated and required greater communication among these elites. Tyack terms this the drive for the "one best system," and it is congruent with the efficiency movement and with the desire to expand the rationalization of life nationally, in the interests of expanding industries and markets.

A leading feature of the corporate model was the role of the superintendent, specifically that individual's power to influence major school-board decisions. A 1901 survey of 233 towns and cities of Massachusetts found that superintendents were taking on duties formerly handled by the school board, though the prerogatives of the school managers were by no means firmly established. They could generally design the course of study, call and chair teachers' meetings, promote pupils, and supervise the work of teachers. While they selected all the textbooks in 92 systems and could nominate teacher candidates in 95 districts, the power to appoint or dismiss teachers was still firmly held by the boards. By 1923, managers had won the power to initiate board actions on staff hirings and firings, new educational policies, shaping the curriculum and selecting textbooks (Tyack, 1974: 144–145).

Those favoring the corporate model of school administration portrayed conflicts of value, debate, and representation of the interests of particular groups as "inefficient" and undesirable. Hence, reports that school board meetings were conducted in conversational tones and concluded quickly were viewed favorably. What lost out was the bargaining among different groups in the ward system, the "lay influence through subcommittees of the board, the contests over cultural and tangible values that had characterized the pluralistic politics of many large cities," and in its place was a "modern and rational" bureaucracy buffered from popular vagaries (Tyack, 1974: 147); the very bureaucratic monster that was to come under attack in the 1960s as being unresponsive and inefficient (cf. Gittell and Hollander, 1968; Rogers, 1968; Schrag, 1967).

In this process, education was defined as an institution that should be above politics, since political parties and politicians were not to be trusted.

Thus the common school, a prime agency for the perpetuation of democracy, was led by persons who made it a matter of principle to distrust one of the central institutions of democratic government, the political party. [But] . . . in urging the corporate form of external school governance and internal control by expert bureaucrats, the centralizers were, of course, simply exchanging one form of "political" decision-making for another. They were arguing for a relatively closed system of politics in which power and initiative flowed from the top down and administrative law or system took the place of decisions by elected officials [Tyack, 1974: 146 –147].

Business leaders sought and gained control over the parameters of education—that is, over who was hired and fired and what was taught. With the superintendent responsible for these matters, accountable only to a small group of wealthy business and professional people, it seems reasonable to assume that the wealthy could veto positions or personnel that they found objectionable. Hence, even if they never intervened directly in the conduct of the schools (and we really have very little evidence about the role they did play; Charters, 1974), their presence in a position of ultimate authority over the superintendent may help to explain the consistent conservatism of school managers that Curti (1935/68) found so remarkable. This assertion does not need to deny the skill and ability of many superintendents to manage and negotiate the situation so as to accomplish their purposes, as Kerr (1973) so interestingly observed. Since the reform business leaders and the new educational executives were generally in agreement, it is not surprising that the objectives of efficiency, differentiation, and control were as likely to be articulated by one group as by another.

The efficiency movement in education received its major impetus from Taylor's new system of industrial management, known as "scientific management" or the "Taylor System" which appeared in 1910 and rapidly captured the imagination of the public, including many school superintendents. Scientific management was management based upon the measurement of time, motion, and money. It sought to determine the one best method for doing a task and to do it in the best possible time, thereby using labor as efficiently as possible. In the popular mind, according to Callahan (1962), it took on almost magical proportions, offering a means of increasing production, raising wages, and lowering prices. Taylorism was associated with the movement for efficiency in education as early as 1911 (Curti, 1935/1968). The efficiency of the schools was to be increased by introducing specialized classes, tests, measurement, and new administrative methods, to reduce the waste, speed up the rate of promotion, and increase the efficiency of the schools. A major contribution to the efficiency of schools was made by Thorndike, who devised objective measurements to determine the efficiency of methods of teaching reading, arithmetic, algebra, writing, and spelling. It is pointless, Thorndike (1912: 289–99, cited in Curti, 1935/1968: 489) wrote, to keep accounts of only time and money expenditures for teachers, books, supplies, buildings, courses of study, and methods of teaching; the credit side, the results achieved, the products of this expensive education, must be measured if we are to know what we are actually getting and where we are going. Education should be put on a more businesslike basis.

The hegemony of business-industrial thought is illustrated in the analogies used by the influential author of *Public School Administration*, Cubberley (1916), writing:

> Our schools are, in a sense, factories in which the raw products (children) are to be shaped and fashioned into products to meet the various demands of life. The specifications for manufacturing come from the demands of the twentieth-century civilization, and it is the business of the school to build its pupils to the specifications laid down. This demands good tools, specialized machinery, continuous measurement of production to see if it is according to specifications, the elimination of waste in manufacture, and a large variety in the output [quoted in Callahan, 1962: 152].

The analogy of the school as a factory captured the imagination of many school administrators at the beginning of the century.

This theme was developed further by George D. Strayer, of Columbia University's Teachers College, who felt that no detail of the administrator's work was too minute to be studied by doctoral candidates. Thus between 1924 and 1930 dissertations were done on such subjects as janitor service in elementary schools, administrative problems of the high-school cafeteria, economy in public-school fire insurance, and public-school plumbing equipment (Callahan, 1962: 187). By striving to improve the efficiency of small aspects of the educational system, this approach completely overlooked the goals of education. For what ends was the system being made more efficient? With so much time and attention being devoted to trivial matters, Nicholas Murray Butler, himself a successful administrator at Columbia University, was led to remark as early as 1915 that there was "some measure of truth in the cynical suggestion that administration may best be defined as the doing extremely well of something that had better not be done at all [quoted in Callahan, 1962: 195]."

While new school administrators were busy learning how to be more efficient, the goals of education and the functions of education in society were perceptibly shifting. Whereas once education prepared for a religious life, increasingly it came to be seen as preparation for work. The active participation by business leaders suggests that the direction of change was not accidental. As we have already seen, business models were taken as guides for how schools should be organized and run. They should be rational and efficient in attaining the ends set by others (either "experts" or "successful men"). They should not be concerned with the ends defined by other participants in the system (whether teachers, pupils, or parents).

As preparation for work and efficiency came to dominate, the schools found themselves in a value bind. The objective of equal education for all, as essential preparation for life in a democracy, began to erode. The attack was based on studies showing the large numbers of school dropouts, "leftbacks" or "overage" students, which were considered indicators of inefficiency. Furthermore, as more and more immigrants arrived in the United States, and the schools proved least effective in keeping, teaching, and promptly promoting their children, demands came for changes in the undifferentiated structure of public education and changes in the prevailing philosophy of equal education for all. The factory model and efficiency criteria were increasingly extended to the selection and training of the human "raw materials" that were to go into industrial production. Thus began the vocational-education and vocational-counseling movements. As Tyack (1974) notes:

> Many of the innovations designed to offer differentiated schooling in the nineteenth century stemmed not so much from career educators as from wealthy philanthropists, merchants, and industrialists. Influential people . . . founded private kindergartens for poor children in cities as far apart as Boston and San Francisco; in a number of cities they privately funded the first public trade schools and commercial high schools, as well as 'industrial schools' for the children of the poor; they supported the first program of vocational guidance [p. 186].

Thus, kindergartens and industrial schools took children off slum streets; commercial or trade schools taught skills which industrialists or merchants wanted; and vocational counselors in settlement houses helped boys and girls find jobs. "In city after city businessmen decided that the regular school curriculum did not provide skills they needed in industry or commerce. They gave large sums to establish special schools. In New York, for example, J. P. Morgan endowed the New York Trades Schools with $500,000 [Tyack, 1974: 189]."

Often these "philanthropies" were subsequently adopted by the public-school system. As Lazerson and Grubb (1974) argue, the vocational-education movement's greatest significance lay not in the numbers of students actually enrolled in it (normally under 10 percent), but in the way it reflected growing concern that "the primary goal of schooling was to prepare youth for the job market [p. 32]."

Cohen (1968) develops the radical significance of industrial education further, arguing that advocates " . . . were calling for the transformation of the school system along industrial lines; for the displacement of the traditional general education by an industrial education; or, if this proved unfeasible, for the establishment of a 'differentiated' system of public education [p. 106]." A vital part of American democratic ideology was the availablity of free quality education for all. Moreover, a common school experience was to be prolonged as late as possible for all children, thus putting off the separation of students according to their future life work (Cohen, 1969).

Contrasting the American system with the European one, Charles W. Eliot, president of Harvard, declared in 1905: "In a democratic society the classification of pupils, according to their so-called probable destinations, should be postponed to the latest possible time of life [quoted in Cohen, 1968: 107]." But within three years, Eliot was advocating trade schools for children "who are unfortunately obliged to leave the regular public school system by the time they are fourteen, or even earlier." Therefore, he said, elementary school teachers ought to assume the responsibility of sorting out the pupils, and "sort them out by their evident or probable destinies [quoted in Cohen, 1968: 107–8]."

In these words, we see an early articulation of what was to become a major function of the schools in industrial America, to sort and classify pupils according to their destinations. Moreover, a society which had previously been portrayed as relatively open and classless was now being depicted in 1908 by Eliot as " . . . divided into layers whose borders blend, whose limits are easily passed by individuals, but which, nevertheless, have distinct characteristics and distinct educational needs [quoted in Tyack, 1974: 129]." By seeking talented children in the lower layers, the school might assist mobility between the layers, but the schools should be reorganized to serve each class "with keen appreciation of the several ends in view [quoted in Tyack, 1974: 129]," that is, to suit the education to the layer being served.

Therefore it is no surprise that a leading educator of school administrators, Cubberly (1909), would advise:

> Our city schools will soon be forced to give up the exceedingly democratic idea that all are equal, and that our society is devoid of classes, as a few cities have already in large part done, and to begin a specialization of educational effort along

many lines in an attempt better to adapt the school to the needs of those many classes in the city life. . . . The new and extensive interest in industrial and vocational training is especially significant of the changing conception of the school and the classes in society which the school is in the future expected to serve [quoted in Cohen, 1968: 108].

In Cubberley's writings we see a new view of how education should be structured, a new recognition of the class structure of society, and a call to abandon the democratic idea of equal education for all.

By the 1920s, Boston's Superintendent of Schools would declare that the public schools "until very recently, have offered equal opportunity for all to receive *one kind* of education, but what will make them democratic is to provide opportunity for all to receive such education as will fit them *equally* well for their life work [quoted in Lazerson, 1971: 189]." But while the concept of equal education for equal participation in democracy was being transformed into the concept of "equal opportunity" for all "within their personal and social capacity," according to the then future Massachusetts Commissioner of Education David Snedden, " . . . equality of opportunity can only be secured by recognition of differences which [while] theoretically individual, may nevertheless, for practical purposes, be regarded as characterizing distinguishable groups of children [quoted in Lazerson, 1971: 200–201]," the unequal rewards of the various positions individuals would fill, and hence the school's role in allocating people to those vastly unequal positions, were apparently of no concern. By World War I, Lazerson finds, Massachusetts schoolmen were increasingly committed to the ideology of categorization and separation. Elementary school children who were "retarded academically," "practical-minded," or came from socioeconomic backgrounds that made continued schooling unlikely were placed in special classes. At the same time, educators began to develop vocational guidance programs. Boston's Superintendent of Schools Brooks felt that people needed more reliable information "showing what vocations are open to children, what conditions prevail in each, and what the rewards of success may be [quoted in Lazerson, 1971: 190–1]."

The initiative for vocational guidance in Boston came from wealthy philanthropists. Vocational guidance emphasized information and job placement, and its guiding motive was how to fit the child to the job. An early director of Boston's Vocation Bureau, Meyer Bloomfield, had a broad social vision of reforming the work place, but when vocational guidance moved from private philanthropy to the public schools "its primary concern became placement in particular educational tracks [Lazerson, 1971: 197]."

When we contrast the ideas that are accepted with those which are ignored, we begin to get a better sense of which groups must have been more influential. Reformers who wanted to alter actual working conditions or expose inadequate conditions were not heeded, while industrial conceptions of increasing the productivity of future industrial workers by selection and special training came to prevail. Indeed, as Lazerson (1971) notes, "vocational guidance, which had initially sought to rationalize educational and career choices, was rapidly losing its commitment to the broader goals of social and industrial reform and was merging with psychological testing and intelligence measurement to categorize students as its predominant concern [p. 198]." For all of these educational changes, we need to separate the stated objectives from the actual consequences, and then ask whose interests were served by what happened.

From Lazerson's study of Boston, we see that curricular differentiation and its attendant, vocational guidance, developed prior to educational testing. Early selections were based upon teacher evaluations and examinations and were highly correlated with ethnic origin and social class. Thus, differences in academic abilities were defined as existing, even before they could be "objectively" measured.

Curricular assignments that were so highly related to ethnic origin or social class, however, had a somewhat illegitimate cast to them, even in the early twentieth century. Therefore, it is not surprising that the fledgling objective-testing movement was so readily embraced by American education, especially urban education, despite its technical difficulties and immaturities. By 1921 the president of the National Association of Directors of Educational Research observed that educators readily adopted the new group intelligence tests as a way to sort children: "Teachers, administrators, and supervisors . . . have received the adaptations of the group intelligence examination to school uses with open arms and all too often with uncritical acceptance of what has been made available [quoted in Tyack, 1974: 207]." The U.S. Army alpha and beta tests had been revised by a group of psychologists who received a grant from the General Education Board. Stanford psychologist Lewis Terman estimated that at least 2 million children had been tested in 1920 to 1921 (Tyack, 1974).

The support of test development by major industrial foundations such as the General Education Board (Chapman, 1972, cited in Tyack, 1974) and the Carnegie Foundation (Karier, 1973) and the rapid acceptance of standardized tests by school personnel illustrate well the convergent interests of several structures of dominance. Industrialists undoubtedly believed that selecting by IQ was a more efficient way of allocating people into the labor market. Moreover, by focusing upon selection into the occupational structure, testing diverts attention away from the structure of ownership, which is not allocated on the basis of merit or IQ. And having selection based upon "scientific criteria" makes the whole process seem considerably more legitimate. By continuing to result in classes segregated largely on the basis of ethnic origin and social class, IQ testing must have pleased many middle-class parents concerned about the heterogeneity of urban public schools. Finally, educators were bolstered in their desire to gain professional stature because their practices were "objective" and scientific. Thus all of the dominant groups in the situation benefited, with only the lower-class and ethnic-minority children being affected adversely.

In large urban school districts, students were grouped and taught according to their class of origin and class of destination (which were very often the same; cf. Counts, 1922). Thus, as Cohen (1968: 105) states, vocational guidance was one mechanism assuring middle-class parents that their children would obtain academic training that prepared them for further education. Another mechanism was the "neighborhood school" concept. The relative homogeneity of many neighborhoods, reinforced by neighborhood schools that tailored their course of study in elementary school to the socioeconomic status of the neighborhood, served to assure parents that their children would receive the appropriate education, as well as associate with the "right" children. Differentiation by neighborhood was noted by William H. Elson, Superintendent of Schools of Cleveland:

> It is obvious that the educational needs of children in a district where the streets are well paved and clean, where the homes are spacious and surrounded by lawns and trees, where the language of the child's playfellows is pure, and where life in general is permeated with the spirit and ideals of America—it is obvious that the educational needs of such a child are radically different from those of the child who lives in a foreign and tenement section [quoted in Cohen, 1968: 106].

In this statement there is a clear indication of the desire to differentiate education on the basis of ethnic and economic position. Educators like Elson saw their role as mirroring the relative positions of groups in society. They illustrate the taken-for-granted nature of stratification in American society. This concept came to fruition in the latter-day suburban enclaves (which are discussed below).

Today the school systems of older, larger, and more heterogeneous suburbs and cities lack both political and economic resources. The large urban school systems have become highly centralized. School-board members are generally elected on a citywide basis, and they have little knowledge about or power over the daily operations of the system. Professional educators are even more strongly established than in suburban systems, often buttressed by bureaucratic procedures and by unionization of teachers and administrators. School-board members are often "concerned members of the community" who send their own children to private schools. The system has been described by at least one observer (Rogers, 1968) as one of organizational paralysis, rather than governance.

Economically, the large city school systems are equally powerless. Their shrinking tax bases make them dependent upon nonlocal sources (state and federal monies) to balance their budgets. Moreover, the property tax base of American public education results in vastly unequal resources for urban, suburban, and rural schools, and for major regional variations in educational expenditures.

The community-control movement in a number of large American cities in the 1960s was addressed to the inert governance structure. While economic issues have been debated, no sweeping reforms have been effected.

Private Boarding Schools[4]

In marked contrast to urban schools, private boarding schools are formally governed by self-perpetuating boards of trustees, representing dominant-class interests, religious interests, and perhaps educational interests. Considerable authority over daily activities is delegated to headmasters, who in both Great Britain and the United States have often been very strong, and long-lived, leaders. The trustees are responsible for investing the endowment of the institution and for raising more money if needed. Thus both political and economic control rests in the hands of relatively few, generally similar trustees who have similar class backgrounds. Kinship ties between trustees and students are strong (cf. McLachlan, 1970).

As secondary schools were being infused with the "common school" ideology, a number of new private boarding schools emerged in America. Early examples were Round Hill (founded in 1823) and the Flushing Institute (founded in 1828), but the big growth period was from 1880 to 1906. During this time, Phillips Exeter, Lawrenceville, Groton, Taft, Hotchkiss, Choate, St. George's, Middlesex, Deerfield, and Kent were either founded or reorganized. As McLachlan (1970: 195) notes, a number of factors contributed to the rapid rise of boarding schools. American higher education was changing at that point, and the first American universities were emerging. Prior to that, even Harvard and Yale had been little more than advanced secondary schools, and students still had to go to Europe for university training. In addition, the enormous influx of immigrants during this period made the cities even more crowded and heterogeneous than they had been earlier. The well off and well educated were often distressed by the diverse student body and the egalitarian social goals of contemporary education, as well as by the low academic standards and educational ineffectiveness of local schools. The emerging professionalization of teaching and the growing educational bureaucracies were apparently perceived by many wealthy parents as unresponsive to their interests. It is not surprising, in light of these developments, that Adams' (1903) survey of family boarding schools[5] stated that they were

---

[4]Private day schools are not discussed here, in part because they vary considerably in their goals, exclusivity, selectivity, and costs. Most have the general objective of providing academic education and they tend to segregate students according to certain shared characteristics such as wealth, occupational background, religion, aspirations, and race.

[5]Family boarding schools refers to the atmosphere schools claimed to create. Ostensibly the headmaster and his wife treated the boys as though they were part of a large family.

being founded partly because of parents' feelings that " . . . in certain localities the companions of the boy in all but the higher grades of day school are, from their nationality, objectionable personal habits, or what not, undesirable [quoted in McLachlan, 1970: 214]."

Many of the family boarding schools were founded by the leaders of early Yankee society, such as Endicott Peabody, of a Boston banking family. Despite their "old money" ties, the founders realized that most of their students were sons of "new money" merchants and manufacturers. Thus, Muhlenberg (the founder of the Flushing Institute) could write in 1828 that " . . . we want intelligent merchants and manufacturers as well as lawyers and doctors, sensible and pious laymen, as well as learned and orthodox clergy-men. To furnish these, education must be loosed from the trammels of the monastery, and be girded as a handmaid to the practical spirit of the age [quoted in McLachlan, 1970: 128]." Indeed, a consequence of these boarding schools may have been the creation of a common culture, shared by old and new wealth owners alike. The new fortunes dwarfed the old ones, but the new rich were not considered gentlemen by the older groups.

Given that the stated purpose of many of these schools (nowhere more apparent than in the influential St. Paul's School) was to produce Christian gentlemen and scholars, it is no surprise that the new fortune makers sent their sons to such schools. "The family boarding school was well established among the rich of antebellum America [McLachlan, 1970: 212]." The growth of girls' finishing schools with some social connection with the boys' boarding schools furthered the integration of old and new wealth so that by the 1870s, observes McLachlan, there was a kinship network of families from Georgia to Maine, New York to San Francisco. While educational leaders of the time expressed some ambivalence about educating only the sons of the rich, mostly they reconciled themselves to the task.

With this brief view of the historical and social function of private board-ing schools, what can we say about the structure and nature of the institution itself? To begin with, the schools were socially and spatially isolated, insu-lated from the rest of society. Virtually all were in the countryside. Even the Flushing Institute was in the then rural meadowlands of Jamaica. Most of the others were in small towns or were established on the country estates of wealthy donors. Only Phillips Exeter was part of the town of Exeter, with students boarding in homes in the community, and when the town grew more industrial and began to lose the small-town community bonds and control it had previously exercised, the school erected its own buildings and estab-lished social distance between its students and the town (cf. McLachlan, 1970). Indeed, the bucolic atmosphere was one of the boarding school's appeals to parents. Not only was it more healthy physically than disease-infested cities, but it was thought to be more pure morally—a place where innocence and virtue could be maintained longer, away from the temptations and corruptions of city life. Isolation served to protect the boys from the undesirable companions they might encounter in the diversified cities.

The physical isolation of the schools facilitated their becoming total institutions, since relatively few distractions were available (cf. Wheeler, 1966). The policies of the school also contributed to its nature as a total institution. A distinctive feature of Round Hill, the Flushing Institute, and St. Paul's was the way in which they controlled the *time* of students enrolled there (McLachlan, 1970: 87, 126, 168). Almost every minute of every day had a planned activity, usually to be done in the company of others. Thus, the school could and did know what every boy was doing virtually all of the time. This was one device used by headmasters to keep boys out of trouble. A number of schools also required students to wear uniforms. While this practice was defended on egalitarian grounds—it prevented boys from sartorial competition—the adoption of uniforms also meant that boys would be recognized if they were off limits (like in town) or misbehaving.

The boarding schools also had a distinctive authority system. Early founders, such as Muhlenberg, saw the authority of the school as based upon the principle of parental kindness rather than coercion. Early schools were small and contact between boys, teachers, and headmaster was very close. The early headmasters knew all of the boys well; tutors and headmaster played sports together and spent a great deal of time together outside of class and chapel services. The successful early headmasters are described as strong personal leaders. Hence we can characterize the form of authority as personal and charismatic rather than bureaucratic. One indication of this might be the collapse of three early schools, Round Hill, Flushing Institute, and St. James, shortly after their first headmasters left. Even today, the headmaster is the most powerful person in the situation (Baird, 1976).

The teachers too were selected for their personal qualities as well as for their scholarship. In 1893 a team of evaluators from Harvard came to St. Paul's School, and noted that the " . . . masters are distinctly above the average of secondary-school teachers in personal qualities. They have the characteristics of leaders of boys [quoted in McLachlan, 1970: 279–80]." Just as the school was a total institution for the boys, it was a nearly total institution for the instructors as well. Not surprisingly, in 1916, an observer at St. Paul's concluded, "the masters have too heavy a program." It is not that their duties in themselves were particularly taxing; it was the fact that "a master can rarely let down completely and be away from his charges [that] entails a nervous strain [quoted in McLachlan, 1970: 279]." Then, as now, many of the faculty were themselves alumni (cf. McLachlan, 1970, and Baird, 1976).

Close faculty–student relationships and low student–faculty ratios permitted a highly personal educational experience. Often, classes were sessions with private tutors. In 1894 Andover and Exeter had a student–faculty ratio of 13:1, while St. Paul's was 8.5:1 (McLachlan, 1970).

Although the term "mastery learning" did not exist in the nineteenth century, I was struck when reading about the educational program at Round Hill by how much it sounded like Bloom's (1971) concept of mastery learning:[6]

> No classes were formed; instead, each student was assigned a book which the instructor thought equal to his knowledge. The student was allowed to prepare as much material as he wished and was expected to report to the teacher whenever he felt ready to recite. When he was ready, he was questioned closely by the teacher; if he failed, he was sent back to continue until he had mastered the lesson [McLachlan, 1970: 84].

Here we see evidence of a pedagogy based upon individualized instruction and mastery of the material studied.

Another very critical element was the absence of competition with other students. "The advantage of . . . [Round Hill's] system," Bassett has suggested, "was that no boy studied with reference to the progress of another boy [i.e., no emulation], and while he was allowed full opportunity to learn all that his interest prompted him to learn he came to esteem excellence in his studies for its own value [quoted in McLachlan, 1970: 84]." The goal, then, was the development of individual talents to the fullest, with no desire to differentiate the boys. At the Flushing Institute, Muhlenberg felt that competition or emulation was particularly hard on the average boys and disrupted the familial, organic social order he was trying to create at the school [McLachlan, 1970: 84, 126–7, 172]. McLachlan sees Muhlenberg's condemnation of emulation as a response to the strenuous competition and social disintegration which characterized Jacksonian America. Although coded ranks in class were sent to students and parents monthly, Muhlenberg felt that students should study what they were good at, rather than impose the same traditional program on all children. "Why," Muhlenberg asked, "should a boy grow double over the conjugation of verbs, to which neither argument nor punishment can compel his attention, and then be dismissed as a block-head; when, had he been directed to some department of natural science, to the arts, or even to practical mechanics, he might have won the distinction of a lad of talent [quoted in McLachlan, 1970: 127]."

Thus were the sons of the rich protected from the personal or social consequences of failure (cf. Goode, 1967, on the "protection of the inept"). Boys were dismissed from boarding school for misbehavior, but not, that I

---

[6]Drawing upon the work of Carroll (1963), Bloom (1971) uses the term "mastery learning" to mean attainment of a predetermined level of competence in a given subject matter. Thus, the task of instructors is to define what they mean by mastery of a subject and to discover methods and materials to help the largest possible proportion of students reach it. Bloom believes that most students (about 90 percent) can master what they are taught (1971). He suggests that students with different aptitudes will need to have the kind and quality of instruction and learning time allowed be made appropriate to their individual characteristics and needs.

know of, for slowness. One wonders, but finds little evidence, whether certain boarding schools still serve to protect the sons and daughters of the wealthy from competition with social "underlings."

Historically, boarding schools had two curricula—a college-preparatory study of the classics, mathematics, natural science, modern languages, and literature, with some schools (like Exeter) also having a "terminal" or English course, designed to discharge pupils immediately into the business world. With the growth of universities in America, the curriculum changed entirely to college preparation, its content largely influenced by what colleges and universities wanted. Thus, as the public high schools were diversifying their curricula, the boarding schools' curricula became more homogeneous. By 1916, all the boarding schools had two major objectives: to prepare their students for entrance to college, and to build character (McLachlan, 1970). The son of a St. Paul's headmaster described the schools as "self-sufficient and insular communities, providing for [their] rather narrow clientele just what was expected—a conservative, gentlemanly preparation of body and mind for the Ivy League colleges and for support of the economic, political and religious status quo [quoted in McLachlan, 1970: 217]." To this view McLachlan (1970) adds:

> The family boarding schools of the 1880s and 1890s were founded in response to many motives, and would be shaped by a complex of often conflicting ideological and social traditions and pressures: among others, by a reaction against the rigidity of the emerging urban school bureaucracies, by the admission standards of the new universities, by the needs and aspirations of the urban and suburban rich, by much the same Victorian notions of childhood innocence and isolation as had molded St. Paul's and St. Mark's, and, not the least, by many parents' undefined hope that they provided the "best" education available for their sons [p. 217].

To this many-faceted interpretation, Baltzell (1958) adds that the growth of "national" boarding schools paralleled the rise of the national corporation. Thus, the shift from local academies to national prep schools reflected the move away from regionally isolated economic elites toward the development of a national elite based upon large national (later international) corporations.

In the early years, very few graduates of boarding schools went into politics or government service. By the Progressive era, however, Theodore Roosevelt, and his friend Endicott Peabody of Groton, were urging students to enter public service. The rise of government regulation of industry, the growth of international business, and the rise of imperialism may have been related to this enhanced interest in public service. As McLachlan (1970) notes, "Politically, the ideal product of Christian nurture was the nineteenth-century liberal, while the ideal product of Progressive nurture would be the twentieth-century social democrat [p. 291]." At home, social discord would be handled with Progressive social reforms, under the guiding hand of boarding school patricians, while abroad, foreign affairs were increasingly directed by old boys from the playing fields of Groton.

To summarize, the emergent structure of boarding schools can be seen as one based upon the personal, charismatic authority of the headmaster, close personal social relations between tutors and boys, and relatively egalitarian conditions among the boys. The curriculum was traditional and college preparatory, and teachers stressed individual development of competence and mastery. The schools were total institutions, demanding both instrumental and affective conformity.

In keeping with its nature as a total institution, even the contemporary boarding school has both academic and personal goals for its students, and it is open about its noncognitive aims: "character development," "leadership," and "social responsibility." To accomplish these aims, it continues to sequester students, although many schools have become coeducational. Schools and classes are small, facilitating close personal relationships between staff and students and among peers.

These are the stated goals of the preparatory schools, and their stated ways of achieving them. What actually happens in practice is very hard to discern. While numerous sociological studies exist dealing with British public (boarding) schools (e.g., Bamford, 1967; Kalton, 1966; Wakeford, 1969; Weinberg, 1967; Wilkinson, 1964), I am unable to find studies of contemporary American boarding schools. On the basis of available information, the formal and informal structure of the private boarding schools appears to be dramatically different from that of the large, urban bureaucratic educational system attended by so many lower-income and minority students.

Suburban Schools

There is every reason to believe that, as are the boarding schools, upper-middle-class suburban schools are quite different from urban schools in their governance, economics, structure, and interactions. As cities grew and the more well-to-do gradually pushed their way to the outer rings and then into newly developing suburbs, these residential patterns were reflected in educational structures. The concept of the neighborhood school meant that as new residential areas grew, residents could form their own schools, geared to their own values and objectives.

Upper-middle-class suburban school systems are formally governed by locally elected school boards. How much formal power they have in relation to the highly professionalized school administrators usually hired to run suburban systems is called into question by Kerr's (1973) study of how new school-board members are coopted by old members and the superintendent. Whatever their real power, the boards tend to give parents the feeling that they have some control over the nature of the school attended by their children. The board and the superintendent make up the school budget.

The resources available depend upon local taxing power and the tax base. The largest source of income for schools is local property taxes, which differentiates sharply among districts with varied real-estate values (Wise, 1967). States also vary with respect to the amount of aid they provide to schools. Federal monies for education are limited to "federally impacted" regions employing large numbers of federal employees or, more recently, to schools with a certain proportion of low-income students. Suburban school districts have the option of proposing bond issues to raise money for capital improvements in school facilities. These are subject to referendum and are one of the few taxes that voters have the chance to veto directly. Thus, while economic control is subject to a number of strictures, suburban parents, who share a common interest in providing a "good education" for their children (though they may differ about what that is), may feel they have some control over the economic resources available.

Parents in such suburban schools are generally quite abreast of "current" practices in education and expect their schools to be following the most "modern" practices. As a result, suburban schools have tended to follow more strongly the current winds of innovation, from Progressivism in the 1930s, "excellence" in the 1950s, to the "open classroom" of the 1970s (cf. Litwak and Meyer, 1973). Practices in upper-middle-class suburban schools probably reflect the contemporary mood in education more closely than do practices in most large urban schools. If this is the case, it may be because authority in suburban schools tends to be based more upon "professional" than bureaucratic criteria. Thus position is based upon expertise, one feature of which is keeping current.

Some people have suggested that the vulnerability of school officials, especially in such suburban districts, results in demands for "relevance" that become almost faddish. Innovations are demanded even before they have been fully tested out (Sieber, no date). Such school systems pride themselves on getting the best-trained teachers and on paying them better than do surrounding districts. Even within city school systems, the teachers working in predominantly white, middle-class schools are sometimes paid more than those in mainly black lower-class schools (Hobson v. Hansen, 1967).[7]

By rewarding teachers better, suburban school districts can look for the best people available and expect a lot from them. Just as private-school parents seem to hold the attitude, "We're paying a lot of money, and we

---

[7]This is still true today in many large cities, largely due to the practice of relating teachers' salaries to their education and experience and to the relatively smaller number of experienced and highly educated teachers in ghetto schools (cf. Ritterband, 1973).

expect you to teach our children," suburban parents may feel that if teachers are well paid results can be expected.[8] In city schools these dynamics are less accessible to parents.

The structural feature of tracking may well vary in upper middle-class suburban schools and urban schools. Tracking has been well defined in an excellent book by Rosenbaum (1976), who sees it as "any school selection system that attempts to homogenize classroom placements in terms of students' personal qualities, performances, or aspirations. Thus tracking is a general term that includes both ability grouping and curriculum grouping and emphasizes their social similarities [p. 6]." In suburban upper-middle-class schools, track placement may affect which college one attends (cf. Cicourel and Kitsuse, 1963), whereas in urban lower-middle-class and working-class schools track placement will influence whether one has a chance for college or not (Rosenbaum, 1976).

The recent survey by Findley and Bryan (1971a) of tracking around the United States suggests that it is more prevalent in districts with larger school populations, which means mostly urban districts. In the three districts with more than 500,000 children, all reported using tracking, and of the 17 districts with from 100,000 to 500,000 children, 88 percent reported using tracking in some or all of the schools in the district. Among smaller districts (under 100,000 students) the proportion using tracking ranged from 91 to 74 percent.

These contemporary findings are consistent with the historical ones reported by the U.S. Bureau of Education. In 1926, 37 out of 40 cities with populations of more than 100,000 used tracking, and in 1932, three-fourths of the 150 largest cities followed the practice (Tyack, 1974: 208). Neither of these studies compared suburban and urban schools with respect to tracking.

Despite such structural differences, suburban schools may share some of the experiential characteristics of urban schools. Jackson (1968) finds upper-middle-class schools to be characterized by crowds, evaluation, and unequal power between teacher and child. Because of crowding, much of the pupil's time is spent waiting, denying desire, facing petty interruptions, and trying to resist social distractions. Hence Jackson feels the quintessence of virtue in most such institutions is *patience*. Evaluation comes primarily from the teacher, although some use is made of peer and self-evaluations as well. The evaluation may be communicated secretly, privately, or publicly. What gets evaluated varies somewhat from teacher to teacher, but Jackson writes that attainment of educational objectives, student adjustment to institutional expectations, and possession of certain character traits (like motivation), are important.

[8]While national statistics on private-school teachers' salaries are not available, it is my impression that they are considerably lower than those of public school teachers. The difference may be that parents hold teachers accountable in the suburbs, while they rest responsibility upon the entire school when they are paying tuition for a private education.

Jackson interestingly analyzes how power and authority were used in the classes he observed. Unlike the parent, the teacher is a relative stranger to the child. While the parent's authority over elementary aged children is more restrictive than prescriptive, the teacher's authority is both restrictive and prescriptive (do this, do that). Teachers require the attention of pupils and very often want to substitute their plans for the students' agenda. One of the forms this takes is the distinction between work and play. A good deal of the pupils' task in the early years of school is to adjust to their first "boss." This process is vividly portrayed by Gracey (1972) in "Kindergarten as Academic Boot Camp." Beginning her analysis at an even earlier part of the educational process, Kanter (1972) examines the total experience provided by one upper-middle-class nursery school, which, she argues, is based upon principles that are quite congruent with life in modern bureaucratic organizations.

Looking at the higher grades, critics of education (e.g., Silberman, 1970) have deplored the competitive, mindless, joyless, stifling atmospheres of American schools, apparently including the suburban schools in their attack. While all American public education stresses individual competition, the suburban schools may show it to the greatest extent, insofar as the parents and children feel that the child's status must be earned through individual achievement, independently of the parents' position. To the degree that the parents' position is nontransferable, we would expect both parents and children to feel pressure for achievement.[9]

In brief, upper-middle-class suburban schools seem to be less bureaucratic and more politically and economically responsive to parents, making such schools more likely to implement educational innovations.

Conclusions

In the past 150 years, American education has changed its goal of preparing to live a religious life to preparation for work. As the concept of education changed, so did forms of educational organizations. But these changes were not universally supported. Certain groups tended to favor certain ideas, while others had competing visions. Thus, compulsory education expanded, under the leadership of Yankee brahmins and new educational leaders, despite resistance from farmers, workers and ethnic minorities. Differentiated curricula and vocational education triumphed in a way that was

[9]How this pressure is handled varies. It may lead to greater effort and competition, or it may lead to withdrawal, as one of my students observed in a participant-observation study of an upper-middle-class New York suburb. Many of the children of highly successful professional parents were anxious that they could not attain the same level of success as their parents, and one reaction observed was the abdication of desire to achieve and compete. This does not mean, of course, that everyone who rejects the upper-middle-class view of success is an unsuccessful competitor.

efficient for industrialists, despite the existence of some participants hoping to reform the work place. Gradually the concept of equality in education, originally conceived of as equal education for all, was redefined as equal opportunity. While the "Common School Ideology" of one education for all flourished and sustained the expansion of compulsory education, private boarding schools were being founded at an unprecedented rate. Consequently, American education consists of different types of aggregates, with different histories, forms of governance, economic support, authority relations, classmates, interactions, and curriculum.

In sum, the structure of dominance influenced the broad direction of educational changes. Different types of educational experiences emerged. These structural differences may contribute in major ways to the educational processes and results which occur in America. They are highly related to prevailing educational concepts and assumptions.

5

Educational Assumptions

MANY EDUCATIONAL CONCEPTS could be examined to see if they are related to the structure of dominance, but in this chapter we consider only two: IQ and "cultural deprivation." These two are selected, first, because they dominate explanations of differential school achievement. Considerable behavioral and social-science research and debate has centered around them, and they largely set the terms in which questions are posed. Their implications are not confined to academic debates, however. As we demonstrate in subsequent chapters, they significantly influence educational practices and processes, pervading almost every school in the United States. They are central to both educational explanations and experiences. Therefore, if it is possible to see even a shadow of influence between the structure of dominance and these concepts, the model advanced here gains plausibility.

Excellent historical studies demonstrating the role of corporate capital (primarily through industrial foundations) in the growth of IQ and other forms of testing have been conducted by Karier (1973) and Chapman (cited in Tyack, 1974). They illuminate how the three most significant developments in the use of testing in American society were all generously supported by such foundations: (1) the spread of aptitude testing nationwide in the 1920s; (2) the consolidation of numerous college testing units into the Educational Testing Service in 1947; and (3) the national assessment of educational progress, a national program of educational evaluation. The transfer of Army's alpha and beta tests to American schools was underwritten by a grant from the General Education Board of the Rockefeller Foundation after World War I (Chapman, cited in Tyack, 1974: 207). Test specialist Edward L. Thorndike received about $325,000 from the Carnegie Foundation between 1922 and 1938 to work on a variey of aptitude and achievement tests (Karier, 1973: 123). Following such "seed money" as this, test publishers found the development of IQ tests sufficiently profitable to do it themselves.

In 1946–47 the Carnegie Foundation for the Advancement of Teaching recommended consolidation of a number of testing units into one. Thus began the Educational Testing Service (ETS), launched with a grant from the Carnegie Corporation.[1] Tests from ETS now screen applicants to many selective colleges, universities, and professional and graduate schools.

Most recently, the Carnegie and Danforth Foundations initiated a national testing program in 1965, called "A National Assessment of Educational Progress," to measure the "progress" of American schools, under the direction of Francis Keppel, John Gardner, and James B. Conant (Karier, 1973: 133). The two foundations provided $300,000 of a $318,000 budget (Raubinger and Hand, 1967, cited in Karier, 1973: 133). The national assessment developed a "Compact of the States" to oversee the program, which "provided the 'quasi-public' vehicles through which national testing could proceed without too much public interference [Karier, 1973: 133]." Thus, major foundations initiated the growth of national mechanisms for testing IQ, aptitude, and achievement. Whether or not this was justified depends, at least in part, upon the validity of those tests themselves, and their consequences.

These correspondences between large foundations and the spread of testing are well documented. In addition, the historical relationship between the old American desire for ethnic dominance and the rise and decline of interest in genetic explanations of intelligence has been demonstrated by Kamin (1974), who documents the role played by testing and the eugenics movement in restricting immigration to the United States beginning in 1924. (In contrast with the thrust of this analysis, Kamin does not really consider how economic interests may have benefited by restricting the influx of "radical" or "socialist" Eastern European immigrants.)

Given this extremely interesting and important work on the emergence of testing, I have chosen here to focus upon the educational concepts of IQ and "cultural deprivation," both of which are intimately related to educational testing. After reviewing the evidence adduced in support of these concepts, I consider whether the widespread beliefs and practices based upon them are warranted.

Intelligence Quotient

Challenges to the concept of IQ have been based upon test content, test procedures and practices, and the claimed heritability of intelligence. Gen-

---

[1]Schudson's (1972) fascinating study of the growth of the College Entrance Examination Board (now combined with ETS) completely ignores the role of corporate wealth in stimulating the CEEB's development. He places the locus of causality on the elite Eastern colleges. We need not deny their interest in the growth of the CEEB to note that its expansion was also perceived as important by industrial foundations.

erally unchallenged is the central premise of IQ testing, namely the assumption that early selection and differentiation are necessary and desirable. But the necessity for selection rests upon several unresolved questions. To what extent are selection and differentiation necessary to develop talent and skill? Who decides what kinds of talents, skills, and social characteristics should be identified and developed? To what extent should the primary goal of education be selection with the purpose of allocation to economic positions? These are issues of public policy that should be publicly debated and decided. Many would argue that this happens. I would disagree, feeling that while these issues are debated in the normative realm, in the sphere of decision making they are not. People discuss what should be, but have little real influence over what is. For example, while the merits of selection by means of standardized tests are continually debated, in practice most children take a number of such tests which play some (perhaps major) role in determining the educational experiences they encounter.

As selection mechanisms, IQ tests are used to justify variations in education, achievement, and rewards, on the basis of individual differences. The rationale is that since some people are more "intelligent" than others, they are entitled to more of other things as well. (This is a moral assertion, which was rationalized by Thorndike's (1920) famous maxim that people who are more intelligent are also more virtuous.)

But IQ tests are designed to *differentiate* people, that is, to measure only their differences. Another kind of test could be developed to stress similarities, thus justifying the similar treatment of all children (or all but discernably brain-damaged children), but this alternative was either not proposed by test advocates or was proposed but not supported by major industrial foundations.

Exactly how are tests designed to differentiate people? The psychometric principles used to develop individual aptitude or achievement tests require that items answered correctly by all sampled respondents be dropped from the test. Thus, in the development of such a test, about 60 percent of the items initially proposed will be answered correctly by all respondents, but these will be discarded from the final test because they do not discriminate among individuals. This may happen even if those rejected items represent the best possible measure of achievement or aptitude (Carver, 1975: 79). Clearly the requirement for differentiation is so deeply embedded in our educational system that it is built into the structure of tests themselves. Then, when differential performances result from this type of test (as they must if the subjects sampled during test development in any way resemble the ones subsequently tested), that differential performance is used to justify selection. Noting the circular reasoning involved in this justification does not mean that we deny the existence of individual differences. They undoubtedly exist. But what we do with those differences, how we stress and enhance them, use them as the basis for differential curricula and rewards—these are the interesting questions.

So far we have identified three core assumptions underlying the concept of intelligence and the practice of IQ testing:

1. Efficiency is highly desirable.
2. Selection of talent and skill in elementary or secondary school is necessary for efficiency.
3. IQ and other standardized tests measure talent and skill.

Most critics of IQ and other forms of standardized testing accept the first two of these premises and begin their challenge on either or both of the following grounds: (1) IQ testing selects the wrong talents and skills; and (2) testing is inefficient, that is, too much talent is lost, either because of failure to measure creative thinking or failure to identify "late bloomers," or because of problems of cultural bias in the content, norming populations, and administration of tests. It may also be inefficient because of the negative consequences it has for the people who are mislabeled as a result of any of the above problems. If testing is considered to measure something innate, it may be inefficient because it labels certain individuals hopeless (not responsive to any serious educational efforts); consequently no efforts will be made.

A number of critics have suggested that IQ tests do not measure important features of intelligence, such as creative or divergent thinking, logic, critical reasoning, and so on. In fact, some have gone so far as to suggest that the tests measure conformity to prevailing cultural values more than they measure "intelligence."

An additional question concerns the predictive validity of tests for grades in school and for success in jobs. In reviewing the evidence, David McClelland (1974) notes that IQ and aptitude-test scores are correlated with school and college grades—not surprisingly, since they are often similar kinds of tests. Binet, in fact, took some of his original test items from exercises teachers used in French schools (McClelland, 1974: 165). But the real question, as McClelland suggests, is how valid the grades are as predictors. McClelland's own small study found no correlation between grades and success in life. More extensive work by Hoyt (1965), who reviewed 46 studies relating college grades to success in many different occupations; Berg (1970), who reviewed studies of factory workers, bank tellers, and air-traffic controllers; Taylor, Smith and Ghiselin (1963), who studied scientific researchers; and studies by Cohen (1970), Collins (1974), Gintis (1971a), and Holtzman (1971) find little relationship between educational achievement or attainment and performance in a variety of blue- and white-collar jobs. None of these studies demonstrates a relationship between grades and work performance.

But perhaps IQ scores are correlated with job performance or income even if grades are not. In 1959 Thorndike and Hagen correlated the aptitude test scores of more than 10,000 respondents with their occupational success (12,000 correlations altogether). The number of significant relationships did not exceed what would have been expected by chance. Holland and Richards (1965) and Elton and Shevel (1969) found no consistent relationships between college student aptitude-test scores and the actual accomplishments of students in social leadership. Ghiselli (1966) did find that intelligence tests were correlated with trainability and proficiency, but he failed to control for social-class background, which is also related to IQ (McClelland, 1974: 168–70).

Bowles and Gintis (1973) confirm what Bajema reported in 1968, namely that IQ is unrelated to attained socioeconomic status, when original social class and number of years of schooling are held constant. Further, Jencks et al. (1972) found that IQ explained only a very small portion of the variance in income when education and occupational status were similar.

In brief, considerable evidence refutes the predictive validity of IQ or aptitude testing. McClelland (1974) notes that many of these same points were made in 1958 by the Social Science Research Council Committee on Early Identification of Talent (McClelland et al., 1958), but they have been virtually ignored for almost 20 years.

To deal with these problems, McClelland calls for criterion-referenced tests. By this he means tests that measure competence on job-relevant skills. To do this, performance must be analyzed into its important components, and then test items designed to measure those behaviors (McClelland, 1974: 179–80). Such tests should be static over time, but should reflect increased learning. How one can improve on the characteristics tested should be made public and explicit, says McClelland. He offers other suggestions as well.

What is particularly interesting is the way McClelland's quite reasonable suggestions have been ignored. These ideas were first presented at an Educational Testing Service conference, but ETS test practices have not changed. As McClelland himself is aware, his tests are likely to reflect growth over time; therefore they are less justifiable as a method of selection. This may be a method for selecting very competent people for doing particular jobs (assuming the criteria are carefully selected), but it is hardly a method designed to exclude people from jobs or for justifying large inequalities between jobs. If nearly everyone can acquire the skills needed for doing certain high-paying and prestigious jobs, how can gross inequalities of status and income be justified? Do these issues lie behind the selection of certain kinds of tests rather than others?

Others have concurred that present practices of IQ testing run the risk of being inefficient for the society. This criticism has been leveled from both an "efficient manpower allocation" perspective and from a social-justice view. Discussing the emergence of the new curriculum in the physical sciences, Bruner (1960) hinted at the dangers of a meritocracy based upon standardized national examinations: "The late bloomer, the early rebel, the child from an educationally indifferent home—all of them, in a full scale meritocracy, become victims of an often senseless irreversibility of decision [p. 77]." Thus, too early, or too decisive a selection procedure would be inefficient and might eliminate someone who could contribute importantly to science. As Spring (1976) notes in this regard, the "meritocracy was feared because it might result in a wastage of talent and not because of its potential elitism [p. 136]."

More extensive criticisms of testing have been leveled by those charging that the tests are culturally biased and discriminate against ethnic minorities or lower-class students. These arguments focus upon test content, procedures, and consequences.

IQ or scholastic-aptitude tests measure verbal and reasoning skills. They essentially require mastery of "standard" American English and grammar. They are designed to test present facility in verbal and sometimes nonverbal skills, and, from that, to infer a student's capability for future learning. As well summarized in Hobson v. Hansen (1967),

> . . . the inference is expressed in the form of a test score which is a statement of how the individual student compares with the [mean] score of the norming group. The [mean] reflects an average ability to learn, a score above or below that average indicating superior or inferior ability. A crucial assumption in this comparative statement, however, is that the individual is fairly comparable with the norming group in terms of environmental background and psychological makeup; to the extent the individual is not comparable, the test score may reflect those differences rather than innate differences [p. 16750].

To demonstrate his presumed future ability to learn, a student must have had the opportunity to learn those skills relied upon for prediction (Hobson v. Hansen, 1967: 16748). Most particularly, the student needs to have learned white American English. The importance of this skill for one's IQ score is apparent on the individual version of the Wechsler Preschool–Primary Scale of Intelligence (WPPSI). One section of that test requires the child to repeat sentences verbatim to the examiner. A test written in one language may be taken by students who grow up speaking a different dialect of that language. Such children, who prove quite skilled at rendering a simultaneous translation of the sentence read by the examiner, are heavily penalized for not repeating the sentence *exactly*. They have demonstrated a far more difficult skill than rote memory by showing that they both understand the meaning of the statement and can rephrase it immediately in their own dialect, but this skill is a handicap rather than an advantage in the test scoring.

Even the nonverbal components of the test may be viewed as designed in ways that work to the relative advantage of children coming from certain kinds of homes. For instance, again in the WPPSI, children are given small blocks to stack, and shapes to replace in a board. Many middle-class homes have such educational toys around for children to play with, while many lower-class homes cannot afford them, but the children may be able to differentiate a number of keys that look very much alike, or may be able to do other tasks that demonstrate the same underlying skill. In short, even nonverbal test items may be culturally loaded.

Efforts have been made to develop test materials that are "culture free" or less "culturally loaded," but the results so far are generally disappointing according to Findley and Bryan (1970c), and Samuda (1975), and I concur.

Most IQ and scholastic aptitude tests used in schools are nationally standardized on white middle-class populations. The serious limitation of tests normed only on whites was perceived by Wechsler (1944), the creator of the Wechsler Intelligence Scale for Children (WISC):

> We have eliminated the colored [versus] white factor by admitting at the outset that our norms cannot be used for the colored population of the United States. Though we have tested a large number of colored persons, our standardization is based upon white subjects only. We omitted the colored population from our first standardization because we did not feel that norms derived by mixing the populations could be interpreted without special provisions and reservations [p. 107].

The greatest validity in test results is found when the tested student closely resembles the typical norming student, who is white and middle-class. Average white middle-class students may be assumed to have had the same opportunities to develop verbal and nonverbal skills as their peers. Under that assumption, the national mean or norm could be seen as an accurate summary of what the average American student

> . . . ought to have learned in the way of verbal and nonverbal skills by a certain age and what can therefore be considered average intelligence or ability to learn. For this reason, standard aptitude tests are most precise and accurate in their measurements of innate ability when given to white middle class students. When standard aptitude tests are given to low income Negro children, or disadvantaged children, however, the tests are less precise and less accurate—so much so that test scores become practically meaningless [Hobson v. Hansen, 1967: 16750].

Vivid documentation of the inaccuracy of standard tests is revealed in a study conducted at Lorton Youth Center, a penal institution in the District of Columbia. Students there working for a high-school equivalency diploma were tested before and after instruction. Ninety percent of the students were school dropouts; 95 percent were black. On the Otis test (a verbal test used in a number of school systems), their average score was 78, substantially below normal. After a year of instruction, however, the average gain for students (as measured by the Stanford Achievement Test) was 1.3 years in reading, and 1.8 in arithmetic, better than normal.

"This study reveals in hard fact that a disadvantaged Negro student with a supposedly low IQ can, given the opportunity, far surpass what might be expected of a truly subnormal student [Hobson v. Hansen, 1967: 16751]." It illustrates how a standardized IQ test can be a faulty predictor of actual achievement for disadvantaged students, and suggests that such tests may be inappropriate for inferring a student's academic ability.

While the problem of inappropriate standardization can be handled by restandardizing scores according to performances in a particular school, in practice it is unlikely that very many school districts are able or willing to do this. Moreover, even a restandardized score does not deal with inappropriate test questions. Another method of improving the predictive validity of a given test is to do a follow-up study of a group of students to ascertain the correlation between actual scholastic achievement and test scores. To prevent contamination, this would require that track placements not be based on the score and that teachers not be informed of the scores. Such a validity study is even more difficult for schools to do.

In an original approach to educational testing, Roth (1974) suggests an additional sociological meaning to the term "standardization." Unlike the psychometric standardization of aptitude tests noted above, in which the individual subject's performance is scored in reference to the mean score of the norming population, the sociological meaning refers to the assumption that "the testing process has a standard organization specified by the rules of the test [Roth, 1974: 152]." (This is the meaning of standardization stressed by Cronbach, 1970.) The interactions that occur between tester and testee are normatively organized, that is, there are rules that both are supposed to follow. It is this condition that attempts to guarantee the uniform administration of tests to all subjects.

For example, testers are supposed to read the rules and statements exactly as they appear on the printed tests, with no variations. Subjects are supposed to follow the stated rules of a particular test, for example, to give an answer for every question, even if they have to guess.

Roth takes the position that we cannot assume conformity by testers and subjects to specific testing rules, because it is difficult and unusual for actors to achieve complete conformity to any rules. He expects that rule variations are likely to occur in testing situations. Thus what happens in the testing situation may vary from occasion to occasion, " . . . even though the outcomes, viewed as products, appear equivalent [Roth, 1974: 155]." Hence, he argues, " . . . we should not take for granted that children of equivalent age with equal IQ scores performed the test the same way [Roth, 1974: 155]." In the process of test giving and taking, it is quite possible that nonrule-bound situations occur. Therefore, the test record should be designed to note unexpected as well as predictable, or "standard," events. However, as Roth (1974) so usefully points out:

> A standardized intelligence test like the Peabody solves the problem of keeping records by taking for granted that the testing process will follow the rules and by arranging in advance to record only whether a child answered any item correctly or not. In other words, the Peabody, and many other tests, "solve" the problem by denying its existence. Because the test record records only standard or anticipated events, the existence of a particular standard test record does not prove that the particular testing process was actually standardized [p. 155].

Roth sees this recording procedure as sociologically naive, since it makes it impossible to ascertain in which situations the rules were followed and in which ones they were not. Hence, he argues, we can never know which test scores are valid and which are not.

Rather than taking the test record as a complete summary of what happened in the testing situation, Roth used audio and video tapes to analyze the entire session. He was able to learn much more about the instructions provided children, how children receive or respond to the instructions, how the children discover in the course of the test that the meanings of the test rules and test items are not what they first thought. He also saw how tester and child handled such unanticipated events as intruders, bells ringing, the need to go to the bathroom, and so on. Finally, certain children recognize the test as familiar, and testers emphasize children's previous experience with tests to help explain what they are supposed to do. Roth (1974) concludes:

> The conception of children's intelligence in terms of measurably limited capacity is not justified by our intelligence test data. Instead of being a measure of the children's intrinsic capacity, the test cut-off point on the Peabody imposes arbitrary limits on our knowledge of the children's abilities. This is true of the lowest-scoring black child and the highest-scoring white child, as well as all the children in between. This means that both the geneticists and the environmentalists are wrong in treating the IQ tests as measures of children's intellectual capacities [p. 216].

The tests fail to provide an understanding of how a child's mind is working, what background is considered by the child to be relevant to a question or task, and why. Hence, we learn almost nothing about either the child's mental processes or his mental capacities in any dynamic sense.

In sum, problems of test content, norming populations and standardization raise serious doubts about what IQ or aptitude tests are actually measuring. Problems of test administration exist as well.

Test Administration

Problems may exist in the administration of IQ or aptitude tests to all children but particularly to lower-class or minority children. These include problems of student anxiety, motivation, test environment, situational constraints, and examiner effects.

Various factors are recognized as heightening test anxiety, including a strong achievement need, fear of failure or punishment, deflated self-concept and inferiority feelings, negative experiences with school examinations and tests, hostile test-center environment, and unfamiliarity with testing procedures and test-taking skills (Samuda, 1975). Because minority students frequently show such characteristics, they are more prone to anxiety than white individuals (Hawkes and Furst, 1971). It is questionable, therefore, whether intelligence-test scores adequately describe the underlying abilities of individuals who have high anxiety drive in the testing situation (Mandler and Sarason, 1952: 172; Sarason and Mandler, 1952: 817).

Past experience in school and on tests may decrease the minority or lower-class child's motivation in the test situation. Eells et al. (1951:21) noted that to the average lower-class child a test is just another situation in which to be punished, to have one's weaknesses shown up, and to be reminded that one is at the bottom of the heap.

Katz (1968) showed experimentally with a group of Southern black male college freshmen that "the best motivation and performance occurred . . . when the subject was told that he had a slightly better-than-even chance of succeeding. If his chances seemed very low or very high he apparently lost interest [p. 279]."

Turner (1964) suggests that students' attitudes with respect to their future education and occupation affect their performance on intelligence tests rather than the reverse. Turner interprets this causal sequence as showing that students "who have the motivations and attitudes which lead to high ambition may be those who are accordingly motivated to make their best performance in the test [cited in Boocock, 1972: 101]."

Performance may be affected by the test center itself, its location, organization, and supervisors. Samuda (1975: 92) notes that a College Entrance Examination Board (CEEB) Committee on Hostile Test Center Environment was constituted in 1971. Their preliminary report noted that 65 percent of minority students surveyed indicated a preference for a familiar test center conveniently located, and that minority and nonminority students were unanimous in noting that there was no minority person performing the role of supervisor, proctor or examiner.

Experiments with much younger children suggest that they can often raise their scores dramatically if the test is administered in a friendly atmosphere where they are both expected and helped to do well (Haggard, cited in Boocock, 1972: 101). Kinnie and Sternlof (1971) found that familiarizing both middle-class white children and lower-class black and white children with test examiners, the language and materials used on a test to elicit responses, and testlike situations in which questions are asked and performance required led to improved WPPSI scores. However, contrary to the experimentors' expectations, the scores of the lower-class children did not increase significantly more than the scores of the middle-class children. Hence, familiarity alone does not seem to explain all of the difference between the groups.

Other observers of testing situations have remarked that the test situation as well as the test environment may intimidate lower-class or minority children more than it does middle-class white children. Labov's (1973) interview material demonstrates that "the social situation is the most powerful determinant of verbal behavior [p. 33]." Further, he notes that an adult must enter the appropriate social relationship with a child to learn what that child can do.

Even with a skilled adult male black interviewer who grew up in Harlem and knew well the boys he was talking with, Labov observed monosyllabic and nonverbal behavior by an eight-year-old boy. Not until the interviewer was able to break down the social constraints was he able to elicit rich and complex verbal statements from the youth. Labov changed the situation by having the interviewer bring in a bag of potato chips, making it more of a party; by bringing along the boy's best friend; by having the interviewer get down on the floor (cutting his height from 6 feet 2 inches to 3 feet 6 inches); and by introducing taboo words and taboo topics into the conversation, showing that anything could be said into the microphone without danger.

Labov suggests transferring this demonstration of the social constraints affecting speech to other test situations. It should be apparent that no standard tests will come close to measuring verbal capacity adequately. On such tests this boy will appear as "the monosyllabic, inept, ignorant, bumbling child of our first interview [Labov, 1973: 33]." Labov's work suggests that there is no single isolated feature of the test situation that affects the outcome, but the entire asymmetrical power relationship of that situation. Therefore, improving one or another aspect of the test situation is not likely to change it very much. Not even a very sympathetic, supportive individual of similar background is able to alter the situation. The differences are too large. The result is repeated instances of test performances that are deemed inadequate and deficient.

Other studies, however, have found that differences in examiner behavior are related to test performance. Thomas, Hertzig, and Dryman (1973) studied 116 school children from 72 families of Puerto Rican working-class origin residing in New York City. The children ranged between the ages of 6 to 15. The Wechsler Intelligence Scale for Children (WISC) was administered to all of the children by one of two examiners. Both examiners were female, of Puerto Rican origin, fluent in Spanish and English, with comparable experience in administering and scoring the WISC. The children were tested in the examiners' homes, both located in upper-middle-class high-rise apartment buildings adjacent to the lower Harlem area. However, while Examiner B had never met any of the children before testing them, Examiner A had known the children and their families for many years as a result of her participation in other phases of the ongoing research project. Curiously, the mean IQs reported by Examiner A were all at least 10 points higher than those reported by Examiner B. The children tested by the two examiners did not differ significantly with respect to either age or sex.

The two examiners were interviewed in order to obtain a retrospective description of how each had conducted the testing session:

> Careful questioning revealed that, although both examiners had operated within the boundaries of the rules of standardized test procedure, they appeared to differ markedly with respect to the manner in which they made initial contact with the child and sustained his interest in the situation. Despite the fact that [Examiner] A already was acquainted with the children, she reported that she spent considerable time with each child before beginning formal testing. She

greeted the child in a lively and friendly manner, engaging him in conversation at once. She encouraged the child to ask questions about herself, the apartment, and features of the test itself. If the child did not bring up any questions, [Examiner] A made sure to spend time showing him around the apartment and describing the contents. She tried to create the atmosphere of a game, and made every effort to draw the child into the test situation as a joint pleasant activity. In the course of the actual testing, Examiner A reported that she encouraged the child to try again if his initial response was an "I don't know." Moreover, she tried to be sensitive to the child's needs, and she organized breaks and rest periods if she felt the child was tired.

In contrast, Examiner B described herself as being very reserved and quiet. She approached the children seriously. Although she emphasized that she replied willingly to spontaneous questions, she reported that she did so in an impersonal manner and did not pursue conversations unrelated to the formal testing session. She tended to follow a set routine that varied little from child to child. Examiner B reported that she tended to remain silent if the child hesitated or responded, "I don't know." She then went on to the next item without encouraging the child to try, stating that she felt that "encouragement at that time would not bring them closer to the answer. It would be almost an act of cruelty . . . to encourage would continue the child's embarrassment [Thomas et al., 1973: 367–368]."

Thus, while the examiners were similar with respect to some presumably important characteristics (sex, ethnic origin, and language facility), nevertheless some very significant differences existed between them in the way they administered the test, even within the established boundaries of test administration procedures. Nineteen children were tested by both examiners, so it was possible to ascertain whether the same children behaved differently with the different examiners by examining the WISC protocols themselves and comparing responses to the verbal subtest items. Children tested by Examiner A tended to give fewer "I don't know" responses than those tested by Examiner B, and the answers of the former group were significantly longer than those in the latter group.

Thomas et al. (1973) note further, "These differences in examiner–child interaction appear to have contributed significantly to the differences in the level of measured intelligence obtained by the two examiners [p. 372]."

Most "disadvantaged" children do not have IQ tests administered under the "optimizing" conditions described above. Minority students rarely get a tester of their own ethnic origin, or one who is fluent in their language. Further, they seldom have IQ tests administered to them individually. Instead they are given a group administration. All of these factors associated with the examiner and the testing situation undoubtedly affect their "performance."

Thomas et al. (1973) remark that this examiner effect on IQ performance cannot be assumed to operate similarly for all groups of children. In their studies of the cognitive behavior of middle-class children the mean IQ scores obtained by 3 different examiners in the testing of 116 children were identical, despite the fact that the examiners' testing styles and ways of making contact varied considerably. There may be something unique about the sense of unease felt by lower-class children in the testing situation that may affect their performance.

There is an additional interesting aspect to the Thomas et al. (1973) study. The WISC test scores from the two examiners were correlated with the reading achievement scores of the children on a standardized test, and it was found that the IQ scores of Examiner B's group correlated better with reading achievement than did the IQs obtained by Examiner A. The authors suggest that this may occur because group reading tests are not administered under conditions designed to maximize performance. I agree with them as far as they go, but I would also suggest that this study provides a clue that a (perhaps substantial) portion of what is done in schools in the name of evaluation of pupil progress and performance may systematically penalize certain economic and ethnic groups.

Thomas and co-workers conclude that the performance level of disadvantaged children on standardized tests can be raised by employing examination procedures that may be more congruent with their spontaneous cognitive styles.

Procedural issues in test administration may affect the test performance of lower-class and minority students more than that of white middle-class pupils. Such procedural problems, in conjunction with problems of test content and standardization, suggest grave limitations in IQ or aptitude testing. These limitations might be acceptable if tests are insignificant in their consequences. But are they?

Aptitude tests of various kinds are used in at least three-quarters of the public-school system in the United States and in a large proportion of private schools as well (Samuda, 1975). In a study of elementary-school testing programs in New York, Connecticut, and New Jersey, Goslin, Epstein, and Halleck (1965) discovered only 1 school out of 700 that did not use at least 1 standardized test. A similar situation exists in secondary schools on a nationwide basis (Goslin, 1965). Several consequences flow from this widespread use of tests.

Before a testing program can have serious consequences, it needs to be accepted by the school system. I have heard of at least one school (according to a teacher in it) that rejected a testing program that yielded unfavorable results. The school officials changed to a test that made them and their students look better.

This is a very different situation from that of the Washington, D.C. school system prior to 1967. There, the schools accepted test results and made serious educational decisions on the basis of them until the Hobson v. Hansen (1967) case, in which the U.S. Court of Appeals ruled that school personnel were not able to ascertain "with reasonable accuracy the maximum potential of each student [p. 16746, 16751]." This ruling was based upon more than the technical deficiencies of aptitude testing. The court was also concerned with the consequences of misjudgments for the education of disadvantaged children. Because of the false images test scores can create, teachers and principals may underestimate the capabilities of such children, and thus undereducate them.

As evidence for its conclusion about underestimation, the court noted how in one year, 60 percent of the teachers' and principals' evaluations of children were overruled by an outside panel of testing experts. The court (Hobson v. Hansen, 1967) expressed concern for the thousands of youngsters who were not reevaluated so carefully, and judged that a "child's future is entitled to judgments giving better odds than one out of three [p. 16752]."

Related to this consequence of underestimation is the problem of mislabeling minority children as mentally retarded (MR), or as educable mentally retarded (EMR). Dunn (1968) reports that minorities comprise more than 50 percent of those designated mentally retarded in the nation. In California, blacks represent 9.1 percent of the student population, yet they account for 27.5 percent of the educable mentally retarded but only 2.5 percent of the mentally gifted (figures issued by the Bureau of Intergroup Relations of the State Department of Education for the State of California, cited in Samuda, 1975: 113).

Two major cases dramatize the effects of standardized tests on the mislabeling of minority children. Mercer (1971) found that the public schools in southern California were sending more children to MR classes than were any of the 241 other organizations she and her colleagues contacted (such as law enforcement agencies, private organizations for the MR, medical facilities, religious organizations, and public welfare centers). The reason for this discrepancy seemed to be the placing of undue weight upon IQ for placement, a nearly total absence of medical diagnosis, a higher than usual cutoff score (79 compared to the state-recommended score of 69 or below), and a failure to interpret IQ scores in the light of sociocultural factors. Mercer's (1971) study found more than 4 times as many Mexican-Americans and twice as many blacks enrolled in classes for the mentally retarded as their proportions would justify. However, Mercer found that when MR was defined by adaptive behavior as well as IQ, and when those scores were interpreted in light of sociocultural considerations, the racial imbalance in classes for the MR vanished. As a result, she argued, about 75 percent of the children enrolled in MR classes were mislabeled, incorrectly placed, and consequently suffered from stigmatization, lowered self-esteem, and diminished learning opportunities (cited in Samuda, 1975: 114).

Second was the court case of Larry P. et al. v. Wilson Riles et al. (1972). Six black elementary school children claimed that they had been placed in EMR classes by the San Francisco School District, on the basis of IQ tests alone. When the children were retested by black certified psychologists, who took account of the cultural and experiential backgrounds of the students and worked to overcome the children's defeatism in the test situation, all scored above the cutoff point of 75. The District Court ruled that placement in classes for the EMR could not be based primarily upon IQ tests as they are currently administered, if the consequence of using such criteria is racial imbalance in the composition of such classes (Samuda, 1975).

A second major consequence of standardized ability testing is *under-education* of minority children. By differentiating curricula according to children's presumed ability, schools determine the scope of subject matter and the pace of learning. As Judge Skelly Wright (Hobson v. Hansen, 1967) noted, "When a misjudgment does occur, the result will be institutionally to shunt the student into a curriculum [paced] to his presumed abilities, where he is likely to progress only at the speed at which he is taught. A sixth grade student nourished on third grade instruction is apt to finish the year with a third grade education; yet the haunting question: could he have done better? [p. 16753]"

The effect of test scores upon teachers' expectations is considered in Chapter 7, but it is important to note here the likely consequence for undereducation inherent in a teacher's assessment of a child's potential on the basis of test scores. In Hobson v. Hansen (1967), the " . . . defendant's own testing expert, Dr. Roger Lennon, acknowledged this to be the common experience. . . . Although test publishers and school administrators may exhort against taking test scores at face value, the magic of numbers is strong [p. 16752]."

Moreover, the school system can heighten the importance of tests when those scores are the basis for major administrative decisions within the system. By requiring a number of tests, Judge Wright stated, the school system is in effect placing its official imprimatur on these tests. Moreover, when track placement is based upon those scores, "the worth of a test score rises high [Hobson v. Hansen, 1967: 16752]." Thus, the weight an institution places upon test scores may increase the importance of those tests for the teachers' expectations.

If contact with peers of different backgrounds and skills contributes to a child's education, and if the use of test scores isolates children from such contact, then testing may contribute in yet another way to the undereducation of children so segregated. (This issue is treated further in Chapter 6.)

Finally, socioeconomic and ethnic segregation may be accompanied by the assignment of more highly paid and more experienced teachers to predominantly white schools. While national studies (e.g., Coleman et al., 1966) have found teachers' salaries to be unrelated to their pupils' academic achievement, salaries could be related within a particular school district (cf. Ritterband, 1973).

Several additional consequences of underestimation and undereducation can be noted. The testing and tracking practices of Washington, D.C. were accompanied by the persistence of low test scores and indeed even declines in academic achievement. Judge Wright noted that in the third grade, 67.2 percent of students in District of Columbia schools were reading at or above third-grade level, but by the eighth grade fewer than half (45.5 percent) were at eighth-grade level. If ability alone were the determining factor, one would not expect such a dramatic decline in achievement. Instead, educational factors must play a critical role.

Finally, students experiencing these consequences appear to lose self-esteem, become alienated, and be more likely to drop out, although Judge Wright concluded that the evidence on this last charge was confused. In 1963, 37 percent of the 1960 tenth grade did not graduate, making Washington rank 17th among 19 city school systems in the country, better only than New York and Detroit. While the proportional trend in Washington was gradually improving, the number of dropouts was increasing. Most of the dropouts were from the lowest 2 tracks. The mixed findings left the Court unable to establish a clear link between tracking and dropouts (Hobson v. Hansen, 1967: 16753).

To summarize, because of their content and their administrative procedures, standardized IQ or aptitude tests are extremely inappropriate means of ascertaining the "ability" of lower-class and minority children. The prevalent use of test scores for educational decisions has resulted in the misclassification and mislabeling of thousands of minority students, with the apparent additional consequences of undereducation, lower teacher expectations, diminished self-esteem, and increased rates of dropout. (These latter assertions require more rigorous supporting evidence, which is presented in following chapters.)

Given the unexamined assumptions of IQ and aptitude testing, the problems of predictive validity, test content and procedure, the contention of IQ heritability seems to rest on shaky ground. But the difficulties with a largely genetic explanation for differential IQ and achievement-test scores go beyond these points. Jensen (1969) claims that 80 percent of the variation in intelligence is determined by heredity. He bases his assertion upon: (1) studies of identical twins reared apart; (2) studies of similarities between identical twins and fraternal twins reared in the same home; and (3) studies of adoptive children. Because identical twins have exactly the same genetic makeup, observed differences in their IQs should be due to environment. Hence, if only small differences in their IQs are noted, the results suggest that heredity plays a large part in determining IQ. Such an inference is warranted provided that the separate environments in which the twins are reared are totally uncorrelated and that the differences between those environments are as great as those between the homes of unrelated children.

In the available twin studies (Burt, 1966; Juel-Nielsen, 1965; Newman, Freeman, and Holzinger, 1937; Shields, 1962), these assumptions are unsupported. Kamin (1974), who has critically examined these four major twin studies, finds that Burt's work is filled with verbal contradictions and arithmetical inconsistencies, as well as marked by utter failure to provide information about crucial procedural details. Recently, even greater doubt has been cast upon Burt's work. In the London *Sunday Times* of October 24, 1976, the newspaper's medical correspondent, Oliver Gillie, indicated that he had been unable to locate any evidence that the coauthors of Burt's later papers (Margaret Howard and J. Conway) had ever existed (Wade, 1976). Two weeks later the *Times* reported that a Ms. Howard had been a faculty member at London University during the 1930s, but doubts remain about the other coauthor and about Burt's data which have numerous internal inconsistencies. Shields' study provides an appendix rich in procedural detail, which shows that many of the presumably separated twins were actually reared in highly related environments. The Juel-Nielsen twin studies failed to standardize the IQ tests used on a Danish population, and Newman and coworkers' studies used procedures for selecting the sample that rewarded twins who could provide accounts of how widely separated they were from an early age, so such reports conceivably could have been exaggerated. After careful documentation of the flaws briefly indicated here, Kamin (1974) concludes that what limited evidence we can believe from these studies makes the case stronger for environment than the researchers or secondary sources suggest.

Studies of identical and fraternal twins reared together assume the same environments for both types of twins, but recent work shows that parents tend to treat identical twins more similarly than fraternal twins (Scarr, 1968, cited in Bronfenbrenner, 1972: 121). Therefore, estimates of the heritability of IQ based upon such evidence are compounded by environmental differences.

Burks' (1928) study of adoptive families was used by both Herrnstein (1973) and Jensen (1972, 1973) to support their position that intelligence is largely inherited. Critical analysis by Goldberg, however, finds that Jensen "thoroughly misrepresented the content and implications of the Burks study [1947b: i]," while Herrnstein's report of it is "substantially inaccurate [1974a: i]." Contrary to Jensen's assertions, Burks' sample was highly selective, her measures of environmental factors were limited and widely different estimates of heritability can be obtained from her data (Goldberg, 1974a, b). Hence the study does not lend strong support to a predominantly hereditarian view of intelligence.

Earlier, Jensen (1969: 50–51) argued that since the correlation between unrelated children reared in the same home is only .24, the remaining 76 percent of the variance in IQ is due entirely to heredity. The possibility that differences exist in parental treatment, school experiences, peer influences, and so forth, is ignored. Jensen relies heavily upon Honzik's (1957) finding that the correlation between the IQs of adopted children and their true mothers was .40 but was unrelated to their adoptive mothers' educational levels (Bronfenbrenner, 1972: 120). But the study from which this figure was taken (Skodak and Skeels, 1949) revealed that the selective placement of children of more intelligent mothers in better foster homes significantly confounded this correlation. The mean IQ of true mothers was 86, while the mean IQ of the foster children at age 12 was 106. Skodak and Skeels attributed this difference to the "maternal stimulation . . . and optimum security" offered in the foster homes, particularly in those where children showed the most dramatic gains (cited in Bronfenbrenner, 1972: 120). Thus here, too, the original study differs from the interpretation Jensen gives to it, and the evidence suggests the considerable importance of environment in developing IQ.

The importance of environment is also apparent in twin studies conducted by Scarr-Salapatek (1971). She reports greater similarity (and higher heritability coefficients) between twins from advantaged rather than disadvantaged socioeconomic groups and in white rather than black families. From this study we can envision environment as a necessary condition for the development of genetic potential. Further, the type of environment may condition the relative role played by environment and heredity (Newman, Freeman, and Holzinger, 1937, cited in Bronfenbrenner, 1972: 123).

Can we draw any conclusions from these studies about the heritability of IQ? Confirmed behaviorist Kamin (1974) concludes, ". . . there exist no data which should lead a prudent man to accept the hypothesis that IQ test scores are in any degree heritable [p. 1]." Most other psychologists and geneticists do not share this conclusion. The biologist Lewontin (1970) sees the heritability of IQ as ranging from .6 to .8, and differs with Jensen's acceptance of the higher range. Bronfenbrenner (1972) rejects the figure of .8, but feels " . . . there can be no question that genetic factors play a substantial role in producing individual differences in mental ability [p. 124]." Loehlin, Lindzey, and Spuhler (1975) think it safe to conclude that the heritability index is neither 0 nor 1.

The evidence and reasoning presented above suggest that some portion of IQ is transmitted genetically from parents to children, but that we do not know exactly how much. Nor do we know very much about how heredity and environment interact, except that such interaction is likely and probably very significant. But even if IQ were totally heritable, what does it matter? Even traits (such as height) which are highly heritable can change dramatically in greatly different environments (for examples see Bronfenbrenner, 1972; Gage, 1972; Lewontin, 1970). Hence, even very high heritability does not mean total determination.

A critical question remains. If IQ is heritable to some degree, can IQ differences between blacks and whites be primarily attributed to genetic differences between the races, as Jensen (1969) suggests? Lewontin (1970) notes that there is absolutely no evidence on this question. One reason is that the black and white populations are not genetically distinct in the United

States. Berreman (1972) concludes that "socially defined populations perform differently on socially defined tasks with socially acquired skills, and this is attributed by Jensen to biology [p. 391]."

In addition to the problem noted by Berreman, Bronfenbrenner (1972) stresses the importance of economic and social environments in facilitating the development of genetic potential, noting that blacks face more economic handicaps. If differences between the races are largely environmental, then when blacks and whites are reared in nearly identical environments, differences in their IQs should tend to disappear. Since Lewontin's (1970) study, evidence addressing this issue has been presented by Scarr-Salapatek and Weinberg (1975). When they compared black and white children adopted by white parents, they found that the mean IQ of the black children was 106 while that of the white children was 111, a difference of only 5 points compared with the average national difference of 15 points. The black children on the average had lived with their adoptive families for fewer years than the white children. Among those blacks who were adopted at a younger age, the average IQ was 110. It appears that the longer black children live in "advantaged" environments, the higher are their IQ scores. Regarding the small remaining differences, genetic proponents would say they are due to genes, while environmentalists would argue that the total environments (including past histories, school experiences, peer contacts, societal context, and so on) are not necessarily equal for members of different races even when both are adopted by white families. On the basis of my own observations of life in the United States I concur with this latter position.

If IQ and achievement differences between the races are environmental rather than genetic, what features of the environment are responsible? Are the differences due to the "cultural deprivation" of certain ethnic and economic groups, or are there other environmental features which account for differential IQ and achievement?

Cultural Deprivation

Standing in apparent opposition to the genetic school of thought, and stemming from progressive and liberal political and educational ideologies, is the environmental–developmental view. This position argues that individual inequalities are not genetic in origin but sociocultural.

At least four models have been developed: the deficient, depraved, different or bicultural. (Most social policy is based on the first two.) At its extreme, in the *deficit*, or absence-of-culture, model some individuals and their families are so deprived that they are seen as actually having no culture. This view was reflected in the Introduction, by Mrs. Lyndon B. Johnson, to a brochure about Head Start in 1965. The brochure declared that these children are "lost in a gray world of poverty and neglect [and that the program would attempt to] lead them into the human family. Circumstance has stranded them on an island of nothingness [quoted in Stein, 1971: 182]." In a similar vein, Wax and Wax (1971) report an Anglo educational administrator's explanation of the problems of educating the Sioux Indian child: "The school gets this child from a conservative home, brought up speaking the Indian language, and all he knows is Grandma. His home has no books, no magazines, radio, television, newspapers—it's empty! He comes into school and we have to teach him everything! . . . . The Indian child has such a *meager* experience [pp. 129–30]." This "vacuum ideology" of the Indians' educators rationalizes the educators' roles in the schools. Wax and Wax (1971) claim this attitude places responsibility for the lack of academic achievement on the Indian child and family:

> Since the child is entering the school with an empty head, then surely it is a triumph if he is taught anything whatsoever. Moreover, the ideology justifies almost any activity within the school as "educational" (just as it derogates any communal activity outside the school); for if the child is presumed deficient in almost every realm of experience, then the task of the educator can properly encompass anything and everything. Finally, the ideology justifies the educators in their social and cultural isolation from the lives of the parents of their students; if the child actually had a culture including knowledge and values, then the educators ought properly to learn about these and build upon them, but if, on entering school, he is merely a vacuum, then what need to give attention to his home and community [p. 132]?

In the second model the child possesses a culture of some kind, but sees that culture as pathogenic, as in the *culture-of-poverty* view. Low-income or minority children do not achieve in school and in life, in this argument, because of deficiencies in their home environments: disorganization in their family structure, inadequate childrearing patterns, undeveloped language use assumed to lead to deficient cognitive development, maladaptive values including inability to defer impulse gratification, personal maladjustment, and low self-esteem. (These components are examined briefly below along with evidence bearing on their explanatory power.)

In the *cultural difference* model, the lower-class or minority child possesses a distinct, separate culture that is as valid in its own right as the mainstream culture. This view is advocated by Baratz and Baratz (1970), who feel that educational programs should recognize the existence of distinct cultures or subcultures and build upon those unique cultural features to bridge the two cultures, and hence facilitate the learning of "mainstream" culture. This viewpoint may be seen as the basis of many bilingual educational programs. But, according to Valentine (1971a), the central theoretical weakness of the difference model is "an implicit assumption that different cultures are necessarily competitive alternatives, that distinct cultural systems can enter human experience only as mutually exclusive alternatives, never as intertwined or simultaneously available repertoires [p. 141]." More-over, this assumption contains a potential assimilationist bias. If cultures are mutually exclusive, then at some point children must choose which culture they are going to keep. Furthermore, since minority cultures are always at a power disadvantage, it seems inevitable, to me, that power differentials will creep into the interactions between members of the different cultures. Thus, when I hear New York City school officials talking about "mainstreaming" the Spanish-speaking children in bilingual programs I feel that the very choice of terminology connotes the superior power and position of the white Anglo culture. In the cultural-difference model there is one monolithic, homo-geneous culture that all blacks or all members of any ethnic group share. But in fact, there is rich variation within such cultural groupings (Valentine, 1971a: 141).

Because of the difficulties he sees in the cultural-deficit and cultural-difference models, Valentine (1971a) proposes a *bicultural model*, which he sees as helping to make better sense out of ethnicity:

> The collective behavior and social life of the Black community is bicultural in the sense that each Afro-American ethnic segment draws upon both a distinctive repertoire of standardized Afro-American group behavior and, simultaneously, patterns derived from the mainstream cultural system of Euro-American deri-vation. Socialization into both systems begins at an early age, continues through-out life, and is generally of equal importance in most individual lives. . . . The idea of biculturation helps explain how people learn and practice both mainstream culture and ethnic cultures at the same time [p. 143].

Since so many social and educational policies are predicated on the deficit model, we examine the principal themes of that view along with the evidence bearing on them.

The "deficiencies" in the home environment have been increasingly specified over the past decade as researchers have become aware of the need to locate specific experiences that affect developmental processes, rather than merely trying to explain observations by means of an unspecified blanket concept-like deprivation. The Plowden Report (1967) in Great Britain dis-tinguished two kinds of social-background variables that might be related to intellectual development and school achievement: material circumstances in the home and paternal attitudes; and found that the latter was more im-portant. American researchers have imputed importance to both. Extrap-olating from animal research on sensory stimulation (e.g., Kretch, 1962), a number of American psychologists have suggested that "deprived" homes provide "inadequate sensory stimulation" (e.g., Hunt, 1961). McCandless (1952) suggested that there might be less material available for learning in some homes than in others. The first adherents of this view suggested the total absence of sensory stimulation. More recent researchers suggest that the amount of stimulation may be similar for lower- and middle-class chil-dren, but that this stimulation is not as "distinctive" for the lower-class child

(Kagan, 1968, cited in Baratz and Baratz, 1970). Or, in another reversal of the prior interpretation, lower-class ghetto life is seen as providing too many stimuli at too high a level for normal development (e.g., Deutsch, Katz, and Jensen, 1968), thus providing a perfect environment in which to learn inattention.

A major tenet of the culture-of-poverty thesis is that the family structure is extremely, even uniquely, unstable and disorganized (Lewis, 1966a, b; Moynihan, 1965). As Valentine and Valentine (1975) note, however, "solid bodies of evidence and trenchant analyses are emerging to demolish the myths of Afro-American disorganization, incapability and pathology [p. 122]" (e.g., Billingsley, 1973, 1968; Hill, 1971; Kunkel and Kennard, 1971; Murray, 1970; Valentine and Valentine, 1974; Young, 1970).

On the individual level, the culture of poverty is said to produce personalities that are weak, disorganized, restricted, and low in self-esteem. As Lewis described it, "On the level of the individual, major characteristics are a strong feeling of marginality, of helplessness, of dependency, and of inferiority . . . weak ego structure [Lewis, 1966a: xlvii, quoted in Valentine, 1971: 209]." For people holding this view, then, Keller's (1963b) finding that "fifth-grade Negro children showed more negative self-evaluations than did white children (80 percent unfavorable self–other comparisons compared to 30 percent for white children) [quoted in Bloom, Davis, and Hess, 1965: 129]," comes as no surprise.

If it were the culture of poverty that produced low self-esteem, we would expect very young children to show the same differences in self-esteem that older ones do. But the reverse is the case. The older the children and the more time they spend in school, the more their self-esteem plummets. This has recently been documented by Bridgeman and Shipman (1975), who found that " . . . through the first grade the self-esteem of nearly all the children in the Head Start samples and in the comparison samples was uniformly high. . . . However, self-esteem scores in third grade were well below ceiling levels, and there also was evidence for significant race–SES [socioeconomic status] differences, at least in girls. . . . [Teachers in the early elementary grades,] especially teachers of economically disadvantaged children, should be particularly aware of their behaviors which may decrease the initially high levels of children's self-esteem [p. 73]." These findings suggest that something happens to the initially high self-esteem of youngsters as they encounter predominantly white middle-class teachers and institutions. Hence, it is not the pathology of their homes but something else that seems to affect their self-esteem.

Integrally related to the "pathological" family and personality structures is the assertion that "culturally deprived" families have values and attitudes that perpetuate the cycle of poverty. Lewis suggests that such families really do not share the standard values of society. Their knowledge of the dominant values is contradicted by their actual behavior. As Lewis (1966b) says,

"People with a culture of poverty are aware of middle-class values, talk about them, and even claim some of them as their own, but on the whole they do not live by them [p. xlvi, quoted in Valentine, 1971b: 206]." As Valentine argues, the poor share many or most of the values associated with the dominant strata of society. In addition, what Lewis terms values may be seen as ideologies by more critical social scientists (cf. Huber and Form, 1973). Finally, the conditions of existence that shape peoples' lives may lead them simultaneously to accept alternative values when their experience contradicts the cultural ideals (see Rodman, 1968, 1965, cited in Valentine, 1971b: 206).

Two specific types of differential values are often stressed by adherents to this view: time orientation and the inability to defer gratification. In Banfield's (1960: 23–44) formulation these two are combined. Thus "class subculture" is a function of two factors: (1) ability to imagine a future; and (2) ability to discipline oneself to sacrifice present for future satisfaction. In Banfield's (1960) view, "the lower-class individual lives from moment to moment. . . . Impulse governs his behavior, either because he cannot discipline himself to sacrifice a present for a future satisfaction or because he has no sense of the future [p. 53]." This lack of future orientation is assumed to influence success in school and in later life. An alternative analysis of the same phenomena, by Liebow (1967), focuses upon the realities of life as the causal agent, rather than the derivative attitudes:

> . . . what appears as a present-time orientation to the outside observer is, to the man experiencing it, as much a future orientation as that of his middle-class counterpart. The difference between the two men lies not so much in their different orientations to time as in their different orientations to future time or, more specifically, to their different futures. . . . As for the future, the young streetcorner man has a fairly good picture of it. . . . It is a future in which everything is uncertain except the ultimate destruction of his hopes and the eventual realization of his fears. The most he can reasonably look forward to is that these things do not come too soon [pp. 64–68].

Thus, from different life realities may come different futures and different adaptations to them. LeShan (1952) found that time orientation varies systematically with social class, but no one has demonstrated that cultural differences in the concept of time impede intellectual growth. LeShan recommends that the differences she observed should be considered in educational efforts with lower-class children, but nowhere does she suggest that such differences make it impossible for them to learn.

The allegedly disorganized family life of minority and lower-class individuals is putatively responsible for their inadequate childrearing practices. But our knowledge of how ghetto mothers rear their children is based upon interview data or laboratory experiments rather than upon observational studies. These former ways of data gathering are familiar to most middle-class mothers. Such mothers are also more likely to know what responses and behaviors the researchers might be seeking. Keeping these difficulties in mind, it is perhaps not surprising that middle-class mothers showed "better" teaching behavior for block sorting and design-copying tasks than did lower-class mothers (Hess et al., 1968). Middle-class mothers are also more likely than lower-class mothers to report frequent reading aloud to their children (Irwin, 1960). While these differences may be real, they do not show that lower-class children are unable to learn to think, read, write, and cipher (cf. Baratz and Baratz, 1970: 37).

In the cultural-deficit model, family disorganization, maternal childrearing styles, and over- or understimulation affect the linguistic competence of the child. Writing about such parents, Hunt (1964) notes, "The variety of linguistic patterns available for imitation in the models provided by lower-class adults is both highly limited and wrong for the standards of later schooling [p. 238]." Deutsch (1963) reported similar problems. The linguistic-deprivation view is well stated by Bereiter and Engelmann (1966), who write: "The language of culturally deprived children is not really an underdeveloped version of standard English, but is a basically non-logical mode of expressive behavior [quoted in Clark, 1975: 347]."

This linguistic incompetence is not limited to black children and families, however. In Great Britain a similar formulation has been applied to the speech differences between middle-class and lower-class families. The middle class, according to Bernstein (1961), demonstrates an *elaborated* linguistic code facilitating the verbal development of subjective intent and sensitivity to the implications of separateness and difference, and providing a complex conceptual hierarchy for the organization of experience. The *restricted* code of the lower working class is distinguished by the rigidity of its syntax and the limited and restricted use of structural possibilities for sentence organization. Thus, from the family's social-class situation, children learn a particular linguistic code, which in turn is assumed to influence their cognitive development and style. Chandler and Erickson (1968), however, found that the use of restricted or elaborated linguistic codes was not so highly related to the social class of speakers as Bernstein's work suggests:

> Both inner city and suburban groups . . . were found to shift back and forth between use of relatively "restricted" linguistic codes and relatively "elaborated" codes. These shifts were closely related to apparent changes in the degree of shared context between group members. Examples of extremely abstract and sophisticated inquiry among inner-city Negro young people were found in which a highly "restricted" linguistic code was employed [quoted in Tulkin, 1972: 328].

Extensive studies demonstrate that black American English is just as complex, highly structured, and conducive to abstract thought as white American English, suggesting that assumptions of inadequate language development and linguistic skills are invalid (Birren and Hess, 1968; Dillard, 1972; Labov, 1973; Stewart, 1969). For example, Labov found that the concept of verbal deprivation is far from the reality of lower-class black children. He witnessed them immersed in verbal stimulation from morning until night, participating fully in a highly verbal culture. Labov (1973) observed many speech events that "depend upon the competitive exhibition of verbal skills: sounding, singing, toasts, rifting, louding²—a whole range of activities in which the individual gains status through his use of language [p. 33]." Labov suggests further that middle-class language may be seen as only stylistically different, although it may be dysfunctional, appearing sometimes as "turgid, redundant, bombastic and empty" rather than superior. He noticed that black speakers shared the same basic vocabulary, the same capacity for conceptual learning, and used the same logic as anyone else who learns to speak and understand English.

That differences in language exist is undeniable. But whether these differences reflect inferiorities or result in cognitive defects, as is so often asserted, is not substantiated. Carroll (1964) suggests that we really know very little about the relation between language style and cognition. To say that one language results in inferior cognitive ability requires that speakers of that language be compared with speakers of another language on a non-linguistic task. Therefore, the oft posited link between linguistic "incompetence" and cognitive impairment has yet to be upheld.

In brief, the features of "cultural deprivation" have often been assumed to exist without substantiating evidence. Furthermore, existing differences are asserted to be causes of inadequate educational attainment, when in fact no such causal evidence exists. One reason that causality is inferred may be due to the comparison with an implicit "ideal type" of middle-class life.

All middle-class children are assumed to receive "adequate" mothering, receive profuse linguistic stimulation, and have just the right orientation toward the future (and never buy now and pay later). As Tulkin (1972) notes, however, middle-class culture has not been "objectively evaluated." Doing so might support Coles' (1968) observation that middle-class children are "nervous and worried," Kagan's (1968) observation that middle-class children are more anxious about failing than other children are, and Maccoby and Mondiano's (1966) remark that people socialized into the modern industrialized world often lose the ability to *experience*.

In short, the "culture of poverty" view is largely unsupported by sound scientific evidence. Where differences do appear, they are not demonstrable causes of school failure. Finally, and most importantly, the differences which appear are rooted in the economic, political, and social inequalities of the society, not in the failings of individuals. By locating the source of deficiency and failure in individuals, however, rather than in economic and social inequalities, both researchers and reformers demonstrate the degree to which legitimating ideologies saturate our society.

²These terms describing various verbal behaviors are illustrated in Labov, Cohen, Robins, and Lewis, 1968, section 4.2.

Conclusions

Ideological saturation is perhaps even more apparent when we consider certain shared assumptions and consequences of the environmental and genetic-deficit theories. While to me their commonalities outweigh their apparent differences, the conflict between them is perceived as very intense and meaningful by the adherents (Valentine and Valentine, 1975). However, this conflict may itself serve positive functions for dominant groups in society (cf. Coser, 1956), by diverting attention from the premises and consequences that both approaches share. The vast, and somewhat technical, literature bearing on these issues contributes to this smoke screen. The nature–nurture controversy rests upon a bedrock of common assumptions about the importance and validity of test performance. Both the genetic and the cultural-deficit adherents assume that IQ is important for "success" in life and appear to agree with the necessity for early selection in schools. In brief, they are united in their support of the instrumental-meritocratic ideology. They do not question the *need* for performance on tests *designed to differentiate*. Given these commonalities, it is no surprise that they have many similar consequences as well.

Supporters of both theories place the locus of blame for failure on children and their families. They divert attention from the entire educational system and how it operates to produce certain outcomes, including failure. Moreover, they absolve educators from the responsibility for children's failures. Accepting these theories justifies whatever educators do and rationalizes their isolation from the students they teach. A rationale is provided for intervention by trained experts, who understand the "problem" and how to deal with it. For these reasons it would be hard for educators not to believe in either genetic or cultural deficits or both.

These concepts also have self-fulfilling potency. As teachers, schools, the larger society, and perhaps children and their parents come to believe them, these assumptions begin to insure that the child will not learn. (How this works with respect to educational structures and teachers' expectations is considered in subsequent chapters.) These results, in turn, tend to corroborate the validity of the models.

In addition to diverting blame for educational failure from teachers and schools to students and families and having self-fulfilling potency, these concepts offer compensatory education as the solution to poverty, thereby diverting attention from structural inequalities of power and wealth. Such a solution is likely to take generations. So, while the cultural-deficit view is not quite so immutable a view of poverty as the hereditarian view, the eradication of poverty is still seen as a long, slow process. However, the process is seen as being possible within the existing system (usually as a result of economic growth). Therefore, it has strong appeal for liberals who deplore existing inequalities but equally dislike the idea of radical changes to eliminate poverty. Both views leave unchallenged the existing structure of inequalities, requiring only that the credo of equal opportunity be met. As Willhelm (1971, 1973) and Valentine and Valentine (1975) have noted, "equal opportunity" is another slogan (ideology) for denying equality and justice to the racially and economically dispossessed. "Equal opportunity" is offered *instead of* the equalization of wealth and power (Valentine and Valentine, 1975: 127).

By focusing so exclusively on deficiencies within the child or family, the revived nature–nurture debate has also diverted attention from questions and research about how different kinds of children do learn things and what kinds of cognitive skills they have. Finally, these models leave unexamined questions about the nature of knowledge to be taught and learned. Adherents of the cultural-deprivation, deficit, and difference models, as well as the genetic-deficit model, posit a certain view of knowledge. Individuals are seen as lacking the mental capacity or the conceptual tools for comprehending the "bodies" or "forms" of knowledge which have historically come to count as school knowledge (cf. Keddie, 1973: 15). Hence the curriculum is seen as socially prescribed knowledge, external to the knower, to be mastered, rather than as a series of possibilities for making sense of life and the world (Greene, 1971, cited in Keddie, 1973: 15).

Greene's and Keddie's views approach those espoused by progressive educators, who think education should be child centered, with children learning from experience. This perspective, carried to its extreme, limits children to the experiences they have already had, rather than building upon that experience to add new insights and understanding. This aproach also tends to deny that any knowledge is essential for all to participate in a common life. In a society or a world in which some have more knowledge and power than others, those without such knowledge may find themselves subject to the greater power of those with it. This issue requires that the symbolic value of education be distinguished from its use value. While certain groups acquire certain kinds of education for its status value, clearly certain kinds of educational experience provide people with skills or qualities they value. If the concept of "mastery learning" (Bloom, 1971) with its attendant optimism about human potential is going to be significant, we need to focus more on what it is important to learn. Issues such as these are rarely debated, perhaps because of nature–nurture controversies.

The foregoing does not imply that intellectual or cultural differences between individuals are nonexistent. But what is done with these differences, how they are regarded and treated, may contribute to the educational and social outcomes observed. It is not necessary to deny the existence of initial differences to suggest that such differences by themselves are not an adequate explanation of differential school achievement. Bloom (1971) has convincingly argued that mastery learning of basic skills in reading and arithmetic is possible for 90 percent of children, including all but severely brain-damaged youngsters. In China and the USSR, where quite different concepts of individual intellectual abilities and cultural variations prevail, visitors report that "slow learners" are worked with until they learn (Bronfenbrenner, 1970; Stein, 1975).

As Feinberg (1975: 204) notes, the Chinese also accept differences in ability but emphasize the similarity of growth processes. He quotes Galtung's (undated) interview with leading members of the Revolutionary Committee of a middle school in Peking:

> Of course people differ in ability. But a student who is weak in one field may be strong in another. And these abilities are not something innate and unchanging. Abilities grow when they are made use of, through practice. . . . As abilities grow by being used they are not constant, and it does not make any sense to say that a given individual has so and so much ability. Hence we do not have final examinations and diplomas with grades on them in our school. We do make use of examinations during the school year, as a pedagogical method, as a check on students and teachers [quoted in Feinberg, 1975: 204].

If virtually all children in societies which have different conceptions of the meaning of intellectual and cultural differences learn the substantive material required, and if so-called disadvantaged groups of children in the United States can demonstrate "mastery learning," then an alternative explanation of differential achievement needs to be considered. Differences in intelligence or culture may be related to the speed with which certain things can be learned, or to what are more effective pedagogical approaches. But, as currently formulated, the concept of intellectual deficits, whether due to genes or culture, itself helps to depress the intellectual growth of some children.

To conclude, the differences between the seemingly warring genetic and cultural-deficit explanations of differential school achievement are more apparent than real. They share many premises and consequences and are both marred by serious evidentiary flaws. Why, then, do they persist, indeed prevail? The shared assumptions and consequences of the concept of intellectual inadequacy (whether due to genes or culture) benefits all of the more powerful participants in the situation. This concept serves the interests of wealth owners by deflecting attention from their dominant positions, justifies the superior rewards of the occupationally privileged, buttresses the positions of behavioral scientists in the structure of dominance and rewards, and rationalizes the unequal results of the educational system. Both the genetic and cultural-deficit theories support the instrumental-meritocratic ideology. Apparently diverse interest groups are united in their support of this ideology, which benefits all but the under class. One of the educational structures which rests heavily on these assumptions is the practice of tracking.

6

Tracking

IF LEADING PARTICIPANTS in the societal structure of dominance perceive educational differentiation as desirable, we would expect them to be involved in developing structural means for achieving it. Indeed, we have seen that major industrialists were a moving force behind the concept of diversified education. Furthermore, when such differentiation did not occur in separate schools, strong efforts were made to differentiate pupils within the same school. Hence, the practice of tracking, which places children together in a class on the basis of similar aptitude, achievement, or aspirations.

The first recorded example of tracking was the Harris plan introduced in St. Louis in 1867. William T. Harris, superintendent of schools in St. Louis and later U.S. Commissioner of Education, has been described by Curti (1935/1968) and Tyack (1974) as perhaps the most influential American educator between the time of Horace Mann and John Dewey. Moreover, Curti (1935/1968: 336) describes him as a great "champion of industrial capitalism."

While historically tracking was promoted by industrial capitalists and their supporters, it has followed a curious pattern of popularity and disuse. In the 1920s and 1930s, a time when large numbers of foreign immigrants needed to be incorporated into the labor force, tracking greatly increased. Then it fell into disuse until the late 1950s when it was revived, apparently in response to the Russian launching of Sputnik and American competitive concern with identifying and educating the "gifted." That period was also marked by the increasing migration of rural Southern blacks to Northern cities and by an influx of Puerto Rican and Mexican-American migrants. Thus the prevalence of a major form of differentiation, the practice of tracking, seems to be correlated with the ethnic composition of urban schools.

As practiced today, educational differentiation is widespread, particularly in large, racially and economically diverse school systems and in schools serving primarily lower-class or minority students (Coleman et al., 1966; Findley and Bryan, 1970a).

In a recent survey, Findley and Bryan (1970a) note that 76 percent of elementary- and secondary-school administrators report some degree of ability grouping (one type of tracking). In 1958 the National Education Association (NEA) survey found that tracking was practiced in 78 percent of elementary schools and 91 percent of high schools. This figure may somewhat underestimate its extent, since Heyns (1971, cited in Rosenbaum, 1974) found that administrators reported less of it than did teachers or students.

In terms of its historical emergence and where it occurs, tracking appears to be related to the structure of dominance. Those in dominant positions are more likely to favor the practice, and those in subordinate positions are more likely to experience it negatively. These historical and ecological differences notwithstanding, the theoretical model proposed here anticipates that position in the structure of dominance is related to track placement and that different educational processes are associated with being in different tracks. How does available evidence bear on these expectations?

One conceptual clarification that is usually missing from research on this issue is the distinction between ability grouping and curriculum differentiation. The distinction involves two dimensions: flexibility and curricular content. Proponents of ability grouping stress flexible subject-area assignment. By this, they mean that students are assigned to learning groups on the basis of their background and achievement in a subject area at any given moment, and that skills and knowledge are evaluated at relatively frequent intervals. Students showing gains can readily be shifted into another group. Furthermore, according to this portrayal, it would not be unusual for students to be in different-level ability groups in different subjects, according to their own rate of growth. This practice suggests a common curriculum shared by all students, with only the mix of student abilities being varied. It also assumes that, within that curriculum, all groups are taught the same material.

In practice, it seems that students are infrequently assessed, that their group placement becomes self-perpetuating, that they are very often grouped at the same level in all subjects, and that even a shared curriculum may be taught differently to different groups. The inflexibility of ability grouping is compounded by the frequent assignment of different ability groups to different courses of study, resulting in differentiation by curriculum and ability simultaneously. It is here that Rosenbaum's (1976) conceptual insight is so helpful. He notes that while ability grouping and curriculum grouping may appear different to educators, in fact they share several important social similarities: (1) Students are placed with those defined as similar to themselves and are segregated from those deemed different; (2) Group placement is done on the basis of criteria such as ability or postgraduate plans which are unequally esteemed. Thus group membership immediately ranks one in a status hierarchy, formally stating that some students are better than others. Following Rosenbaum (1976), the general term of tracking is applied here to both types of grouping. Since ability grouping and curricular differentiation share important social characteristics, studies which have considered either or both are relevant to investigate the questions of whether position in the structure of dominance is related to track assignment, and whether track assignment is related to the educational experiences encountered.

Three major criteria for allocating students to homogeneous ability groups have been noted in the vast literature: (1) standardized test scores; (2) teacher grades, recommendations, or opinions about pupils; and (3) pupil race and socioeconomic class.

The NEA survey of 1962 found that achievement tests and IQ tests were the primary basis for tracking in secondary schools. Findley and Bryan (1970a) reported that 82 percent of the districts reporting ability grouping indicated that they used tests as the sole basis or as a partial basis for placement, although only 13 percent indicated they used test scores alone. In a reanalysis of the Coleman et al. (1966) data, Heyns (1974) learned that tested verbal ability explains 17.6 percent of the variance in curriculum placement in secondary schools (which is 65 percent of the total variance explained). Thus, she concluded, curriculum placement is primarily dependent upon test scores. But there is a large amount of variance in placement that is unexplained.

In Washington, D.C., the track system was based completely on "ability" as judged by standardized tests (Findley and Bryan, 1970b: 51). However, track placement was "directly related" to social class, in the eyes of Court of Appeals Judge Skelly Wright, in the Hobson v. Hansen (1967) case, the first to raise the issue of ethnic and social stratification that so often accompanies tracking. (This consequence is considered below.) Carter (1970) found that tracking was widely practiced in Southwestern U.S. schools, where there are large numbers of Mexican-American children. Track placement rested upon the appraisal of intellectual capacity and academic achievement (through tests or other means). In short, standardized tests of academic ability, with all their limitations and biases (discussed in Chapter 5), are a major basis for tracking. Additionally, even where ability or achievement tests are indicated as being the primary basis for track assignment, there are gross discrepancies in the actual way that track assignments are made (Rosenbaum, 1976).

Teacher recommendations are used by some school districts instead of, or in addition to, standardized test scores (Findley and Bryan, 1970a). The NEA survey (1962) found that elementary school group placement was based primarily upon teachers' judgment. Rist (1970) reports that the teacher's judgment was the basis for assigning children into learning groups on the eighth day of school. Mackler and Giddings (1969) suggest that teacher judgments may be based on other grounds than academic achievement. In their observations of Harlem schools, they noticed that the price for success (high group placement) is behaving in a way that the school finds acceptable. Thus behavioral elements may play a considerable role in grouping when assignment is mediated by teacher recommendations.

In a study of three junior high schools in the Midwest, Kariger (1962) found that track placement was based on grades, study habits, citizenship, industry, and social and emotional maturity. He found that this practice resulted in more ethnic and social-class homogeneity within the various tracks than would have occurred if test scores alone had been used as the basis for track assignment. Subsequent changes in track assignment were also patterned. Among upper-class children who were shifted, 93 percent were moved upward; among middle-class children, 68 percent; and among lower-class children, 61 percent. The original track placements were highly related to social class, and the ensuing "corrections" pushed further toward homogeneous groupings with respect to social class.

While few can disagree that race and class are associated with track placement (more evidence on this subject is presented below), many would deny that race or class is a basis for allocation to track. Mehl (1965), for example, found that the pupils in the top two homogenous groups and those in the bottom two groups were segregated along social-class lines. Moreover, he found only a low correlation between social class and IQ or achievement. Unfortunately, he did not analyze class and academic ability simultaneously in relation to track placement. Other research studies, however, have done this. Both Kariger (1962) and Brookover, Leu, and Kariger (1965) found that social class was related to track placement even when student achievement was held constant (data reported in Jones, Erickson, and Crowell, 1972: 347).

Heyns (1974) did an analysis of covariance and found that class explained only 3.2 percent of the total variance in curriculum placement in schools, although the joint effects of socioeconomic status and verbal ability accounted for nearly 25 percent of the total variance explained. Schafer and Olexa (1971) observed that placement in the noncollege track was highly related to both race and class. Even when prior school achievement and IQ were controlled, 40 percent of working class students and 60 percent of blacks with high IQ and high achievement were placed in the noncollege-preparatory curriculum, while 60 percent of the white middle-class students with low IQ and achievement were put in the academic track (cited in Trimberger, 1973: 41). Skeptics might reply that student choice could account for this discrepancy, that fewer working class or black students want the college-preparatory curriculum. As Jencks et al. (1972) report, by the time students enter the eighth grade their educational and occupational aspirations are fairly fixed. (How and why this happens is considered in Chapter 10.) Without knowing more about how track assignments were made, we cannot conclude from the Schafer and Olexa study that race and class were the primary criteria used to place students in the noncollege curriculum.

Work by Baker (1974), however, does show that race was salient for placement into the lower tracks of a specialized vocational high school in New York City. By spending several years at the school, getting to know teachers, sitting in on entrance interviews, and observing decision-making sessions, Baker saw how labor-market criteria relating to race were brought into educational decisions regarding track placement. While we can only assume its generalizability, this work indicates that allocation decisions were made by the school, not by students, and that a major criteria used was race.

The relationship between social class and track placement has also been observed in England. Douglas (1964) found 11 percent more middle-class children in the upper streams and 26 percent fewer in the lower streams than would be expected on the basis of measured ability. Judging from his own observations of schools, he noted that cleanliness and good clothes and shoes were even more important than a child's social class. In that situation, the appearance of gentility was more important than the actual social and economic position of the family. In Sweden Husen found that lower-class students with equal tested ability were not in the "able student" classes as often as upper-class students (cited in Goldberg, Passow, and Justman, 1966: 166). In an analysis of the British educational system, Elder (1965) observed that the lower the child's measured ability, the more salient was the family's social class in determining educational placement. This interpretation is clearly consistent with Kariger's (1962) data about placement and changes in track position.

In brief, standardized test scores, teachers' recommendations, and pupils' social class and race are related to track placement. Tests and teacher recommendations themselves appear to be related to race and class. How these criteria are selected and by whom are questions worthy of further investigation.

Processes Associated with Tracking

At least three different processes have been observed to vary according to track placement: the instruction offered, the student–teacher interactions which occur, and student–student interactions.

While many studies of tracking unfortunately fail to control for the type and amount of instruction offered, a number of instructional differences have been observed. Heathers (1967) found that teachers stressed basic skills and facts and used drill a great deal with "slow learners," while they emphasized conceptual learning and encouraged independent projects with high-ability groups (cited in Heathers, 1969: 566). In a like vein, Squire's (1966) national study of the teaching of English in American high schools revealed that teachers tended to employ dull, unimaginative instructional approaches with so-called slow-learning groups (cited in Heathers, 1969: 566).

Rosenbaum (1976) noted a number of institutional variations by track. While college track students are generally guaranteed better teachers, many teachers instruct lower track students as well. "But," Rosenbaum (1976) emphasizes, "the most important teaching bias is not in the allocation of teachers but in the way that individual teachers allocate their attention. Teachers report that they prepare more for college-track than for noncollege-track classes, and they feel that lower-business and general-track classes are so undemanding as to require little or no preparation at all. Students report the same phenomenon, noting that some lower-track teachers assign a workbook exercise every day and then spend the class period ignoring students and reading the newspaper. Half the respondents say that teachers try harder for the college-track classes and that the college-track students receive a better education. Thus, even when the noncollege-track students get the same teachers as college-track students get, they do not get as much attention, concern, or effort from their teachers [p. 179]." Thus both teacher personnel and effort vary by track.

In a study of a British comprehensive school, Keddie (1971) realized that students in different streams[1] received different educational content, within the same curriculum. Keddie (1971) notes the remarks of one economics teacher who reported that with "A-stream" children, "I'd be much more concerned with how the different types of taxation work," whereas with "C-stream" pupils the teacher would teach, "how to fill in tax forms [p. 148]." Keddie notes that this differential treatment of the economy means that certain categories of analysis are made available to some students but withheld from others. Similar variations in educational content were noted by Leacock (1969) in middle-class compared to working-class schools.

Sørenson (1970) suggests that tracking systems may vary with respect to the amount of choice they allow students among curricula and regarding attendance (he calls this the degree of selectivity), as well as in the range of alternatives they provide. Anselone (in progress) has discovered that "disadvantaged" students tracked into a special university program had a more limited choice of majors, were allowed fewer cuts, and could choose fewer electives. These findings reveal that a tracking program highly related to social class contains differential options within the tracks. In short, available evidence shows that students in different tracks receive different instructional styles, teacher effort, educational content and options, with the alternatives more highly valued by educators and students consistently going to those in higher tracks.

Most research on tracking has not inspected the nature or frequency of teacher–pupil interactions within various tracks. Freiberg's (1970) work is an exception, however. He found that the "higher" group received more empathy, praise, and use of their ideas, as well as less direction and criticism, than the lower groups. As Rosenshine (1970b) has indicated, we do not yet know how behaviors such as these are related to student achievement, but it seems reasonable to expect them to be related to self-esteem at least.

This is exactly what Rosenbaum's evidence suggests. He reports that

[1]Streaming is the British term for educational tracking.

more than one third of lower (noncollege) track students mentioned "blatant insults directed at them by teachers and administrators: 'Teachers are always telling us how dumb we are.' . . . ." One articulate general-track student reported that he sought academic help from a teacher but was told that he was not smart enough to learn that material. Several students reported that a lower-track student who asks a guidance counselor for a change of classes is not only prevented from changing but is also insulted for being so presumptuous as to make the request.

"The reader must feel some skepticism, as I did, at reports of teachers' expressing such degrading insults in front of students. Yet a dozen students report receiving this kind of comment. I heard such comments myself. One of the younger teachers with a more 'liberal' reputation told me, 'You're wasting your time asking these kids for their opinions. There's not an idea in any of their heads.' This comment was not expressed in the privacy of the teacher's room; it was said at a normal volume in a quiet classroom full of students! [Rosenbaum, 1976: 179–180]." Hence, a major result of tracking is differential respect from peers and teachers, with implications for both instruction and esteem.

In addition to variations in curriculum and teaching, track placement may be related to unequal educational resources. Hargreaves (1967) found that poorer teachers were regularly assigned to teach lower streams. Apparently both the teachers and the students knew this. Heyns (1974) reports that curriculum placement was related to differential access to school resources, specifically the number of meetings with school counselors and the amount of encouragement students felt they received from counselors. Armor (1969) and Weinberg and Skager (1966) also note greater use of career guidance services by middle- and upper-class students. Heyns suggests that other school resources, such as science equipment and library facilities, may be differentially distributed by track as well, although she did not measure that possibility. Rosenbaum (1976) found that college track students consistently received better teachers, class materials, laboratory facilities, field trips and visitors than their lower track counterparts. Moreover, lower track students reported being discouraged by both peers and teachers from participating in such extracurricular activities as student government or the newspaper. Rosenbaum also noted that information about the educational and occupational consequences of different tracks was given to high track students and systematically denied lower track students. Indeed, they were deceived about the negative effects their curricular placement would have for them. Finally, students' rank in class was negatively affected by their track placement. Grading curves were lower in non-college tracks (i.e., fewer high grades were given), and high grades counted less when grade averages were computed, thus giving lower track students a double penalty when class ranks were calculated. Students in the lower general track needed an A average to have the same class rank as D average students in the upper college track

(Rosenbaum, 1976). For these reasons, studies of the effect of schooling which treat schools as units of analysis completely overlook the possibility of internal variations in the availability of resources.

The Consequences of Tracking

The extent to which ability grouping is related to segregation by social class and ethnicity has important implications for academic achievement, self-concept, attitudes, subcultures, and teacher expectations. A number of American and international studies have shown that children from the middle and upper classes are found mainly in high-ability groups while children from the lower classes are found disproportionately in low-ability groups. This finding appears in reports by Douglas (1964), Husen and Svensson (1960), Kariger (1962), Mehl (1965), Sarthory (1968), and Willig (1963). Reviewing a number of studies, Eash (1961) noted that at an early age, ability grouping seems to favor unduly the placement of higher-social-class children into higher-ability groups.

Racial as well as class separation has been associated with grouping, as reported by Esposito (1973), Hobson v. Hansen (1967), and *Racial and Social Isolation in the Schools* (1969). Several studies, including Matzen (1965), McPartland (1969), and Wilson (1967), have suggested that such class and racial segregation may reduce the educational stimulation received by low-achieving students. These research studies lend substance to Heathers' (1969) statement that ability grouping may be " . . . an agency for maintaining and enhancing caste and class stratification in a society [p. 566]." Class stratification may also be maintained via the academic outcomes of tracking.

To assess whether tracking affects academic achievement I considered original studies and review articles, examining more than 217 works (Billet, 1932; Daniels, 1961; Eash, 1961; Ekstrom, 1961; Findley and Bryan, 1970b; Goldberg, Passow and Justman, 1966; Goodlad, 1960; Miller and Otto, 1930; National Educational Association, 1968; Rosenbaum, 1976; Yates, 1966). On the basis of this literature, it is possible to conclude, as Findley and Bryan (1970b) did, that separation into ability groups has no clear-cut positive or negative effect on the *average scholastic achievement* of the students involved. There is a slight trend toward improving the achievement of "high ability" groups, but that is offset by substantial losses by the average and low groups.

A number of studies, however, indicate that gains for the "higher ability" group appear only when the content, materials, and teaching methods are enriched for them and when they are "pushed" (Eash, 1961; Ekstrom, 1961; Goodlad, 1960; National Educational Association, 1968). Thus it is not ability grouping per se that explains the gains of the "higher ability" groups, but the differentiated teaching and curriculum they receive. This conclusion is consistent with the finding by Douglas (1964) that "higher ability" students in the "A stream" improved, while students of comparable ability in the "B stream" deteriorated. Similarly, "lower ability" students in the "A stream" gained while like pupils in a lower stream lost. We cannot tell from the Douglas (1964) study whether there were curricular differences involved or unequal teacher expectations, or both.

The direct result of the differential gains and losses in academic achievement is increased *academic differentiation* of pupils in schools with ability grouping. Borg (1966), Daniels (1961), and Heathers (1967, cited in Heathers, 1969) found that ability grouping in schools was related to an increase in the dispersion of students' scores on standardized tests of academic achievement. More recently, Rosenbaum (1976) has argued that the variance in IQ scores over time is a better indicator of the effect of tracking on the students in a school than is a change in mean scores. He found that "higher track" students' IQ scores became more dispersed within their group over time while "lower track" students' scores became more homogeneous. In a related vein, Schafer, Olexa, and Polk (1973) report a widening gap in academic performance (measured by student grades) from ninth grade to twelfth grade between the college and noncollege tracks.

This increased differentiation could be one factor helping to support the relative *stability* of track placement. Daniels (1961) found that children were very likely to remain in their assigned ability levels. In his study, teachers estimated that about 17 percent of the students were moved from one level to another each year, whereas, in fact, only about 2 percent were shifted. Schafer, Olexa, and Polk (1973) learned that only about 7 percent of the students moved from the college track to the noncollege track and no more than that moved up. Similarly, Rosenbaum (1976) reports that virtually all of the upper-college-track students stayed in their original grouping as did all of the noncollege students, although many lower-college-track students moved to noncollege tracks. Rosenbaum sees stability as the chief characteristic of the system, with what movement there is mainly downward. Similarly, in the Washington, D.C. system, track placement was permanent for 90 percent of the students (Hobson v. Hansen, 1967: 16760).

A final implication of this system of academic differentiation is the effect it has upon the pursuit of further education. Track assignment tends to become stabilized, and tracking is an important determinant of further education. In a national sample of high-school graduates, Jaffe and Adams (1970) found that track in high school, not ability, was the variable most importantly related to whether students went to college, and whether those who did attended a two- or four-year college.

It is also possible that ability grouping affects one's sense of self. Findley and Bryan (1970b) note that research on ability grouping in the 1920s and 1930s did not study the affective domain but was concerned only with the consequences of grouping for achievement. Studies in the early 1960s were largely concerned with the effects of ability grouping on the "gifted." Today, Findley and Bryan remind us, low- and high-ability groupings have socio-economic and ethnic overtones.

In general, the effects of ability grouping on self-concept are mixed. Four studies have discovered that ability grouping is positively related to self-concept for "low ability" students but negatively related for "high ability" groups (Cowles, 1963; Drews, 1963; Olavarri, 1967; and Wilcox, 1963). At least one (Olavarri, 1967) found that special adjustments were made by teachers of the "low ability" classes to provide increased chances for student success. The "high ability" students only slightly favored the grouped settings.

A few studies find that ability grouping is not related to different self-concepts (Bacher, 1964; Dyson, 1965; Fick, 1962; Goldberg et al., 1966; Lovell, 1960). At least two of these studies (Bacher, 1964; Goldberg et al., 1966) were conducted in predominantly white middle-class schools, suggesting that racial and socioeconomic homogeneity might reduce the relation between grouping and self-concept.

The majority of studies, however, report negative consequences for the self-concept of "average" and "low ability" students (Adkison, 1964; Borg, 1966; Byers, 1961; Kelly, 1975; Levenson, 1972; Luchins and Luchins, 1948; Lunn, 1970; Mann, 1960; Ogletree, 1969). Reviewing numerous other studies in addition to these, Findley and Bryan (1970b) conclude that ability grouping builds (inflates?) the egos of the "high ability" groups and reduces the self-esteem of "average" and "low ability" groups. Findley and Bryan (1970b) remark that ability grouping does not "promote desirable attitudes and healthy self-concepts [p. 24]." Most of the studies mentioned did not consider ethnicity or class, so we do not know whether ethnic minorities and lower-class students are affected in similar ways by ability grouping. This question needs further investigation.

Qualitative data vividly depict the effect of ability sorting on the self-concepts of the children involved. Reporting on the British system prior to its reform, Elder (1965) quotes one headmaster as saying, "I have not found any pupil who failed the eleven-plus exam who has overcome his sense of inferiority at this failure, irrespective of his performance even at university level [p. 184]."

Mann (1960) interviewed 102 fifth graders in one American school, asking them which fifth-grade section they were in, and why they were in that section. She found that children in the highest and lowest groups were most aware of their level, replying that they were in the "best" or "high" or "low" group rather than giving their teacher's name. The reasons they gave? "I'm smart," "We're smarter," "I'm too dumb," "We don't know very much," "We are lazy." She concluded that ability grouping was cruel to all but the top students.

Cottle (1974) gives a very telling account of the effects of grouping on one eleven-year-old black boy:[2]

Ollie Taylor is 11 years old. He lives with his family in Boston. They are very poor even though his father works almost 50 hours a week. For this boy failure is an inevitability. Almost every action he takes ends in convincing him that he is, in his own words, worthless. And from speaking with him for three years, I know that feeling can be traced directly to his school, not to his family, from whom he receives encouragement, love, and respect. His parents and grandparents tell me that the inner strength given him by God, and sustained by their enduring care for him, is going to be shattered by years of schooling and a tracking system which every day pounds into his head the notion that he is dumb, talentless, hopeless. And the assessments, he reminds me every time I see him, are based on scientific tests scored by computers. They cannot, in other words, be argued with.

Here we see how the putative scientific basis of testing and tracking made Ollie Taylor feel that there was no disputing the judgment of his ability. Moreover, as Ollie says, school is very important to him:

"The only thing that matters in my life is school and there they think I'm dumb and always will be. I'm starting to think they're right. Hell, I know they put all the Black kids together in one group if they can, but that doesn't make any difference either. I'm still dumb. Even if I look around and know that I'm the smartest in my group, all that means is that I'm the smartest of the dumbest, so I haven't gotten anywhere at all, have I? I'm right where I always was. Every word those teachers tell me, even the ones I like most, I can hear in their voice that what they're really saying is, 'All right you dumb kids. I'll make it as easy as I can, and if you don't get it then, then you'll never get it. Ever.' That's what I hear every day, man. From every one of them. Even the other kids talk that way to me too."

"You mean the kids in the upper tracks?" I asked, barely able to hold back my feelings of outrage.

"Upper tracks? Man, when do you think I see *those* kids? I never see them. Why should I? Some of them don't even go to class in the same building with me. If I ever walked into one of their rooms they'd throw me out before the teacher even came in. They'd say I'd only be holding them back from their learning. I wouldn't go near them," he grumbled. "And they wouldn't come around us neither, I'm sure."

These words indicate how being tracked with other students labeled "slow" or "dumb" affects this boy's self-esteem and how he sees this designation mirrored in the teacher's behavior and tone. The feeling is aggravated by the attitude he expects the physically and socially isolated upper-track students to show toward him.

But Ollie Taylor did not always feel so negatively about himself:

[2]Quoted from Thomas J. Cottle, "What Tracking Did to Ollie Taylor," in *Social Policy*, July–August 1974, vol. 5, no. 2, 23–24. Copyright 1974 by Social Policy Corporation. Reprinted by permission.

"I used to think, man, that even if I wasn't so smart, that I could talk in any class in that school, if I did my studying, I mean, and have everybody in that class, all the kids and the teacher too, think I was all right. Maybe better than all right too. You know what I mean?"

"That you were intelligent," I said softly.

"Right. That I was intelligent like they were. I used to think that all the time, man. Had myself convinced that whenever I had to stand up and give a little speech, you know, about something, that I'd just be able to go to it and do it." He tilted his head back and forth. "Just like that," he added excitedly.

"I'm sure you could too."

"I could have once, but not anymore."

For a time, when he had been assigned to a higher track, he had done all right in the class, until the school told him he had to change classes:

"Just last year before they tested us and talked to us, you know, to see what we were like, I was in this one class and doing real good. As good as anybody else. Did everything they told me to do. Read what they said, wrote what they said, listened when they talked."

"How long was this?"

"Almost two weeks," he answered proudly. . . . "Then they told me on a Friday that today would be my last day in that class. That I should go to it today, you know, but that on Monday I had to switch to this other one. They just gave me a different room number but I knew what they were doing. Like they were giving me one more day with the brains, and then I had to go be with the dummies, where I was supposed to be. Like my vacation was over. So I went with the brains one more day, on that Friday like I said, in the afternoon. But the teacher didn't know I was moving, so she acted like I belonged there. Wasn't her fault. All the time I was just sitting there thinking 'this is the last day for me. This is the last time I'm ever going to learn anything,' you know what I mean? Real learning."

. . . "From then on," he was saying, "I knew I had to go back where they made me believe I belonged. I didn't even argue. I was just sitting there thinking I was like some prisoner, you know, who thought he was free. Like they let him out of jail and he was walking around, like you and me here, having a great old time. Then the warden meets him on the street and tells him they made a mistake and he has to go back to prison. That's what I was thinking of in that class.

"So then the teacher called on me—and this is how I know just how not smart I am—she called on me, like she always did, like she'd call on anybody, and she asked me a question. I knew the answer 'cause I'd read it the night before in my book which I bought, and then my mother read the book to me, too, after I'd already read it. So I began to speak and suddenly I couldn't say nothing. Nothing, man. Not a word. Like my mind died in there. And everybody was looking at me, you know, like I was crazy or something. My heart was beating real fast. I knew the answer, man. And she was just waiting, and I couldn't say nothing. And you know what I did? I cried. I sat there and cried, man, 'cause I couldn't say nothing. That's how I know how smart I am. That's when I really learned at that school how smart I was. I mean, how smart I *thought* I was. I had no business being there. Nobody smart's sitting in no class crying. That's the day I found out for real. That's the day that made me know for sure."

Of course we cannot generalize from a sample of one. But if even a few children feel this devastated as a result of an educational practice that has no visible academic benefits, we cannot ignore such painful utterances. They suggest that schools may have a very powerful negative effect on the self-concept of some children, particularly of ethnic minorities and lower-classes. Lennards' (1969) study of the social consequences of streaming in the Netherlands found that school differentiation is directly related to pupil attitudes toward stratification. In that country there are no comprehensive schools at the secondary level. Students are selected at age 11 by a test of academic ability, and segregated into three different types of schools, each aiming at a different level in the occupational hierarchy. Teachers from different educational backgrounds present different curricula. In this system, Lennards observed, only 20 percent of students in all types of schools reject the principle of deferring to the opinions of an educated elite, and 40 percent feel that less-educated people should not earn more than better-educated people (1969: 25). He suggests that this type of school structure "causes" these attitudes. While this is merely a suggestion, it indicates fruitful lines for further cross-cultural research into how school structures create attitudes and values consonant with a society's stratification system.

Attitudes toward school are also related to one's ability-group position. Griffin (1969) found that comprehensive-school children in England had more positive attitudes toward school than did grammar-school students.[3] Levenson (1972) reported that ability grouping in the teaching of reading was related to negative attitudes toward reading. Similarly, Adkison (1968) noted that being in a "low ability" group was related to negative attitudes about one's ability group, and Peterson (1966) remarked that students in "low ability" sections felt that their teachers enjoyed teaching their classes to a lesser extent. (This may well be an accurate perception, since most teachers like ability grouping and prefer working with average or better sections. See, e.g., Lunn, 1970.) Furthermore, students in a "middle" group felt that they could have learned more in a higher section (Peterson, 1966). Thus it is not surprising that Lesyk, Katzenmeyer and Hynes (1971) found higher achievers more favorable toward grouping than lower achievers. Such sentiments may be related to school success and to attitudes about continuing in school.

In addition, students in the lower group tend to develop their own subculture, which becomes increasingly antagonistic toward teachers and school (Hargreaves, 1967). Knowing the school's opinion of them and perceiving their life chances, the boys Hargreaves studied felt little desire or

[3]Comprehensive schools are most like middle-class and lower-class American secondary schools. They combine academic (or college-bound) curricula with general education programs and vocational curricula. Secondary modern schools in Great Britain are comparable to vocational schools in the United States. They teach more "practical" courses, including such subjects as woodworking or metalworking. Grammar schools, on the other hand, are entirely college preparatory.

need to conform to the school's demands. Indeed, they received much more ego support from their peers in the opposition subculture than from the school. Just as Lunn (1970) noticed how the structure of the school affected students' attitudes, Hargreaves (1969) saw this continuing and leading to the development of an alternative structure of values and rewards.

Summary

Ability-group and track placement relies heavily upon standardized-test scores, although teacher recommendations and pupil race or social class may also influence a student's assignment. While we lack systematic evidence about the educational processes that occur in different tracks, there is reason to believe that the curricular content, type of instruction, degree of selectivity, frequency and type of teacher–pupil interaction, and available educational resources tend to favor higher over lower tracks. Since tracking practices so often result in racial and economic homogeneity within classes, these differences in content and experience may help to explain variations in academic achievement by race and class. But as Rosenbaum's (1976) research so vividly demonstrates, tracking differentiates students even in a school that is homogeneous with respect to race and class.

Most research studies show no clear-cut effect of tracking on the *average* academic achievement of students. There is a slight trend toward improving the achievement of "high ability" groups, but this is offset by the substantial losses of the "average" and "low" groups. Moreover, the observed gains appear to be due to differences in the content, materials, and methods of teaching rather than to tracking per se. With respect to the range of academic achievement, tracking seems to increase the dispersion of student-achievement scores. This seems to be because the top scorers go up somewhat while students in "lower" groups decline.

Perhaps as a result of such dispersion, the stability of ability-group placement increases over time. What changes there are tend to be downward rather than upward. A further academic consequence is the effect of track placement on continued education.

Tracking appears to reduce the self-esteem of many students and build up (inflate?) the egos of only a few chosen students. This outcome has interesting implications, perhaps explaining why substantial inequalities in society are accepted, as Lennards (1969) suggests. The structural feature of tracking may socialize the children exposed to it so that those in lower tracks come to feel that they deserve less from life, while those in higher tracks, like those in private schools, come to expect more for themselves out of life.

Tracking may also influence achievement, self-concept, and attitudes via the expectations teachers hold for different students. Hargreaves (1967) notes that teachers have lower standards for lower-stream children, but most studies of tracking have not measured the possible consequences of tracking for teachers' expectations. Therefore we need to analyze the effects of track placement and other factors on the genesis of teachers' expectations. In doing this, we can begin to see the connection between structural forms and interpersonal relationships.

7

The Genesis of Teachers' Expectations

How DOES POSITION in the structure of dominance influence participants in educational settings? In Chapter 2 I suggested that structures of dominance in society are related to societal ideologies (such as the instrumental–merito-cratic ideology), which in turn are related to educational assumptions (in-cluding the IQ and cultural deficit theories). These educational concepts, along with selection and differentiating structures in schools, may impinge upon teachers and students in the situation.

To explore this issue, consider the question of whether a student's posi-tion in the structure of dominance (indicated directly by race and social class, and indirectly by appearance, language, behavior and test scores) is related to the expectations teachers hold. If it is, why do teachers hold lower expec-tations for lower class or minority students? I consider four possibilities:

1. Teachers have certain personality traits that predispose them to have lower expectations for certain children.
2. Teachers are exposed to certain socializing experiences and societal prejudices that shape their perceptions of students.
3. Educational concepts, such as those concerning IQ and cultural deficits (considered in Chapter 5), influence teachers' expectations.
4. Educational structures, including tracking, affect teachers' expecta-tions.

A number of pupil characteristics may be viewed as indicators of position in the structure of dominance, including such relatively direct indicators as ethnicity or social class and indirect ones such as test scores, pupil ap-pearance, language and behavior. The frequency of research on such student characteristics and the comparative lack of research on teacher or structural characteristics reflects the hegemony of the individualistic ideology (discussed in Chapters 3 and 5), which guides the formulation of research topics with respect to what is taken as the problem to be explained. Because of their underrepresentation in the research literature, certain analytic categories tend to be overlooked or underplayed when explanations are offered. Having recognized this ideological bias, we can nevertheless peruse the content of such research and consider how pupil characteristics influence the genesis of teachers' expectations.

Pupil Characteristics

Although many researchers report that pupil race is related to teacher expectations, I discovered two (Deitz and Purkey, 1969; Roeber, 1970) who found no relation between pupil race and teacher expectations.

Deitz and Purkey studied 147 white graduate students in the College of Education of the University of Florida who had been employed as classroom teachers within the previous 24 months. Each respondent was given a paragraph describing a hypothetical adolescent boy: his economic and family background, likes and dislikes, and prior year's discipline record in school. The "experimental" and "control" paragraphs were identical except for the inclusion of the word "Negro" before the word "boy" in the first sentence of the former. The paragraphs were randomly distributed to the subjects, who were asked to read the material and then estimate the boy's future academic performance on a 7-point scale ranging from "far below average" (1), to "far above average" (7). The researchers report that the mean rating of the "Negro" paragraph was 3.82 ($SD = .75$), while for the "unqualified" "boy" paragraph it was 3.95 ($SD = .87$). The difference between the means was not significant at .05. Deitz and Purkey (1969) conclude that these results " . . . question the commonly held assumption that teachers enter the classroom with differential expectation levels for students based on the variable of race [p. 694]."

What we do not know from their report is how they described the socioeconomic and family background, likes and dislikes, and school-discipline record for the two boys. It is quite possible that certain descriptions might minimize the salience of race for teachers. For example, if the boys were described as coming from upper-middle-class professional families, as having intellectual or scientific interests and no disciplinary problems in school, race might be unimportant. Under less favorable circumstances it is possible that race might become more salient for teachers.

Roeber's work (1970) enables us to specify some of the conditions under which race is *not* salient to teachers. Studying 30 female elementary-school teachers in a school district near Detroit, he found that their expectations for student ability and achievement were influenced by test scores, record of achievement, and comments of former teachers, but not by the race or the socioeconomic status of the students. The subjects were given "student-information files," apparently constructed by the researcher, containing information on those characteristics. The race and social class of student were presented ecologically, by describing the school district and elementary school. Possibly for some teachers, having other "objective" information about a pupil is a decisive influence, and thus race no longer *directly* affects the expectations they hold for children. Roeber's work confirms the observation by Guskin and Guskin (1970) that "labels and stereotypes can have an important impact on perception when more reliable information is absent, but tend to have little significance when more directly observable and relevant cues are present [p. 30]." But if expectations are influenced by comments of former teachers, record of achievement, and test scores, which may themselves be related to race, then the "reliable information" may provide an illusory scientific objectivity in support of a stereotype. (The issue of bias in assessment procedures is discussed in Chapter 5.) In any event, Roeber's (1970) work suggests that the presence of other information may minimize the effect of race on expectations.

Three of the seven studies finding positive relationships between pupil race and teacher expectations asked teachers to listen to tape recordings of black and white students reading a sample passage (Guskin, 1971; Pugh, 1974; Williams and Whitehead, 1971). Both Guskin and Pugh found that white student speakers were perceived in more favorable terms. The 41 black and 41 white teachers in Guskin's (1971) study agreed on the greater ability of the white speakers to succeed in present and future educational settings. Some might argue that this was a realistic appraisal given the success rates of black students in school, but it is nevertheless significant that both black and white teachers in this study had lower expectations for black students. In addition, the teachers tended to perceive black speakers as being of a lower social class than they actually were, which suggests that the teachers may be perceiving the blacks in biased terms.

In a similar vein, Pugh (1974) found that both male and female teachers judged the academic ability and school behavior of white students more favorably than those of black students, even when the students were matched for social-class background.

Williams and Whitehead (1971) found that teachers' evaluations of the stereotypes of a particular ethnic group tended to be related to their ratings of children belonging to that particular group. Thus a teacher, rating a stereotypical Anglo example as relatively high on the confidence–eagerness scale the researchers developed or low in ethnicity–nonstandardness, tended to rate the videotaped child from that group accordingly. Thus, teachers may evaluate individual children relative to their stereotypes for particular groups. Williams and Whitehead (1971) suggest, " . . . stereotypes may mediate in the differentiation of the speech samples, but the teacher-rater nevertheless is still somewhat sensitive to individual differences *within* ethnic categories [p. 112]."

Rosenfeld (1973) also addressed the question of whether teachers stereotype students of different ethnic and class backgrounds, using actual classroom evaluative criteria, and audio, visual, and audiovisual cues to elicit teacher stereotypes. Teachers were presented with audio, visual, and audiovisual materials portraying students from different ethnic and social-class groups and were asked to evaluate the students using a semantic-differential scale. Rosenfeld found that teachers do stereotype students on the basis of ethnic and class cues, and that these cues are transmitted through both audio and visual modes, the former providing more information for making judgments. This suggests that the language practices of ethnic children may stimulate less favorable expectations in the minds of their teachers. As Baratz and Baratz (1970), Dillard (1972), Labov (1973), and Williams and Whitehead (1971) remind us, differences in language habits have all too often been considered as *deficits*. Hence, Rosenfeld's (1973) work suggests that language may be one of the factors that mediate between pupil race and teacher expectations.

The possible mediating effect of language on the relationship between pupil race and teacher expectations may underlie Buford's (1973) finding that teachers expected greater achievement from Anglo-American students than was warranted by objective predictions, and significantly underexpected for Mexican-American and black students. Buford studied 15 third- and fourth-grade teachers in Title I schools in a central Texas city. During the two years of the study, those teachers taught 715 students. Buford asked the teachers to indicate their expected achievement for the children. Buford then, independently, computed an "objectively predicted achievement" for the same students, based upon information in the students' cumulative records. Thus, by comparing the "objective" predictions with the teachers' expectations for different ethnic groups, Buford could assess the degree to which teacher expectations were affected by race. Since the "objectively" predicted achievement was based upon information that was itself probably somewhat biased against blacks and Mexican-Americans, it is all the more remarkable that she obtained significant differences for the various ethnic groups. Moreover, the use of cumulative records containing grades, teacher evaluations, and student test scores may have helped indirectly to control for social class, which was not introduced as a formal variable in the study.

It is apparent, however, that language alone does not fully explain why teachers often seem to have lower expectations for black pupils. Harvey and Slatin (1975) studied 96 elementary teachers from 4 schools serving lower- and middle-class neighborhoods. Teachers were given full-length photographs of 9 white and 9 black children and then asked to estimate the performance potential of each child by classifying the child according to 8 categories related to academic performance. They were also asked to indicate their perception of the child's social class. They found that, regardless of the perceived class of the child, teachers more often expected white children to succeed and black children to fail. This study, based solely on the visual cues in a photograph, involved no verbal exposure to the children and controlled for perceived social class.

It appears that when teachers have relatively few cues, as in the Harvey and Slatin (1975) and Buford (1973) studies, they are influenced in their expectations by race. When they have more information, particularly verbal-behavior cues, the effect of race on expectations is directly mediated through that information. Finally, when even more information is available, as in the Roeber (1970) study, the effect of race upon expectations is no longer visible. Roeber, however, did not examine the possibility that race was correlated with teacher comments, pupil achievement, and test scores, which may have effectively mediated the effect of pupil race on teacher expectations.

In short, substantial evidence suggests that teacher expectations may be related to student race. In five of these seven studies, the teachers appear to be from Southern states (Virginia, Texas, Florida, Kentucky); in the other two the state is not indicated. This result may not be typical of non-Southern states. In general, it is dangerous to generalize too strongly to national populations from small, nonrandom samples of teachers in a few experiments. Nevertheless, the frequency with which the relationship between pupil race and teacher expectation appears suggests that student race is probably an important influence on teacher expectations.

At first glance, student socioeconomic status seems to have a mixed relationship with teacher expectations. I located seven studies on this subject; in four teacher expectations were positively influenced by social class and in three there was no relationship. From these apparently conflicting studies, can one ascertain anything about the conditions under which class is independently related to teacher expectations?

One possibility is that class has less effect on teacher expectations when other important information about the student is available. This may be particularly true when other student characteristics are related to class. Thus Pugh (1974) found that 13 teachers, asked to listen to tape recordings as a basis for estimating the academic ability and school behavior of 3 black and 3 white male student speakers, representing upper-middle-, middle- and lower-class backgrounds, were influenced by student race but not by social class. But perhaps in this Florida county, racial differences were more salient to the teachers than class differences.

In the Wise (1972) study race was not mentioned as a possibly confounding factor, but teachers were given information about their pupils' behavior—whether the pupils were "teachable" and "controllable"—in addition to information about pupil class. So perhaps the behavioral data about the students offset any influence of social class and explain the absence of class influence on expectations.

Roeber (1970), as noted, provided teachers with information about pupils' test scores, records of achievement, and prior teacher comments. It may be, as he concludes, that this information is a more important influence on teachers' expectations than social-class data, but I have some hesitation about accepting this interpretation because the pupil's social class was conveyed by describing a school district and a particular elementary school rather than individual data. Therefore, it is difficult to decide from Roeber's study whether the lack of relationship between class and teacher expectations is explainable in terms of the presence of other factors (which might themselves be related to class) or was due to an unconvincing portrayal of the individual child's class background.

At least one group of researchers (Miller et al., 1968) found that social class is related to teachers' expectations. Lower-class individuals were viewed as having more detentions, having less ability in arithmetic, participating less in extracurricular activities, having parents who were less involved in school, leaving school at a younger age, reading fewer books independently, completing fewer homework assignments, and having lower future IQs *even when current IQ and achievement were comparable.* So other student information may not eliminate the relationship between class and expectations under all circumstances.

An additional feature distinguishes the above studies with conflicting results. All of the positive findings appeared in studies in which either real children were the stimulus for teacher perception of social class or the teachers were given information from which they formed a perception of the child's class. In these studies, then, it was perception of class which was related to expectations. For example, Miller et al. (1968) provided case histories containing cues concerning lower-class origins, and Harvey and Slatin (1975) presented teacher subjects with photographs of students and asked the teachers to rank the class of the children. Thus, in both of these studies, *the teachers themselves evaluated the child's social class*, based on either verbal or visual cues. They were not simply presented with the researchers' description of the child as "middle" or "lower class."

Studies of the natural genesis of expectations assume an inference about the child's social class by the teacher, who receives various cues from observing the children. Davidson and Lang (1960) and Rist (1970) gathered indicators to categorize a child's social class. Then teacher expectations were examined in relation to these "objective" class differences. Davidson and Lang divided the 203 children they studied into three groups: the upper group, coming from families of professional people, white-collar workers and businessmen; the middle social class, whose parents were skilled workers, policemen, and firemen; and the lower group, whose parents were semi-skilled, unskilled, or unemployed.

Davidson and Lang measured teacher expectations, or perceived teacher feelings, by asking the children to decide how their teacher felt toward them with respect to each of 35 traits, including "not eager to learn," "a hard worker," "clever," "not eager to study," "smart," etc., and then to rate each of their answers on a 3-point scale as true most of the time, half of the time, or seldom. The researchers then computed an index of favorability, totaling all these ratings, and found that children in the upper and middle social-class groups perceived their teachers' feelings toward them more favorably than did the children in the lower social-class groups. This was true even when pupil achievement level was held constant. Thus, although teacher expectations are measured here by pupil perceptions, the results suggest that teacher expectations and sentiments toward children may be influenced by the child's class background.

Rist (1970) did an ethnography of an all-black kindergarten class. He considered pupil social class to be indicated by the family's income, whether or not they received welfare, and by the educational level of the parents. The pupils from higher class backgrounds were much more likely to be assigned to Tables 1 and 2 and much less likely to be at Table 3. Rist concluded that pupil social class was salient to teachers in their formulation of expectations for pupils, as reflected in the table assignments.

In brief, student class was found to be related to teacher expectations when other factors such as race were not more salient, when expectations were engendered by real children, or when there was a chance for teachers to draw inferences about students' class rather than simply being told their background. Hence, there is evidence to support the inference that pupil race and social class are directly related to teachers' expectations, particularly in natural rather than experimental situations.

Since race and class are related to test scores and to conduct evaluations, they may mediate the influence upon expectations of the pupil's position in the structure of dominance. Eight of 11 (73 percent) studies that examine pupil test scores in relation to teacher expectations report a positive relationship between known test scores and expectations and 3 find no relationship. Studies reporting negative findings are considered first and then those with positive findings, to see if we can understand the conditions under which teacher expectations are influenced by pupil test scores.

Pitt (1956), Fleming and Anttonen (1971), and Sorotzkin, Fleming, and Anttonen (1974) all report no relationship between pupil test scores and teacher expectations. The three studies share some remarkable similarities. First, they all employ induced expectations; the manipulation of test-score data is the only stimulus variable. That is, teachers were given false IQ information about children in their class. A control group of students had no IQ information reported to the teacher. Secondly, in none of the studies were the teachers' expectations measured directly, for example, by asking them what expectations they held for particular students. Instead, teacher expectation was *inferred* from the lack of *effects* on the children whose scores were manipulated. Since José and Cody (1971) report that in 61 percent of the teachers they studied, teacher expectancy had not been modified by the experimenter, there may be a serious problem in "inducing" an expectancy in a teacher. It certainly cannot be assumed that such an expectancy has been induced without measuring it directly.

Pitt (1956) found that inflated or deflated IQ scores reported to teachers were not related to the pupils' achievement scores or to the teachers' marks given to those students. This illustrates the importance of considering expectations and outcomes as two separate concepts, which need to be measured independently. Otherwise, we have no way of knowing whether teacher expectations were affected, and if so, how. All we know is that an *attempt* to manipulate teacher expectations was not related to measured outcomes, but we do not know whether this was because:

1. the attempt to induce an expectation failed;
2. teachers believed the false test scores but did not treat the variously designated children differently; or
3. they believed the scores and treated the children differently, but with no effect.

Fleming and Anttonen (1971) suggest that teachers possibly recognized the inflated scores as inaccurate and may have placed greater credence on their own perception of the academic performance and behavior of this group of children. These are interesting, but basically unanswerable speculations. Fleming and Anttonen (1971) also raise some interesting questions about the usefulness for teachers of group IQ tests, suggesting that the tests may not really assist in the instructional program except insofar as the teacher " . . . feels more comfortable for having had them [p. 250]." They do not try to explain why the teacher might feel more comfortable with tests than without them, and they also do not speculate about possible negative consequences of test information. Finally, they suggest that teachers' knowledge of testing and attitudes toward testing may be critical factors affecting how teachers use test information.

In sum, the three studies that found no relationship between test scores and teacher expectations manipulated only test-score information. Moreover, these studies did not measure expectations directly. Therefore I am not convinced by these studies that IQ or other test scores are unimportant influences on teachers' expectations.

The eight studies finding positive correlations between test information and teacher expectations differ markedly from the negative studies in several critical respects. I thought they might differ in terms of whether expectations were induced or natural. While four of the positive results were based upon natural expectations (Barnard, Zimbardo, and Sarason, 1968; Given, 1974; Williams, 1975; Willis, 1972), four were not (Beez, 1970; Brown, 1969; Long and Henderson, 1974; Roeber, 1970). Significantly, however, in none of these studies was test information the only data available to teachers. In the three natural situations, the teachers knew the students from classes and could use that information as well. In those situations, IQ and other scores were not manipulated. Thus, a question, thoughtfully suggested by Barnard, Zimbardo and Sarason (1968), is whether teacher perceptions and expectations associated with IQ are a reflection of actually occurring behavioral differences among children or whether they are distortions of reality. The researchers found that pupils with high IQ scores tended to be perceived by their teachers as ones who learn quickly, pay attention, retain material, overachieve, and are ambitious relative to children with low IQ. Also, children with higher IQs were viewed as less dependent and daydreamy, and more aggressive, sensitive, mature, sociable, popular, and active. The researchers present and discuss several lines of converging evidence suggesting that the positive traits associated with IQ may distort reality somewhat. Since children were tested on anxiety level as well as IQ, the authors could see that teachers evaluated anxious children who were bright differently from anxious children who were not bright, and did so on traits shown by previous research not to be characteristic of the bright, anxious child. Hence, their evidence suggests a kind of halo effect between IQ score and teacher expectations.

The four positive studies using induced expectations differ from the negative studies in the manner of inducement. Beez (1970), for example, presented similar IQ scores for all the children but presented reports for "low ability" pupils which termed their scores "low average," interpreted the results negatively, and predicted poor school performance. The reports for "high ability" children stressed positive fictional behaviors in the test situation and good prior school adjustment. Brown (1969) gave fictitious psychological reports to teachers with dichotomous classification of IQ scores. After the teachers read the reports, the experimenter reiterated the information. These means of inducing expectations may have greater effect than merely reporting scores without comment.

An additional factor that may affect the genesis of particular teacher expectations is the presence of information about the child in addition to IQ data. In all the studies reporting positive findings, teachers had more than test scores on which to formulate their expectations for a child (Barnard, Zimbardo and Sarason, 1968; Beez, 1970; Brown, 1969; Given, 1974; Long and Henderson, 1974; Roeber, 1970; Williams, 1975; Willis, 1972). In these studies, the teachers either knew the actual children or received a fictional psychological report or student file. It may be that test scores are even more influential when they can be viewed in the context of additional information about a child and that they have less effect when they are presented to teachers by themselves.

A final source of difference between the studies reporting positive and negative results concerns the question of whether teacher expectations were measured directly or inferred from the outcomes. In seven of the eight positive-result studies, teacher expectations were measured directly in some way, often by asking teachers to rate children in terms of expected future school achievement. Alone among the positive-result studies, Brown's (1969) inferred expectation from teacher behavior, which is closer to the source than are measures of pupil achievement or growth. In brief, test scores appear to influence teachers' expectations when they are received in natural situations or when, if induced, they are interpreted for the teacher (cf. Meichenbaum, Bowers, and Ross, 1969). Similarly, teachers appear to be more influenced by test scores when they receive them along with other information about the child. Finally, virtually all the positive studies measured the teachers' expectations directly rather than inferring them from pupil behavior. Given the positive relationship between the structure of dominance and the development of the testing movement (see Chapter 5), these findings suggest an indirect way that the structure of dominance is related to the genesis of teachers' expectations.

The possible mediating effect of behavioral traits is suggested by the work of Lawlor and Lawlor (1973). They gave 72 undergraduate student teachers 2 10-minute video tapes of an elementary science lesson. The sound track was so noisy that there were few audible verbal cues. After seeing the tape, the prospective teachers were asked to rank order the children (5 pupils in the first lesson and 4 in the second) in terms of their ability and to indicate the clues used in making their judgments. The researchers were surprised to find that 86 percent of the subjects did rank the children. Most of the reasons given for their rankings were unsubstantiated inferences, such as saying that a child seemed "interested," "independent," "lost," and so on. In conjunction with these inference statements, 109 factual observations were reported. Of these, 46 percent referred to the speed with which children accomplished the task. Speed was the most common basis for making judgments, in the absence of verbal cues. Lawlor and Lawlor (1973) concluded, "This is consistent with our use of timed intelligence tests, the criteria for the College Quiz championships and the brief 'wait time' exhibited by teachers on all levels [p. 13]." Their work suggests that, given the cultural differences in how time is regarded, children from various backgrounds may show varying rates of speed in task performance, which in turn may affect teacher expectations.

The possibility that the physical appearance of children may affect teacher expectations was noted by Clifford and Walster (1973). They found that the physical attractiveness of children was significantly related to teachers' expectations about how intelligent a child was, how interested in school, and probable popularity with peers. Since concepts of physical attractiveness are culturally defined and very often class linked, we see another subtle way in which race or social status may influence expectations.

Adams and Cohen (1974) agree with Clifford and Walster up to a point. They found that teacher interactions appear to be influenced initially by physical characteristics of the child. They note, however, that facial attractiveness appeared to influence teachers more than overall personal appearance, and they speculate that this might be due to the location of their study in a middle-class school, in which the children were not very differently dressed. They suggest that in certain ghetto schools, in which there might be a wider range of personal appearance and dress, overall appearance may exert more influence. They conclude that their findings provide some support for the view of Adams and LaVoie (1974) that a child's physical characteristics (i.e., facial attractiveness and personal appearance) influence a teacher more during initial teacher–student interactions than later.

Adams and LaVoie (1974) asked 350 male and female elementary teachers in a large metropolitan school district to predict a student's attitudes, work habits, parental interest, and peer relations after studying a student progress report and a color photograph of the student. The teachers' ratings were affected more by the student's reported conduct than by the child's physical attractiveness. Thus, Adams and LaVoie suggest that attractiveness may be influential at first, or when a teacher knows nothing else about a student, but that, subsequently, the student's record, particularly reports of behavior, is most important.

Adams and LaVoie also found that conduct appeared to be the most important feature of the student record. Students who had low grades on personal and social growth were negatively evaluated by teachers on a number of criteria, even though they had received mostly As and Bs in their academic courses. They conclude that the child who does not conform to behavioral expectations is viewed as having less potential for the educative process. They note their finding in another study (LaVoie and Adams, 1974) that students with poor conduct ratings were perceived by teachers as having lower ability. Moreover, such students were less likely to receive post-high-school training or to attain a high-status occupation. This is direct evidence in support of the thesis of Bowles and Gintis (1976) that the social-control features of school are much more important than cognitive aspects. The instrumental-meritocratic ideology focuses primarily upon the cognitive content of education, stressing that schools select and reward people on the basis of their academic achievement and skills. But LaVoie and Adams (1974; Adams and LaVoie, 1974) indicate that behavioral criteria are more important for teachers' expectations and, moreover, that these behavioral criteria vary with the social class of the students.

Additional evidence in this direction comes from Keeley (1973) who investigated whether teacher expectations were affected by the inclusion of the juvenile-delinquent label in the cumulative-record folders of hypothetical delinquency-prone students. Teachers reacted to these cumulative records with their expectations of how these hypothetical students would perform and behave if they were a pupil in the teachers' classrooms. Keeley found that white teachers ($N = 27$) significantly lowered their expectations for academic and emotional maturity for students labeled delinquent, but not their expectations for social maturity. Black teachers ($N = 9$) indicated lowered expectations regarding labeled students' social maturity but not for such students' academic and emotional maturity. In short, teachers held lower expectations for students labeled delinquent than for students who were not so labeled, with some variation in academic expectations according to teacher race.

Thus, not only do teachers form expectations of children based directly upon race and social class, but their expectations are also influenced by pupil test scores, appearance, language style, speed of task performance, and behavior–characteristics which are themselves culturally defined and related to relative position in the structure of dominance. When such traits are not related to teachers' expectations, we notice that often the experimental manipulation (whether of race, social class, or IQ) may appear obvious to teachers. Teachers, like anyone else, do not want to look like dupes. But when the cues are more subtle, or are presented in natural situations, and teachers draw their own conclusions, then race, social class, and test scores seem to influence expectations. Moreover, teacher expectations are more influenced by *negative* information about pupil characteristics than by positive data (Mason, 1973). This is a particularly interesting finding since so much of the information teachers gain about low-income and minority children seems to be negative.

But why do teachers come to view minority or lower-class students in negative ways? Are teachers guilty of flawed characters (as Silberman, 1970, seems to suggest by stopping his analysis at differential teacher expectations), or are there sociological explanations for this tendency?

Teacher Characteristics

A number of personality characteristics of teachers, such as locus of control, trust in self, conceptual system, mental set, and prejudice, have been studied in relation to their expectations, so it is possible to partially test Silberman's explanation. Both Machowsky (1973) and Murray (1972), who studied a combined total of 117 teachers, failed to find any relationship between locus of control, as measured on Rotter's scale, and teacher expectancy. Similarly, Harris (1972) found no relationship between the conceptual system of 81 female education majors and the formation of expectations of students' abilities.

On the other hand, Wise (1972) studied 301 teachers in rural New York State and found that teachers' trust in the validity of their own experiences (TVE) was moderately related to their expectations for 4 of the students in their class. While related to Rotter's scale and other measures of personal competence, confidence, and independence, Wise's measure did not have as high a reliability coefficient as he would have liked (.65 and .43 on samples of 62 and 237, respectively). Moreover, the correlation between TVE and expectation was low (.16). Finally, TVE and information about pupils' behavior interacted in their effect on teachers' expectations. Therefore, it is hard to place much credence in the importance of the TVE factor. To the degree that we do, it may be interpreted as indicating an affective, rather than a cognitive, personality trait.

What might be deemed "mental set" was found by Anastasiow (1964) to be related to teachers' expectations. That study found that teachers perceived their classes' mean reading levels to be at the class grade level regardless of actual reading achievement. A third-grade teacher (teaching eight- and nine-year-olds) assigned books considered suitable for that level to average students in the class, even though they were actually reading at the sixth-grade level!

A number of critics of American education have suggested that prejudice may be an important factor affecting teachers' expectations for children. Prejudice can be examined as a function of teacher personality or conformity and as a response to a characteristic of the children.

According to Guskin and Guskin (1970):

> Prejudice can be said to exist when an individual has a negative stereotype and negative attitude toward a particular group of people. It should be added that prejudice is more often the result of an individual's acceptance of general community attitudes (norms) than a function of his own personality. This was demonstrated in a study by Pettigrew (1958). He administered a measure of authoritarian personality and an anti-Negro questionnaire along with a conformity scale to many people in South Africa and the Southern part of the United States. His findings indicated that while a small minority, in both groups, had an authoritarian personality related to prejudicial attitudes and a stereotype of Negroes, the overwhelming majority of those who had a negative, prejudicial attitude toward Negroes were conforming to general societal standards (norms). When these prejudicial norms are held by the teacher as well as community members, the negative consequences for the Negro pupil are obvious [p. 32].

Both mental set and prejudices may be interpreted in terms of conformity to social norms. Thus while personality traits such as locus of control and conceptual system are not related to teacher expectations, social norms appear to be. And norms are learned in social contexts. Teachers of different races may be reared in different social contexts, and hence, hold different expectations for students. This is exactly what has been noted by a number of observers, with most finding that black teachers hold higher expectations for all students, both black and white (see Keeley, 1973; Krupczak, 1972; Pugh, 1974).

Similarly, Gottlieb (1964) found significant differences between white and black teachers in their attitudes toward pupils of both races from low-income families. White teachers saw such students as "talkative," "lazy," "fun loving," "high strung," and "rebellious" and tended to blame the children and their parents for educational problems. By contrast, black teachers described the same children as "fun loving," "happy," "cooperative," "energetic," and "ambitious" and blamed problems on the physical environment. In short, four studies have found black teachers to be somewhat more favorable than white teachers in their expectations toward all children.

Aside from living in a society characterized by certain class and racial ideologies (see Chapter 3), teachers are exposed to specialized professional training. Does the content of that training in any way influence their perceptions of lower-class and minority children? One aspect of contemporary teacher training is exposure to research on "the culturally deprived" child. This concept has already been discussed in considerable detail (see Chapter 5). Both Stein (1971) and S. Hill (1971) suggest that prevailing models in the behavioral sciences might influence teachers' expectations. Hill did a content analysis of 71 research articles selected from the 1970 editions of *Educational Index* and *Psychological Abstracts* in order to classify the proposed causes of poor academic performance among low-income youth. Articles were coded in terms of three possible models: (1) the clinical perspective, which assumes that poor academic performance is due to cognitive, cultural, or personal deficiencies in the child or his environment; (2) the structural approach, which posits defects in the nature and organization of school processes; and (3) the systemic perspective, which proposes that pervasive structural defects in the schooling process restrict a youth's options to attain cultural, economic, political, or personal competence. She found that the vast majority of research on the education of disadvantaged students was conducted from a clinical perspective. The research literature assumes that disadvantaged youth have: inadequate families (35 observations in the 71 articles), personality deficiencies (27 observations), undeveloped language (21 observations), gaps in perceptual and motor readiness (21 observations), inadequate motivation (18 observations), and/or intellectual deficiencies (11 observations). Hill reports further that far fewer studies were based on even minor alterations of educational structure. Those that did deal with structure were concerned with teacher change (9 observations), classroom grouping (8 observations), and curriculum relevance (6 observations). No studies were predicated on the need for massive system overhaul. While these results may be biased somewhat by the exclusion of *Sociological Abstracts* from the sampling frame, they reflect the general state of research on education at that time (cf. Persell, 1976, who found that less than 9 percent of all the research on education published in the United States in 1967–68 was concerned with education in relation to its societal context).

Moreover, the influence of these research perspectives on teacher-training textbooks is apparent (Stein, 1971), as it is on the way in which many teachers discuss the education of disadvantaged students (see, e.g., Arnez, 1966). Schindler (1970) observed how these processes are filtered into the world views of teachers. Considering the environmentalist position (cultural differences) he notes:

What is being *said* is: the children have problems that hinder learning according to conventional (traditional middle-class) ways of teaching; but what is being *heard* is: the children have so many problems that they can learn only with difficulty, so don't be surprised if they fail at an appalling rate—it's not the teacher's fault; they were "years behind" when they began school [Schindler, 1970: 26–27].

Similarly, with respect to the genetic-deficit view, Schindler (1970) quotes a teacher: "Someone named Jenner [Jensen] from Harvard has proved that the Negro children are not as smart as the white children [p. 27]." While impressionistic, these quotations indicate how the behavioral-science literature is assimilated into teachers' definitions of the situation. These behavioral-science orientations may justify existing prejudices in teachers or may generate biased perspectives where none existed before.

If behavioral-science and education concepts and ideologies fail to socialize prospective teachers completely, more experienced teachers are often ready to step in and fill the gap. Fuchs (1973), for example, presents the following diary entry by a beginning teacher in an inner-city elementary school:

Mrs. Jones (an experienced teacher) explained about the problems that these children have. "Some of them never see a newspaper. Some of them have never been on the subway. The parents are so busy having parties and things that they have no time for their children. They can't even take them to a museum or anything. It's very important that the teacher stress books."

Mrs. Jones tells her class, "If anyone asks you what you want for Christmas, you can say you want a book." She told me that she had a 6-1 [sixth grade, top track] class last year, and it was absolutely amazing how many children had never even seen a newspaper. They can't read Spanish either. So she said that the educational problem lies with the parents. They are the ones that have to be educated [p. 76].

At least two features of this "socializing account" are interesting. First, the more experienced teacher seems to feel very strongly the need to "explain the problem" to the new teacher. It would be interesting to see how widespread this type of socialization is in the lives of all teachers. Is it more frequent in inner-city schools than in suburban ones? Secondly, even if it occurs in all schools that the old initiate the new, does it always take this form—that is, does it always stress the *deficiencies* of the children? Does it ever indicate what they do know, what they are good at, what experiences they have had, so that a new teacher might find ways of relating to those experiences and backgrounds?

This socialization, in terms of what is missing from the lives and experiences of the children rather than in terms of what is positive and present, is also apparent in the accounts of Wax and Wax (1971) about teaching in American Indian schools. They have observed the "vacuum ideology," as they call it, that is articulated by the administrators of the school. No studies, to my knowledge, have been done to examine how this socializing by more experienced teachers may systematically engender particular types of expectations.

In the same diary of the beginning teacher, Fuchs (1973) presents anecdotal evidence about how the new teacher reacts: "It's just a shame that the children suffer. This problem will take an awful lot to straighten it out. I guess it won't take one day or even a year; it will take time [p. 76]." In this instance, the teacher already seems to feel somewhat hopeless about the situation. There seems to be very little that a teacher or a school can do, since the problem is rooted in the homes and lives of the children. Therefore, the teacher may be seen as having relatively pessimistic expectations for the children. In addition, the teacher has no concrete ideas about what to do that might be helpful for the children. Fuchs (1973), again out of the diary, shows how the new teacher wishes she could get some help in learning how to be a more effective teacher:

> I never had a course in college for teaching phonetics to children. In this school we had conferences about it, but I really wish that one of the reading teachers would come in and specifically show me how to go about teaching phonetics. . . . It is a difficult thing, especially when there is a language barrier and words are quite strange to these children who can't speak English. How can they read English? We have a great responsibility on our shoulders and the teachers should take these things seriously [p. 76].

Thus, while other teachers are ready to indicate to the novitiate what the problems of the children are, and thereby perhaps influence expectations for what the children will be able to learn, no one provides assistance in dealing with the situation. Schindler (1970) also observed that one of the main features of the new teacher's socialization is "the taking on of the salient categories of the experienced teachers [p. 32]." This problem is rendered all the more acute by the frequency with which inexperienced teachers are assigned to ghetto schools.

That certain pupil characteristics associated with social position are related to teacher expectations appears to be due less to personal failings on the part of teachers than to prevailing behavioral-science concepts and theories about such children. If teachers are "inadequately" socialized to the structures of dominance in their society, they may be trained to perceive the problem more "appropriately" by their peers. But teachers work in organizational contexts. Could school characteristics influence teacher expectations in any way?

Just as individual teachers may influence a new teacher, the entire faculty of a school may establish a particular climate of expectations (cf. Gigliotti and Brookover, 1975). In *Crisis in the Classroom*, Silberman (1970) identified three elementary schools in New York City that were succeeding in teaching low-income minority children to read at or above grade level. His book suggests one mechanism that may be operating to set a "tone" of high expectations for student achievement within a school. Silberman reports that all three principals of these successful schools were convinced that their students could learn. Given the teachers' past experience and their probable biases, common to many white middle-class Americans, Silberman asks, "How do the principals' positive expectations prevail?" In answer, he cites Merton (1957), who notes that "the self-fulfilling prophecy, whereby fears are translated into reality, operates only in the absence of deliberate institutional controls [quoted in Silberman, 1970: 105]." Silberman (1970) observed that each of the three principals provided such controls by holding " . . . themselves and their teachers accountable if their students fail. . . . One principal tells his teachers, 'There's no excuse for our kids not succeeding. I don't want to hear any talk about apathetic parents or hungry children or sleepy children or anything else. We have enough riches to overcome such handicaps, and we are accountable if these children fail [pp. 105–106]." Silberman (1970) indicates that "the schools are run accordingly: the expectation of success, and accountability for failure, are built into their structure, despite their wide differences in administrative style and approach [p. 106]."

This material suggests for further investigation: (1) the possibility that a principal, or a cadre of teachers, might have very strong positive expectations about the learning potential of all children, which might influence other teachers in the situation; and (2) the need to identify mechanisms and processes that effectively convey these expectations to other teachers. Existing educational practices may all too often contribute to the genesis of negative expectations.

One such educational practice with potentially negative consequences is tracking (discussed in Chapter 6). This practice has been pinpointed as an influence on teachers' expectations in at least seven studies. In Great Britain, Morrison and McIntyre (1969) report that surveys carried out in different educational systems and various types of schools (e.g., Pidgeon, 1970) indicate that "streaming and tracking practices, school objectives and curricula can all have a bearing on teachers' attitudes about what should be taught, how it should be taught and what kinds of responses can be expected from pupils [pp. 181–182]."

In a study of more than 10,000 students in Toronto, Williams (1975) found that the single most important source of teacher expectations was the school's certification of the student's aptitude via ability grouping, even when the student's past performance, current ambition, and academic aptitude were held constant. Hargreaves' (1967) observational study, *Social Relations in a Secondary School*, also noted that teachers in one English comprehensive school held lower standards for the lower-stream students than for the higher-stream ones. Keddie (1971) reports similar attitudes among teachers.

Thus two large-scale surveys and several observational studies have identified a structural source of teacher expectations, independent of student performance and attitudes. It is curious that these studies were conducted outside the United States. Major studies of the effects of tracking in American schools (see Findley and Bryan, 1970a, for a good review of these studies) do not usually examine the effects on teacher expectations. An interesting exception is the work of Flowers (1966), who shifted two experimental groups of seventh-grade students to higher-ability sections than their test scores warranted, without the students' or teachers' knowledge. Two control groups, matched on IQ and achievement scores, were not so shifted. From teacher-questionnaire replies, Flowers inferred that track placement affects the teachers' expectations. Teachers favored the high-ability groups, seemed more aware when high-ability students needed remedial help, and appeared to try to motivate higher-ability students more than the comparable control groups. These findings suggest that track placement somehow becomes another "fact" that influences the teachers' expectations, apparently in addition to other information they have about pupils from test scores, performance in class, and so on.

Schrank (1968, 1970) performed a similar manipulation. He randomly assigned one hundred enlisted airmen at the U.S. Air Force Academy Preparatory School to one of five instructional sections. Instructors were told the sections were homogeneously grouped by ability. When section grade averages were compared at the end of the term, there were significant differences, with the groups labeled "higher ability" receiving higher grades. In a second experiment, he followed the identical procedure, except that instructors knew that the students had not been grouped according to ability. Under those circumstances, there were no significant differences in the average grades among classes. Different outcomes, Schrank concludes, appear to be due to differences in the teacher's perception of pupil ability, which appears to be reflected in the teacher's grading standards and teaching methods. Although teacher expectations per se were not measured, but only inferred from differences in educational outcomes, this work indicates that a critical influence on teacher expectations may be the track to which a student is assigned. This result is consistent with the Tuckman and Bierman (1971) findings.

Tuckman and Bierman moved 421 randomly selected black high-school and junior high-school students in a suburban-city school system into the next higher ability group, while 384 comparable students were retained in their assigned ability groups as controls. By the end of the year the two groups received quite different recommendations for ability-group placement for the next year. Teachers recommended 54 percent of the experimental students for the same (higher) group in the following year, but only 1 percent of the controls were recommended for that group. If we are willing to infer expectations from recommendation for track placement, we can see the potent effect of ability grouping on teacher expectations.

In sum, tracking is repeatedly related to teacher expectations. Teachers expect more from "higher" groups and less from "lower" groups, even when students have actually been randomly assigned to those groups. In view of this evidence that tracking itself affects teacher expectations, independently of student "ability," it is plausible that other institutional practices are important for expectations as well.

In the first section of this chapter, I treated such factors as test scores and school performance as characteristics of children. Here I suggest that they may be viewed in another way, as characteristics that vary by schools and are produced by particular practices. Educational systems vary with respect to how they assess and evaluate pupils. In earlier epochs of American education, grading and testing did not exist or took different forms. Today differences exist between schools in this respect. Hence it is possible that variations in testing, evaluation, and recordkeeping may influence teacher expectations.

Whether or not schools use standardized tests, who receives test information, and what is done with it are procedures that may affect teacher expectations. I know of no study comparing schools that use and do not use standardized tests in terms of the expectations teachers hold for students. Given the substantial influence test scores appear to have on teacher expectations, as observed earlier in this chapter, such a possibility warrants exploration.

Fleming and Anttonen (1971) concluded that "teachers assess children on the basis of previously developed attitudes toward children and tests [p. 251]." Thus, in certain schools, teachers may be very unimpressed by tests, and this factor may affect testing practices and the way tests are interpreted on a schoolwide basis; whereas in other schools, the reverse may be true.

Related to assessment practices are the ways in which assessments are recorded and attached to children as part of their permanent record. Formalized record-keeping practices allow future teachers to learn what past teachers have thought of individual children. Teacher reports influence subsequent teachers' expectations (as noted by Keeley, 1973; Long and Henderson, 1974; Mason, 1973; Roeber, 1970). Therefore, school record-keeping practices probably contribute to the expectations of future teachers. Legislative action and court decisions which have begun to open student records to pupil and parental view are an indication of the growing awareness of the importance attached to such records.

One of the most striking aspects of American education is the requirement that schools evaluate and *differentiate* students, beginning at the earliest age. Lawlor and Lawlor (1973) and Harvey and Slatin (1975) were astounded by teachers' or student teachers' readiness to rate pupils on the basis of a brief video tape or a photograph, although both groups of researchers told subjects that they did not need to do the ratings if they felt they had insufficient

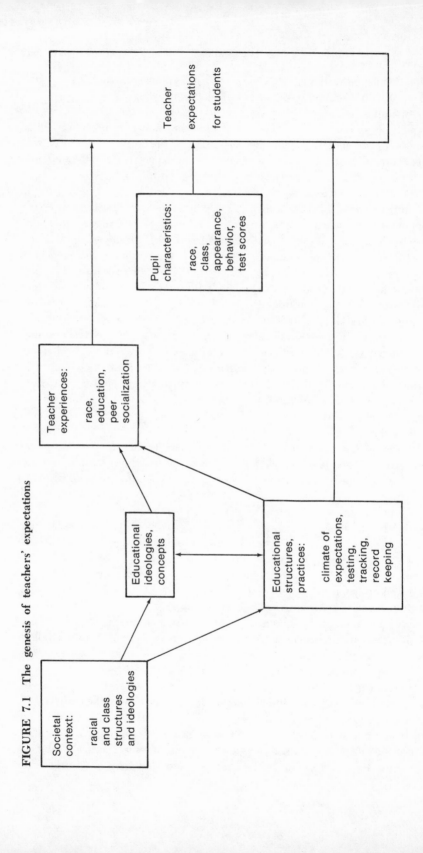

FIGURE 7.1 The genesis of teachers' expectations

Societal context: racial and class structures and ideologies

Educational ideologies, concepts

Educational structures, practices: climate of expectations, testing, tracking, record keeping

Teacher experiences: race, education, peer socialization

Pupil characteristics: race, class, appearance, behavior, test scores

Teacher expectations for students

information. Lawlor and Lawlor (1973) conclude that the evaluative function "is so much a part of the teacher role that the student teacher is very easily pushed into making judgments even when the evidence for judging is extremely skimpy [p. 13]."

I suggest that the requirement to differentiate is so ingrained in the American educational system that it is bound to influence teacher expectations. Specifically, it pushes toward a belief that not all children can learn certain material, that differences are to be expected and are beyond the control of the teacher. Thus, what may be "real" differences in the speed or ease with which certain children learn particular materials or skills may lead to expectations that some children *cannot* learn certain things.

This long review of the genesis of teachers' expectations was designed to ascertain whether the structure of dominance is related to teachers' expectations and, if so, how. Our conclusions are summarized graphically in Figure 7.1. Both experimental and natural studies find that race and social class influence teachers' expectations directly as well as indirectly through language style, appearance, and behavior. The roots of such prejudicial expectations were unearthed in societal norms, social-science concepts, and the attitudes of more experienced teachers. Moreover, the climate of expectations in an entire school, the practice of tracking, and the requirement that schools differentiate pupils all tend to vary by the class and ethnic composition of the school and appear to influence teachers' expectations as well. In these ways the structure of dominance in society appears to contribute to the genesis of differential teachers' expectations. We now need to know whether these differential expectations affect teacher–pupil interactions and educational outcomes.

8

The Consequences
of Teacher Expectations

TEACHER EXPECTATIONS ARE SHAPED by the societal structure of dominance, both directly and indirectly. But are expectations related to teacher behaviors and to student outcomes, as the model suggests? Research addressing these questions has produced seemingly contradictory results. Some researchers report that teacher expectations are related to teacher behaviors and/or pupil learning; others find no such relationship. Methodological controversies (Elashoff and Snow, 1971; Snow, 1969; Thorndike, 1968) and a burgeoning literature on the subject have made it difficult to resolve this controversy. Those who reject the notion simply note the methodological criticisms leveled at Rosenthal and Jacobson's (1968a) *Pygmalion in the Classroom,* and cite a few studies which fail to support their thesis,[1] thus dismissing the possibility that teacher expectations might be a factor in differential pupil learning (e.g., Jensen, 1973a: 260-64). The concept of teacher expectations is a crucial

---

[1]Rosenthal and Jacobson (1968a) tested the children in an elementary school, using a test that they called the "Harvard Test of Inflected Acquisition" (which was actually a standardized, relatively nonverbal test of intelligence. Flanagan's [1960] Tests of General Ability [TOGA]). Rosenthal and Jacobson told teachers that on the basis of the test, they could predict that certain children, whose names were provided, would demonstrate intellectual "blooming" or "spurting" during the year. In fact, the alleged "spurters" were a random sample of about 20 percent of the children in the school. All children were retested with the same IQ test after 1 semester, 1 academic year, and 2 academic years. Gains in IQ from pretest to 1 year retest were computed, and "expectancy advantage" was defined by the degree to which IQ gains by "experimental" children exceeded gains by "control group" children. A significant expectancy advantage was found, particularly among children in the first and second grades. While both experimental and control groups gained in IQ points, 47 percent of experimental group children gained 20 or more IQ points, compared to 19 percent of control group children.

mediating link in the theory offered here. Therefore, these apparently opposite findings warrant careful analysis to see whether they can be reconciled. To do this, we look first at research considering the relationship of teachers expectations to their behaviors (28 studies) and then at studies measuring the effects of teachers' expectations on pupils (61 reports).[2]

Teacher Expectations and Behaviors

While the original Rosenthal and Jacobson (1968a) study did not study teacher behaviors, efforts have been made since then to identify teacher actions that stem from expectations. These studies vary considerably, both with respect to whether the expectations were natural or "induced," and with respect to results. About half of the studies assess the natural expectations of teachers, usually by having them rate or rank their own students in terms of expected academic achievement. Slightly more than half are closer replications of the Rosenthal and Jacobson study, in that they attempt to induce an expectation in the teachers, by manipulating test-score information, by random assignment of pupils to pseudoability groups, and so forth. Most of these efforts to induce expectations do not measure the expectations directly but assume that they have been affected by the experimental manipulation.

There are three studies of natural situations that infer the presence of particular teacher expectations. In studies by Alpert (1974) and Martinez (1973), expectations are inferred from reading-ability group placement or the achievement level of the class. Gabbert (1973) goes further and appears to infer expectations from student social class. In these cases, as in most of the induced-expectations studies, teacher expectations are not measured independently.

The absence of measurement of teacher expectations may help to explain the variation in results. When the origin of teachers' expectations is natural, and those expectations are directly measured, expectations are related to substantial variations in teacher behaviors, in 6 out of 7 studies, and in the seventh study the results were mixed, that is, differences were noted in some teacher behaviors but not in others. Even where expectations were inferred from something such as ability group placement rather than being directly measured, natural expectations were positively related to teacher behaviors in four cases, bore a mixed relation in three, and were unrelated in only one. (See Appendix 1 for a classification of these studies.)

[2] I am grateful to Dan Smith for sharing his very helpful and extensive review of studies on teachers' expectations with me.

Of the 13 studies attempting to induce expectations, 8 had positive or mixed results, suggesting that even relatively weakly induced expectations may influence teacher behaviors under certain conditions. The 5 studies reporting no relation leave us with several questions. Only José and Cody (1971) measured teachers' expectations. In that report, 11 out of 18 (61%) teachers said they expected no more of the experimental pupils than of the others in their classes. Apparently the experimental manipulation failed, and the induced expectation did not "take." This interpretation gains support when we compare how expectations were induced in studies reporting positive results. Meichenbaum et al. (1969) presented the pupils predicted to bloom to teachers with considerable elaboration and group discussion. Kester (1969) also held meetings with participating teachers during one part of the induction phase. Other studies suggest that only expectations which are truly believed by teachers are likely to affect their behaviors. Clearly the naturally induced expectations, formulated by the teachers themselves, meet this criterion.

Having learned something about the conditions under which teacher expectations appear to be related to differential behaviors, what do we know about how behavior varies? Two factors are the frequency or rates of interaction between teachers and pupils, and the kinds of behaviors teachers show toward different children.

Teachers spend more time interacting with pupils for whom they have higher expectations (Adams and Cohen, 1974; Blakey, 1970; Brophy and Good, 1970; Cornbleth et al., 1974; Given, 1974; Jeter, 1973; Kranz, 1970; Rist, 1970; Rubovits and Maehr, 1973, 1971; Silberman, 1969; Willis, 1969). Different studies use different coding schemes for analyzing rates of interaction. Most frequently used are Bales' interaction analysis, Flanders' interaction analysis, and Brophy and Good's (1970) dyadic interaction analysis. The purpose of the coding scheme is to enhance the observer's reliability in coding behaviors of different frequency and type, including who initiates the interaction. For example, Brophy and Good (1970) found that students for whom teachers held high expectations were more frequently praised when correct and less frequently criticized when wrong or unresponsive than were pupils for whom teachers had low expectations. Similarly, Given (1974) found that high-expectancy students received more of Flanders' various modes of verbal interaction than did low-expectancy students. Rist (1970) observed that the teacher initiated many more interactions with pupils for whom she had higher expectations than with other pupils.

Other studies examine how teacher behaviors differ in the type or quality of interactions (Dalton, 1973; Kester, 1969; Meichenbaum et al., 1969; Parsons, 1973; Peng, 1974; Rothbart, Dalfen, and Barrett, 1971). Teachers were more friendly, encouraging, and supportive of students who had been designated particularly "bright" (Kester, 1969). Meichen-baum et al. (1969) found differences among teachers, with some signifi-cantly increasing positive interactions with girls purported to be "late bloomers" and others reducing negative interactions with these girls. While Parsons (1973) inferred teacher expectations from the achieve-ment level of the classes, he observed teachers showing somewhat more praise and acceptance of the better classes, although the differences were not significant. The code category he termed "the restricting behavior index" (measured on the Flanders-Galloway interaction analysis system) was the most responsible for the differences that he did observe. While we do not know whether the classes differed substan-tially in behavior, these results are particularly interesting in light of Bowles and Gintis' (1976) assertion that social-control aspects of school-ing are more important than cognitive-learning features. Bowles and Gintis suggest that schools serve to recreate the social relations of pro-duction by organizing the behavioral requirements of school in different ways for different social classes. While Parsons (1973) does not reflect on his findings in these terms, his work indicates another dimension of interaction that may not be captured in the coding schemes widely used in studies of classroom interaction; namely, the degree of behavioral restriction that occurs.

Rosenthal (1974) believes that there are at least four related ways in which expectancy effects are mediated. He bases this judgment upon his review of 285 studies of interpersonal influence, including at least 80 in classrooms or other natural settings. First, he sees a *general climate fac-tor*, consisting of the overall warmth a teacher shows to children, with more shown to high-expectancy students. While he does not discuss individual studies, I located at least 3 that suggested various nonverbal ways in which teacher expectancy could be communicated.

Johnson (1970) hypothesized that when subjects experience a discre-pancy between their expectations for someone and that person's perfor-mance, they may provide certain feedback that serves to maintain con-gruency between expectations and performance. Specifically, Johnson expected that subjects experiencing expectancy-performance discre-pancy would be more likely to avoid eye contact with the other person. This was confirmed with one confederate testee but insignificant with the other. While not conclusive, this evidence suggests one means—the amount of eye contact—through which teacher expectations may be conveyed.

Further evidence in this direction is provided by Cooper (1971), who found that the amount of eye contact an experimenter showed a subject was related to the subject's feelings about himself. Therefore Cooper also suggests that primary visual cues may be an important determinant of expectancy transmission.

Chaikin, Sigler, and Derlega (1974) examined whether tutors holding different expectations for students in a microteaching situation exhibit different patterns of nonverbal behavior. Chaikin et al. (1974) observed that tutors did behave differently toward designated bright students, showing greater forward lean, eye gaze, affirmative head nods, and smiles—"all indices of approval and attraction, as established by Mehrabian (1971), Exline (1971), Hall (1966) and others. It would seem, judging by these nonverbal behaviors, that bright pupils are liked more by their tutors than are control or dull students [p. 148]."

Rosenthal (1974) identifies a second way in which expectancy is mediated as more praise for doing something right. This differential warmth provides feedback about the pupil's specific behavior, a feature illustrated by Brophy and Good's (1970) findings reported above.

Third, Rosenthal (1974) notes the input factor, or the actual amount of teaching pupils receive. As Beez (1970) noted, tutors taught many more words to students they thought were bright than to pupils designated slow. Similarly, presentation of more vocabulary words to students of alleged higher ability was noted by Carter (1969) and by McQueen (1970). In a natural setting, Martinez (1973) found that teachers spent more time on reading instruction in high-achieving classes than in low-achieving classes. Rist (1970) observed that pupils in the teacher-designated higher group could see more of the material written on the board from the table the teacher assigned them to than could the "lower" group.

Fourth, Rosenthal (1974) indicates that expectancy may be mediated by a response opportunity factor, or an output factor. Students for whom the teacher has higher expectations are called on more often and are given more chance to reply, as well as more and tougher questions. Robinson (1973) found that teachers made a larger proportion (44%) of cognitive demands upon perceived high achievers than upon perceived low achievers (24%).

A fifth way, which Rosenthal does not mention but which has been observed by others, is the different type of curriculum that teachers may present to children for whom they have different expectations. We have mentioned Keddie's (1971) finding that teachers report they present a completely different type of economics to students of differently perceived abilities. Similarly, Alpert (1975b) reports that teachers use more readers and more difficult ones with the top reading group, but concludes that such differences are consistent with differences in group need, as measured by the ability of the pupils to read books at various levels. But need might be evident in other criteria as well, such as interest in the story, need for variety, relevance of the book to one's own life, and so on. By using more books with the higher-ability group, the teacher is increasing the chance that pupils will find a book that they especially like. More work needs to be done on the question of whether and how teacher expectations affect what is taught in a classroom.

In brief, we have seen that teacher expectations are most likely to be related to teacher behaviors in natural situations or in situations that effectively induce an expectation and measure whether that expectation exists. "Higher" teacher expectations are related to more and warmer interactions between teacher and pupil. In particular, Rosenthal (1974) specifies that positive expectancy may be communicated by: (1) a general climate of warmth; (2) more praise for performance; (3) more actual teaching; and (4) more opportunities to respond. To these I add (5) the amount and type of material taught.

There is, then, considerable evidence that teacher expectations affect behavior toward students. But the critical question remains: do these expectations and behaviors actually affect students? Do students think differently about themselves or learn more as a result of the expectations teachers hold? Therein lies the heart of the "Pygmalion effect" controversy.

The Effects Of Teacher Expectations

There are some striking patterns in the findings of studies that measure the effects of teacher expectations. In 16 studies of natural teacher expectations, only 3 were not related to cognitive changes in children (see Appendix 2). The results of induced expectations, on the other hand, are very mixed. Of 42 such studies, 15 report a positive relationship between expectations and cognitive changes, 6 report mixed results, and 21 indicate no relationship (Appendix 2).

The first and most global conclusion from these studies we have already pointed out: teacher expectations always appear to be related to pupil changes when those expectations are "naturally" held by the teacher and only sometimes when the expectations are induced by an experimenter. Of course, the problem with "natural" expectations is that the teachers may be "right;" that is, they may have successfully identified students who will gain more. Because of this difficulty, it is particularly important to try to specify the conditions under which the experimental expectancy effect operates. Having done that, we will be in a better position to consider the consequences of teacher expectations for lower-class and minority children. At least three types of specifying conditions appear to exist: experimental conditions; teacher characteristics and behaviors; and pupil characteristics.

In order for induced expectations to be related to changes in students, the expectations must have been effectively induced. That is, the teachers must believe that children designated positively by the experimenter will in fact make gains (see Anderson, 1971; Goldsmith and Fry, 1971; José, 1969). Only 4 of the 42 induced-expectancy studies measured whether or not the teacher expectancy had been influenced by the experimenter (see Appendix 2). José and Goldsmith and Fry discovered that the majority of teachers did *not* hold the expectations the experimenter had tried to induce. Hence, they were not surprised to observe little cognitive change in students. Anderson (1971) specified that positive cognitive changes were contingent upon changes in teacher expectations. Spielberg (1973), however, suggests that teachers' statements alone may be an inadequate measure of the expectations held, since she found that teachers' statements were not related to their behavior. Thus, teacher expectations may be unaffected by the inducement procedure. Moreover, even if the teachers' stated expectancy changes, that may not modify behaviors. Therefore the lack of results may be due to the nonexistence of an expectancy state in the teachers.

One possible explanation for failure to induce expectancies is offered by Smith (1976). How, he wonders, can teachers believe in a test that claims to predict *future* growth? The notion of gains to come seems implausible to him. A number of teachers may have been similarly skeptical of research purporting to measure something that will happen in the future. Spielberg (1973) feels that there may be a Rosenthal–Jacobson "sensitizing effect" operating now that so many people have heard of the "Pygmalion" study, making it virtually impossible to find naive teacher subjects any longer.

The teacher's skepticism or, conversely, the effectiveness of an induced expectancy may depend in part upon the teacher's prior knowledge of a pupil. A number of induced-expectancy studies reporting no relationship began in the middle of the academic year, allowing considerable time for teachers to form independent expectations (see, e.g., Claiborn, 1969; Fiedler, Cohen and Feeney, 1971; Gosciewski, 1970; Havlin, 1969; Pellegrini and Hicks, 1972).

Teachers' experiences with children may operate any time during an experiment, not only prior to experimental intervention. This possibility may help to explain Spielberg's (1973) finding that teacher expectations are not very stable over time. Even if they are successfully induced at one time, they may be changed with subsequent teacher-student interaction.

Besides factors affecting the credibility of an induced expectation, an ethical constraint operates in experimental situations which may reduce the efficacy of induced expectations. Seaver (1973) suggests that negative expectations may have more potent effects on student cognitive change than positive expectations. Ethical concerns have understandably precluded most experimenters from attempting to induce negative expectations in teachers. As a result, however, the limited range of expectations in induced situations may have diminished the effects of such expectations. These experimental conditions may help to explain why the results of induced expectancy studies are mixed. Teacher characteristics also may mediate the expectancy effect.

As noted in Chapter 7, one basis for forming expectations may be a pupil's test scores. However, teachers' opinions about tests may affect how seriously they value score information (Fleming and Anttonen, 1971; Sorotzkin, Fleming and Anttonen, 1974). Hence, attempts to manipulate expectancies by reporting false test scores may be effective with some teachers and completely ineffective with others, depending upon their attitudes toward test results.

Out of 44 induced expectancy studies, there were 18 in which both teacher behaviors and pupil outcomes were measured. In most of these studies there were consistent relationships between teacher behaviors and cognitive outcomes. In 8 studies teacher behaviors changed in the direction of the induced expectation, and pupils changed as well. In 5 studies teacher behaviors remained constant and pupil test scores showed no significant gains. In 3 studies teacher behavior was modified in a way that was consistent with the induced expectations, but pupils showed no change (Brown, 1970; Gosciewski, 1970; Kester, 1969, Appendix 2). Thus, where induced expectations appear to approximate natural ones, both in credibility and behavioral manifestations, they are most likely to affect children.

What teacher behaviors affect student outcomes? Some general possibilities were suggested by Rosenthal (1974). From the studies reviewed here, we can identify two types of instrumental teacher behaviors: the amount of material taught, and the amount and type of teacher–pupil interaction.

Beez (1970) reported that tutors given higher expectations for a child tried to teach more words than those tutors given lower expectations. Moreover, teachers of children designated "low ability" explained the meaning of a word more often, gave more examples, and spent more time on nonteaching activities than did teachers of "high ability" children. Carter (1969) reported similar findings.

Peng (1974) found that provision of learning opportunities ("the extent and degree of assistance, and amount of time, space and materials provided for the class; the willingness exhibited in helping pupils [p. 5]") was correlated with perceived pupil problem-solving ability. He measured teacher instructional behavior related to the provision of learning opportunities through the perceptions of pupils. Such ratings may be biased by individual pupil variations, Peng cautions, but since he uses classes as the units of analysis he was able to get the mean score from all students in each class, thus assuring higher reliability. Teacher behavior was measured by scales constructed from a 13-item questionnaire, with entries like: "I can always use the books when I need them: Yes   No."

Meichenbaum et al. (1969) found that the amount of positively toned interaction increased and the amount of negative interaction decreased among some teachers after the experimental expectancy had been induced. Blakey (1970), on the other hand, found that the amount and type of teacher–pupil interaction measured on the Flanders interaction analysis scale was not related to achievement gains, even though behaviors were related to expectations and expectations were related to student gains. He concluded that verbal cues alone are probably insufficient to mediate expectancy effectively. This highlights the importance of studies delineating critical nonverbal cues. What little we know of the behaviors deriving from expectations related to cognitive gains suggests the importance of affective tone and of how much teaching occurs.

Psychological and social characteristics of students also affect how pupils respond to teacher expectations. Kohn (1973) suggests that students who comprehend the teacher's message vary in the extent to which they yield to or resist it. He predicts that such differences should generally be greater for negative messages than positive ones. This assertion is consistent with Asbury's (1970) finding that students reporting internal and external loci of control responded differently to different expectancy conditions. Under conditions of positive expectation, student locus of control was not related to performance. Under negative-expectancy conditions, however, pupils with external loci of control performed significantly more poorly than those with internal loci of control. This suggests that at least this one personality trait of pupils is related to their receptivity to expectations.

Kohn claims that the distinction in the persuasion and communication literature between understanding the position of a communicator and yielding to its exists in teacher–pupil relationships as well. Children may vary in their sensitivity to the emotional content of a communication. This is exactly what Conn et al. (1968) discovered.

Peng's (1974) work provides some insight into how teacher expectations and behaviors and pupil self-expectations may interact to produce differential pupil achievement. Congruence between teacher and self-expectations was related to achievement. Students with high teacher- and self-expectations were high achievers and those with low teacher- and self-expectations were low achievers. Teacher behaviors, rated in terms of clarity, provision of learning opportunities, and enthusiasm, were related to pupil achievement only for pupils with high teacher- and self-expectations. This indicates that positive teacher behaviors may produce student gains only when they occur in an already positive situation with respect to both teacher expectation and the student self-expectation.

Sociological factors also modify a student's susceptibility to teacher expectations. Krupczak (1972) found that black pupils were more affected by teacher expectations than were white students. Yee (1968) and Baker (1973) suggest that lower-class students are more vulnerable to teacher expectations than are middle-class pupils. Rosenthal and Jacobson (1968a) found that younger children showed more expectancy effects than pupils in higher elementary grades. All these characteristics (race, class, and age) may be viewed as indicators of pupil efficacy; that is, they may be seen as resources a student can marshall to negotiate the teacher's definition of the situation. These characteristics reflect the student's power, prestige, and experience in the world and are correlated with position in the structure of dominance.

The consequences of teacher expectations for pupil achievement appear when those expectations are strongly held and are related to modified teacher behavior (see Figure 8.1). Specifically, students exhibit more cognitive gains if teachers teach more and show more warmth toward them. Pupil personality characteristics, including sensitivity to verbal communication of emotions, internal locus of control, and self-expectations, seem to interact with teacher expectations with attendant consequences for cognitive gains.

Conclusions

The implications of teacher expectations for lower-class and minority students can now be considered:

1. Teachers are more likely to hold negative expectations for lower-class and minority children than for middle-class and white children (Chapter 7 of this volume; Buford, 1973).
2. Teacher expectations are affected by testing and tracking, procedures which are themselves biased against lower-class and minority children (see Chapters 5 and 6).
3. It is precisely such negative information that Asbury (1970), Kohn (1973), Mason (1973) and Seaver (1973) suggest is more potent in its consequences than positive expectations.
4. Expectations are related to teacher behaviors and to student cognitive changes even when pupil IQ and achievement are controlled.
5. Given the less powerful position of lower-class and minority children in society, they appear to be more influenced by teacher expectations.

FIGURE 8.1 The consequences of teacher expectations

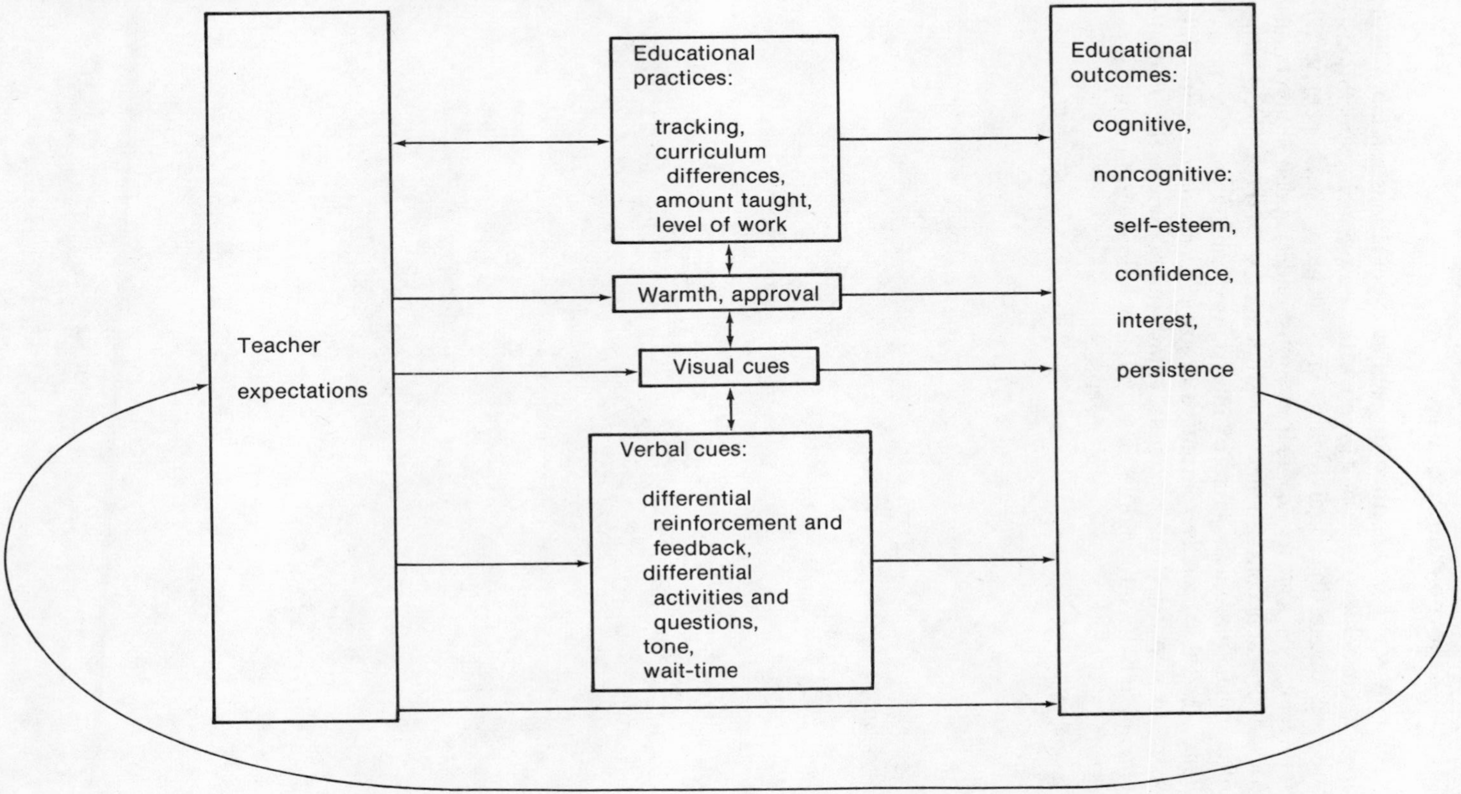

Teacher expectations

Educational practices:

tracking, curriculum differences, amount taught, level of work

Warmth, approval

Visual cues

Verbal cues:

differential reinforcement and feedback, differential activities and questions, tone, wait-time

Educational outcomes:

cognitive,

noncognitive:

self-esteem, confidence, interest, persistence

Pupils who are receptive to teacher expectations are more likely to have their achievement negatively affected by such expectations than are less suggestible individuals. To conclude, teacher expectations influence the learning of many pupils under specifiable conditions. Moreover, their consequences for students low in the societal structure of dominance are intensified by interrelated and cumulative processes. Thus, the educational experiences of lower-class and minority children work to depress their academic achievement, while the educational encounters of white middle-class students help them to achieve.

9

Educational Outcomes

As ALREADY CONSIDERED, societal structures and ideologies have a dual influence upon (1) the conceptual realm of education and (2) the structural features of education. It remains to be seen how conceptual and structural characteristics of educational systems operate in concert to produce unequal educational outcomes.

Definitions Of Educational Outcomes

The hegemony of the instrumental-meritocratic ideology is revealed nowhere more clearly than in the way educational effects are defined and measured in contemporary studies of schools. By confining their study to scores on standardized cognitive achievement tests, such influential works as Coleman et al. (1966) and Boocock (1972) provide a restricted view of education. Similarly, even studies such as those by Jencks et al. (1972) and Averch et al. (1972), which acknowledge the likely importance of noncognitive results of education, dismiss the subject by denying the existence of reliable evidence. But there is a considerable psychological literature on the influence of educational experiences upon self-concept and self-esteem.

What the psychological literature does not do (and what I hope to accomplish here) is to link the effects of educational practices on conceptions of self with the larger social context in which they occur. While many lists of aims of education exist (see Boocock, 1972, and Goslin, 1965), it is curious that the most influential research on education in the last decade has focused almost exclusively upon cognitive achievement. Why has this been the case? The instrumental–meritocratic ideology sug-

135

gests that economic development and prosperity are largely dependent upon the development of cognitive skills (increasingly through formal education) and that those who are most proficient in these skills will advance farthest in the occupational and rewards hierarchy. In view of this ideology, it is not hard to see why cognitive outcomes have been stressed.

Moreover, if this ideology is widely assumed, there may be more consensus in the population on cognitive development as an important goal of education than upon such (apparently more value-laden) noncognitive objectives as self-development, character, leadership, and so on. Given the vulnerability of education to outside intervention, observed by Callahan (1962), Henry (1972), and Sieber (no date), among others, it may be better for the institution to focus on ends which are widely shared rather than on those that might arouse controversy.

Finally, the noncognitive results of education may be more difficult to measure, partly as a result of the lack of consensus as to which ones are important. But the relative ease of measuring cognitive achievement may be largely illusory, as demonstrated below. We consider how cognitive achievement has been measured in studies of educational outcomes, and then turn to the inadequacies of those measurements. Finally, we reflect on why these measurements are so widely used, given all their limitations, and what we can do with them as we attempt to assess the effects of educational concepts, structures, and interactions upon educational outcomes.

Cognitive achievement in education is increasingly being measured (in both research and educational practice) by standardized multiple-choice tests. According to testing expert Cronbach (1970), ". . . a test is a systematic procedure for observing a person's behavior and describing it with the aid of a numerical scale or a category-system [p. 26]." A major feature of early tests was the effort to *standardize* them, so that results obtained at one time or place could be compared with those obtained at another. Hence, Cronbach (1970) can remark, " . . . a standardized test is one in which the testing procedures can be followed at different times and places [p. 27]." (Another, more sociological meaning of standardization is discussed in Chapter 5.) The *objectivity* of a test refers to the degree to which it permits every observer of a performance to arrive at exactly the same report. Significantly, as we indicate below (and have discussed in Chapter 5), objectivity does not refer to the *content* of a test, which may affect different children in very different ways.

Achievement tests are predicated on the assumption that the test items actually measure how well the subject matter that has been taught has been learned. Very often normative scores are provided, so that the meaning of "raw" test scores can be interpreted. (Raw scores indicate the actual number of correct responses, in terms of a simple or weighted count of correct answers.) Raw scores are converted to percentiles by comparing them with sets of scores achieved by some reference, or norming, group, either local or national. Thus, the percentile rank indicates a student's position relative to others in the reference population. Percentile scores can be transformed into grade equivalents or other types of normative scores. Despite their wide use, age- and grade-equivalent scores have been severely criticized (Cronbach, 1970; Angoff, 1971, reported in Averch et al., 1972: 20). Cronbach (1970: 98) recommends the use of standard scores, percentiles, or raw scores for research and for reporting on pupils and classes. In this context, however, he is using the term "standard score" to refer to a raw score that has been converted to a common scale, based upon the mean and standard deviation of scores (again, from a norming population). All scores except raw scores encounter the problem of norming populations. Raw scores still have problems of validity. (Both are discussed below.)

Even where raw scores are used to measure achievement, it is invariably the average, or mean, that is used, generally with no reference to the standard deviation or variance in the score. As Rosenbaum's (1976) work suggests, when this is done it obscures the differentiating function that schools are actually performing. Moreover, when the overall distribution of achievement scores is examined, it reveals that inputs usually found to have no effects actually have positive effects (Brown and Saks, 1975). Thus, the use of mean scores only may conceal relationships between school characteristics and outcomes.

Finally (as noted in Chapter 5), the content of such tests is selected to maximize the differences among individuals taking the test by dropping items that are answered correctly by everyone in the norming population (Carver, 1975).

Given these characteristics of the tests used to measure cognitive achievement, it is not surprising that many people have come to view contemporary testing as inadequate (e.g., Anastasi, 1967; Averch et al., 1972; Hoepfner, 1970; Klein, 1971), for a number of reasons: its limited view of education; poor congruence of program and test content; questionable validity; administration; and cultural bias.

As Averch et al. (1972) note, ". . . one very serious criticism of standardized tests is that they engender perverse incentives by overemphasizing some outcomes at the expense of others," while they enable schools to compare themselves to other schools, the tests run the risk of ". . . suppressing desirable outcomes that are not measured by standardized tests (abstract reasoning, creativity, and so on) [p. 19]." Hence many important cognitive outcomes may be overlooked or diminished because they are not measured.

In a related vein, all the objectives of an educational program may not be captured by items included in the standardized test used to evaluate it. This has been offered as an explanation for the apparent failure of many innovative educational programs (see e.g., Cohen, 1970; Klein, 1971; Lennon, 1971, cited in Averch et al., 1972: 24). Even when the test covers some of a program's objectives, there may be poor agreement between specific program goals and test content. Averch et al. (1972) comment, "Tests are not designed with specific programs in mind, and poor overlap is to be expected between the objectives a test measures and those an education program aspires to [p. 24]."

What exactly is the test measuring? How well does it measure it? Even when test items appear to coincide with program objectives, current methods of test construction lead to tests of low validity. Test items are selected by test writers on the basis of their response to the instructional material. Hence the student's score is a function of the test writer's responses and has no known relationship to actual instructional content (Bormuth, 1970, cited in Averch et al., 1972: 25).

To these problems, Anastasi (1967) adds the misuse and misinterpretation of achievement-test results, difficulties that are compounded by "inappropriate test instructions and directions, and confusing test designs and formats [Klein, 1971, cited in Averch et al., 1972: 23]."

Cultural bias may affect test results through the content of test items, the sample used to establish test norms, and test administration. Efforts to develop "culture-free" tests have not offered significant improvement (Chapter 5, this volume; Samuda, 1975).

In light of all these inadequacies in achievement testing, why is testing so widely used? Problems with objective testing existed from the outset, but that did not stop testing's rapid spread within school systems. Testing was adopted as schools were being called upon to prepare people for the stratified world of work. Standardized tests provide an apparently "scientific and objective" basis for differentiating people. They are critically important for making the differentiations schools are required to perform seem legitimate. Since placement in different curricula is not completely correlated with achievement-test scores, and since curricular differences are related to the available educational and career options (with their attendant inequalities of reward), it is extremely important that such decisions appear to be objective. In fact, however, there are a great many patterned inadequacies in the tests. By "patterned," I mean to suggest that while they can have negative effects for any child, they are more likely to have negative consequences for lower-income or ethnic-minority children. It is their programs that will be canceled because they fail to show positive gains, it is they who are most likely to be placed into a track leading only to low-paying work. It is they whose families lack the resources to neutralize the negative consequences of low test scores. (cf. Elder's, 1965, finding that IQ scores were much less importantly related to educational attainment for higher-class youth than for lower-class youth.)

Families have different levels of resources they can bring to an educational situation, for example to neutralize negative test scores or other educational evaluations. Higher-class families have: greater knowledge of the system and how it works, more confidence and knowledge to help them ignore or refute test results, more capacity to make complaints that are taken seriously by the schools, and if ignored, more resources for changing tests, counselors, classes or schools. In a study of working-class compared to middle-class students in a British grammar school, Jackson and Marsden (1962) found a similar situation. Middle-class parents were better able to work the school system to the advantage of their children. They carefully selected the primary school with the best record of placements in grammar schools, they worked on the child's educational problems, and they were able to intervene successfully and support their children, even in the face of opposition from the school. By contrast, working-class parents chose less successful schools, had trouble gaining access to educational authorities, did not understand the system, and felt uneasy talking with teachers with different accents. The feature of parental potency in managing the situation of their child's education is largely ignored in American sociology of education.

Besides their obvious congruence with the structure of dominance in society, tests are widely used because they satisfy the "efficiency" criteria so widely transferred from business to education (see Chapter 4). Tests conveniently give a number, the appearance that outcomes have been measured. Tests make the work of both researchers and educators seem more scientific and objective, and facilitate the production of interpretations and conclusions. Tests improve the appearance of rationality and thus strengthen the position of both researcher and administrator. Observers predict that the use of standardized achievement tests will increase if the practice of accountability continues to spread (Averch et al., 1972), since presumably the criteria must be as reliable and "objective" as possible.

Finally, testing is an industrial operation in its own right, one that is very profitable for the producers. It seems safe to say that testing continues to be popular, despite its limitations, because of the convergence of interests among wealth owners, occupational elites, educational administrators, researchers, and test producers.

Should we then ignore studies of educational effects which use tests to measure achievement? I think not, for several reasons. The knowledge of what affects "school achievement" may be of strategic value for certain groups, at least on a short-term basis. These measures are frequently used by the educational system to make critical decisions. Therefore, while I doubt their validity, it is important for immediate policy questions to know what affects so-called academic achievement. For example, if lower-class or minority children "do well," it will be more difficult to discriminate against them in a way that appears legitimate.

Moreover, some people will be convinced that schools affect children only when results are apparent on measures they value—such as achievement-test scores. Thus, I present available evidence to answer whether or not schools contribute to poorer academic achievement among minority and low socioeconomic-status children, not only with respect to the definitions of achievement used, but also in terms of educational processes that affect prevailing measures of achievement.

Finally, strategic reasons notwithstanding, we can refuse to confine our examination of outcomes to those reflected in standard-test scores and consider other measures and other outcomes as well. Therefore, we turn to a consideration of how educational concepts, structures, expectations, and interactions are related to educational outcomes.

Influences on Educational Outcomes

Six interrelated features of schools that are related to societal structures of dominance appear to influence the cognitive and noncognitive results of schooling: (1) the economic and political resources of schools; (2) schools' bureaucratic structure; (3) the degree to which they are total institutions; (4) the selective functions of the school; (5) the climate of expectations within schools; and (6) the patterns of interactions occurring within them.

Schools vary considerably with respect to the amount of money available to them and the relative control different participants have over how that money is to be spent. While Coleman et al. (1966) concluded that resources have no direct effects on learning, he controlled for resource allocation at the district level. Since a number of analyses show that resources are unevenly distributed within districts (Hobson v.Hansen, 1967; Summers and Wolfe, 1975), especially in large urban districts, and that the allocation of economic resources is related to academic achievement (Brown and Saks, 1975; Gutherie et al., 1971; Ritterband, 1973; Summers and Wolfe, 1975) and attainment (Byrne, Williamson, and Fletcher, 1973), it seems more plausible to conclude that economic resources may be related to learning outcomes, and proceed to see how (see, e.g., Ritterband, 1973), than to conclude that they are not related.

The sources of the economic support of schools may also be related to learning, although I know of no systematic studies of this variable. The sources of economic support are undoubtedly related to the constituencies schools must serve. Thus, if aid to schools is based upon attendance figures, schools will tend to be concerned about attendance rates. If aid is related to the proportion of students achieving below a certain level, we might expect schools to be concerned accordingly. (The negative implications of pegging rewards to failure have been suggested by organization development consultant Billie Alban, 1976, who knows teachers who have been told not to raise the reading level of children too greatly, so as not to lose the Title I money coming to the school. The effects of such negative rewards on the operation of an educational system are impossible to measure, but the matter certainly warrants further investigation.)

Related to the sources of money for schools is the degree of control participants have over how the money is to be spent. As large urban schools become more bureaucratized, the participants in the situation— whether they be parents, students, teachers, or administrators—have increasingly less to say about how economic resources are to be allocated. Thus, teachers with interesting curricular ideas are constrained by economics, space, and available equipment. By contrast, it is not unusual in small, private, or suburban schools for teachers, principals, and parents to discuss new educational programs and materials and implement their ideas within the year.

The governance of schools is related to their economics. We have noted (see Chapter 4) that different types of schools have very different structures of governance, from the self-perpetuating boards of trustees of private schools to the locally elected boards in upper middle-class suburban districts, and the relatively powerless school boards of large urban areas, elected on a districtwide basis. While we know little about how governance structures are related to educational outcomes, Berube (1971), Hamilton (1971), and Levin (1972) have theorized that community, or local, control of school boards is related to increased learning. In a systematic study in New York City's Intermediate School 201, Guttentag (1973) found that compared to similar schools in a neighboring district, the community-controlled schools tended to have a climate characterized by intellectual activity, social action, individual responsibility, and open-mindedness. Teachers described themselves as having intellectual aspirations and competitiveness, and indicated that the school climate supported these personal needs. Intermediate School 201 teachers saw themselves as more able to accept criticism, and more purposeful, organized, and self-reliant compared with the self-descriptions of other New York City teachers (Guttentag, 1973: 244–5). Parents were more likely to help out in the schools in a variety of constructive ways. In this atmosphere, teacher-student interaction differed from that in comparison schools, and teacher race, which was related to teacher verbal behavior in those schools, was not so related in the community-controlled schools. In Intermediate School 201 the teachers were more likely to follow student-initiated talk with praise or acceptance of the students' ideas (using the Flanders interaction scale) than were teachers in the comparison schools. Guttentag suggests that a social climate had been created in the newly organized schools that overcame individual characteristics of teachers, such as their race. Unfortunately a lack of procedural details in Guttentag's (1973) report prevents us from answering several important questions. Were the teachers selected or self-selected in any way? Did the observers know which districts the schools belonged to, or were they "blind" to the district differences and their implications? These factors could compound the findings.

Several measures suggest that children in Intermediate School 201 improved their academic achievement as a result of being in the school. Children in the district for three years had significantly higher mean achievement scores in reading and math. One school in the district had a mean score significantly above national norms. Intermediate School 201 students did not decline during the three-year-observation period, as students in many other New York City schools did. The kindergarten and first-grade children did the best, children in second to sixth grade were somewhat better than those in comparison schools, but seventh- and eighth-grade children did not differ from comparison-school children. (This could be due to the effects of prior schooling.) But we do not know on what tests these children improved or whether comparisons between three-year and more recent students in the district controlled for initial performance levels, ethnicity, or length of residence in the city. While answers would provide a stronger basis for inferring causality, this work suggests fruitful avenues for further exploration and evaluation.

The social and economic context of a school is related to the level of bureaucratization in it (B. Anderson, 1971). Moreover, level of bureaucratization is related to student alienation (B. Anderson, 1973: 330). Since level of alienation is inversely related to student achievement, Anderson suggests that a less bureaucratic mode of school organization might produce higher levels of student achievement. Supporting evidence is offered by Bidwell and Kasarda (1975), who learned that the more administrative positions there were in a district (surely an indicator of bureaucratization), the lower the achievement scores, while more people in teaching positions was associated with higher pupil-achievement scores. The pupil–teacher ratio, in turn, was contingent upon the resources available to a district.

While the evidence on class size and pupil learning is mixed, and generally indicates no relationship (cf. Boocock, 1972: 155–8), these recent data from Bidwell and Kasarda suggest that the ratio of pupils to teachers in an entire system is somehow related to achievement. Perhaps that ratio measures some underlying concept such as commitment to teaching. Furthermore, it is quite likely that teaching style and amount of control behavior are strongly influenced by pupil–teacher ratios. The average number of pupils per teacher in metropolitan-area elementary schools is 30.5 compared to 26.3 in nonmetropolitan areas (Coleman et al. 1966: 68). This figure should be compared with private schools, in which the pupil–teacher ratio is very low. In 1970-71, the ratio of number of pupils per teacher in all elementary and secondary non-religious private schools (both boarding and day schools) was 12.6, in those with religious affiliations other than Roman Catholic, it was 17.8, and in Catholic schools, the ratio was 27.5. Thus, private schools of all types consistently have lower student–teacher ratios than public schools, on the average (Grant and Lind, 1976). Obviously classes can be organized and conducted very differently if they consist of 12 rather than 30 students. While these differences may not be related to cognitive achievement on standardized tests, they may very well be related to creative thinking, ability to express oneself orally or in writing, self-esteem, and sense of control over one's environment.

It may be significant that of the 21 Operation Head Start programs that Hawkridge et al. (1968) found showing cognitive gains, none had a pupil-to-adult ratio of more than 7:1. (Because they did not study "unsuccessful" programs, it is impossible to say that size was definitely related to results.)

Unfortunately class size is almost impossible to measure in isolation, and experimental variations do not approximate life conditions closely enough. Several months of attendance in small classes might not affect one's thinking ability and life outlook, but 12 years might. Therefore, until creative strategies for studying the effects of class size are developed, these are only informed speculations.

Schools vary with respect to how closely they approximate total institutions. Goffman (1961) uses the term in *Asylums* to mean "a place of residence and work where a large number of like-situated individuals, cut off from the wider society for an appreciable period of time, together lead an enclosed, formally administered round of life [p. xii]." Schools differ in terms of the amount of time students spend in them, from 24 to just 2 or 3 hours per day. Within that time period, institutions vary with respect to the amount of control they exercise over individuals. Does the institution wish to control only cognitive behavior or affect morality as well? Effects are more likely in total institutions, although they might be negative ones. If individuals and peers share the organizational goals, personal change is more likely (cf. Bronfenbrenner, 1972, on the use of peer groups by schools in the USSR).

The permeability of institutional boundaries is another important dimension of a school's totality. How much do events or people from the "outside" enter the institution? How readily can the individual leave, either for short periods or permanently?

Degree of totality will be related to the consequences—either conformity or primary and secondary adaptations that are not in conformity. The extent to which a school approaches a total institution to the child is related to its effect on the child. Urban ghetto schools are more nearly total institutions than are upper-middle-class suburban schools, especially for elementary children. They are generally less permeable by the parents and the community, they try to control more aspects of the child's behavior, and there is less chance for parents voluntarily to remove their children from the situation. The child and the parents have less chance and capacity to negotiate with the teacher or the school over their definitions of the situation (because of economic, social, and symbolic resources available to the respective parties; cf. Lacey, 1970). If the school has aims and practices that the child finds very antithetical we would predict both individual and group responses in opposition to the goals and practices of the school (the formation of a strong peer culture that becomes increasingly antischool; cf. Hargreaves, 1967; Lacey, 1970; Schindler, 1970). The involuntary nature of school makes all schools into total institutions to some degree.

The degree to which a school is a total institution contributes to the effects it has on children and helps to explain the attitude changes among Bennington College students in the 1930s (Newcomb, 1943) and Himmelweit and Swift's (1969) discovery that certain British boarding schools were able to launch even their lower-class graduates into higher occupations, while social class of origin was much more important for comprehensive, nonboarding-school graduates, even when curriculum was held constant.

Selectivity is the third characteristic of schools that influences their consequences. Selectivity is reflected in criteria for entrance as well as in internal practices and structures. Lennards (1969) studied the effects of the eleven-plus examination in Holland which serves to divide children into three types of schools, and found that selection was related to political and social attitudes about the stratification system. Benitez (1973) found that being selected into a status-conferring school had a "knighting effect," making students feel that they were members of an elite. The positive effects of selection somewhat masked the effects of an internal competition that made some students feel inadequate in relation to their highly selected peers [what Davis, 1966, calls the negative effect of being a small frog in a big (or competitive) pond].

The bulk of American elementary and secondary school "selection" is obscured by the concept of neighborhood schools and residential segregation. While this practice takes many forms, none has been studied more than racial segregation and desegregation. Debate rages over the question of how racial integration affects the achievement and self-conceptions of the children involved. There is a wealth of literature on this subject, fortunately well reviewed by St. John (1975) and by Weinberg (1975). Two general conclusions seem warranted by the dozens of studies they reviewed. First, desegregation very seldom lowers the achievement of nonwhites and quite often raises it. Second, there is virtually no evidence that desegregation lowers the achievement levels of whites (St. John, 1975, Chapter 2; Weinberg, 1975: 243). Under what circumstances is desegregation related to achievement? Achievement gains for racial minorities, according to Weinberg (1975: 269) seem most likely when the following conditions are met:

1. There is relatively little racial hostility among students.
2. Teachers and administrators understand and accept minority students, and these characteristics are encouraged by effective in-service training programs if necessary.
3. The majority of students in any given class are from middle or upper socioeconomic classes.
4. Desegregation occurs within the classroom, not just at the schoolwide level.
5. Rigid ability grouping and tracking do not occur.
6. The community is not inflamed by racial conflict.

St. John (1975, Chapter 2) feels that:

1. Younger children (especially those of kindergarten age) seem to benefit more than older children.
2. City size or region is unrelated.
3. The length of exposure to desegregation has not proved to be an important variable so far, perhaps because so many experiences are of such short duration.
4. Findings do not seem to depend upon the definition of desegregation (that is, what proportion of different races constitutes desegregation).
5. The method used by a community to achieve desegregation (whether bussing, demographic changes in neighborhoods, school-board rezoning of districts, voluntary transfer of selected pupils, or districtwide desegregation) does not determine whether academic gains result.

More work needs to be done to identify how school practices and personnel shape the results of desegregation. How, for example, do teachers and other students behave? What curriculum is taught, in what ways? How bureaucratic is the school? As we have seen earlier, these factors can interact with race and have important consequences for pupil learning. Desegregation is only one of a number of variables in a complex situation.

Some of these factors may influence the effects of desegregation on the self-concepts of minority-group members. These effects are more likely to be negative or mixed than positive in the short run, albeit higher in the long run (St. John, 1975). On the other hand, Rosenberg and Simmons (1971) found that sense of control is never negatively related to desegregation, and that it is sometimes positively related. One of the problems with such studies is that they generally ignore classroom processes and interracial climates. Rosenberg and Simmons (1971), however, did not. They found that desegregated black children in their sample were exposed to racial prejudice, cultural dissonance, and stiff academic competition.

The importance of the conditions of integration is supported by Wessman's (1973) study of secondary school boys undergoing an intensive summer program in the Dartmouth ABC (A Better Chance) Program prior to attending 39 independent boarding schools in the Northeast. Two years after beginning the program, 16 of the 80 students had dropped out. Of the remaining boys, 80 percent reported that they worked harder at boarding school but had smaller classes, more individual help, and better teaching than at their previous schools. Most (88 percent) felt that they were treated no differently by the faculty than other students, while 8 percent felt they received some special attention or help, and 4 percent felt they received unusual attention or were not held to the same standards as other students (Wessman, 1973: 274). With respect to their new schools, 60 percent of the students felt they really belonged, 30 percent felt somewhat apart, and 10 percent felt very apart and alone. About 40 percent indicated that they had experienced major incidents of prejudice and racial discrimination involving other students, but 35 percent reported none (Wessman, 1973: 275).

Overall, the program appreciably improved the academic performance of about one third of the students. About a quarter had been good students intially who continued on that path, and about half did average or poor academic work, which, for some, represented a decline. Noncognitive changes were more dramatic, however, with more than half of the boys reporting major beneficial changes from prep school, 17 percent indicating mixed feelings, and 6 percent viewing the experience as harmful. The faculty also reported observing positive changes in about three-quarters of the boys, but we do not know if they constituted the same group whose self-reports were favorable. Faculty saw the students as becoming more at ease and confident, improving academically, becoming more experienced, broader, more aware and perceptive, and more articulate. They felt, however, that at least 10 percent of the boys were more tense and anxious, discouraged and defeated, alienated and cynical, and more complacent and snobbish. Wessman (1973) reported that the positive students said they had changed a great deal in the direction of "increased academic competence; greater social awareness; more direction and higher goals in life; wider cultural background; greater social ease; more self-awareness; more political awareness; increased tolerance; and increased articulateness [p. 275]." But 26 percent reported greater tension and anxiety; 15 percent discouragement with their limitations; and 10 percent less drive and dedication.

It would be particularly interesting to know the content of their increased political and social awareness. How was this Rockefeller Foundation-sponsored program socializing them? In what ways were they coming to see the world differently? Obviously this program includes more than just an integrated educational experience. It contains the possibility of sponsorship for upward mobility (as did the schools in Himmelweit and Swift's, 1969, study). Could any of the tensions experienced have centered around the process of cooptation in the course of sponsorship? This is a fascinating but unexplored aspect of Wessman's study. The selective nature of the program and its concomitant "knighting effect," the near-total nature of the institutions, and the close personal contact between students and instructors undoubtedly contributed to the changes reported by the boys. How lasting they will be remains to be seen.

When selection is not accomplished by restricted admission or ecological segregation it often appears to occur through tracking. Particularly prevalent in large urban schools, tracking affects the ethnic and class composition of school classrooms and influences academic achievement and self-concept (as discussed in Chapter 6).

An additional structural characteristic of schools related to their selectivity is the rate of failure in the school. Obviously, if a school makes an administrative decision that only so many students can pass or receive certain grades, that decision is going to affect the rates of success and failure in the school. Both Rosenbaum (1976) and Schindler (1970) document specific rates of failure. I have heard of such decisions being linked to position in the track structure, as in one large metropolitan school system in which teachers are told to give no grade above 80 to students in the lower tracks (Wexler, 1976). Cicourel and Kitsuse (1963) and Rosenbaum (1976) report that grades in honors courses were weighted more heavily in computing pupils' grade-point averages. In such ways as these, school selection policies and practices can affect not only achievement outcomes but aspirations as well. Breton, McDonald, and Richer (1972) found that the rate of failure within a school was negatively related to the educational and occupational aspirations of students in the school, even among students who did not themselves fail. Administrative policies about acceptable rates of success may very well affect the expectations engendered in teachers, although I know of no studies that have examined this linkage.

Gigliotti and Brookover (1975) suggest that the climate of expectations within a school may be an important feature distinguishing high-achieving lower-class schools from the more usual low-achieving ones.

The pervasive climate of low expectations for student achievement in lower-class minority schools was noted by Leacock (1969), Massey, Scott and Dornbush (1975), Schindler (1970), Silberman (1970), and Rist (1970). Given the relationship between expectations and achievement (documented in Chapter 8), it may be that lowered expectations permeate certain schools, with negative consequences for student learning, while much more positive expectations get built into other schools.

Brookover and Schneider (1975) examined middle-class, predominantly white schools with lower than average achievement levels and found that teachers and administrators generally held lower expectations for students in those schools. This is a critical study because it documents that the usual relationship of race, class, and achievement disappears when the climate of expectations is held constant. The evidence that white middle-class students achieve poorly when expectations are low while black lower-class students achieve well when expectations are high totally contradicts an explanation of achievement based upon genes or culture.

The potency of peer expectations, particularly for educational aspirations, has received a great deal of attention in the literature. Early studies inferred the climate of peer expectations from the socioeconomic status of the students in a school (e.g., Boyle, 1966; Michael, 1961; Wilson, 1959) with ensuing debates (e.g., Hauser, Sewell, and Alwin, 1974; Sewell and Armer, 1966). As Cohen (1975) points out, one of the problems with these studies may have been their lack of a direct measure of the school normative-audience climates. When peer "value climates" have been directly measured (as in Kandel and Lesser, 1969; Krauss, 1964), the educational plans of peers are related to an individual's plans. Students who are highly esteemed by their peers are also more likely to have college plans than those held in lower esteem (Coleman, 1961; McDill, Meyers, and Rigsby, 1966).

Several qualitative studies suggest that peers may reinforce the expectations held by teachers, with intensified consequences for the achievement and self-esteem of affected children. Researchers found that other children in the class picked on children who were negatively evaluated by the teacher, showing physical abuse (Rist, 1970) and verbal abuse (Schindler, 1970) without being sanctioned by the teacher. Moreover, after the students had been separated into reading groups, Rist (1973) noticed that each group of pupils began to emulate the teacher's treatment of the other groups: middle-class youngsters were ". . . learning to control the poor, and the poor students were learning to shuffle [p. 245]." The implication here is that students are learning their place in society, both from the teacher's treatment of them and from the treatment they receive from peers.

Teacher and peer expectations may have a number of cognitive consequences as well. One subtle feature noted by Hargreaves (1967), Lacey (1970), and Schindler (1970) is that students in the lower tracks began to form antischool subcultures, perhaps in an effort to counteract the negative evaluations placed upon them by the school. These students increasingly come to esteem ones who most effectively subverted the goals of the school. Hence students are rewarded by their peers for poor performances, for distracting behaviors, and for upsetting the teachers. While such behavior may help to preserve the self-respect of those who manifest it (cf. Schindler, 1970), it has self-fulfilling potency as regards the academic learning that occurs within the school. By reinforcing the teachers' expectations that students are unwilling or unable to learn, such peer dynamics ensure that even less learning occurs, leading teachers to expect even less, and so on.

One of the assumptions underlying studies of teaching styles is the belief that teachers spend most of their time in the classroom engaged in teaching behavior. But a number of very interesting observational studies (Jackson, 1968; Lortie, 1976; Rist, 1970; Schindler, 1970; Smith and Geoffrey, 1968) suggest that even in upper-middle-class schools (Jackson, 1968) teachers spend an inordinate amount of time on control and management activities. Indeed, it was this feature of the teacher's role that led Smith and Geoffrey to conceptualize the teacher role as that of a manager. Jackson added the dimension of evaluation as critical to the teacher's role, but in the upper-middle-class schools he observed, evaluation was primarily in terms of holding out carrots to students rather than in the use of sticks. Negative comments and even physical punishment were more often observed in large urban schools populated by lower-class minority students (Kozol, 1967; Rist, 1970; Schindler, 1970). Schindler added another feature to the teacher's role: haranguing students for what they did not know or could not do. Instead of teaching them what they needed to know, the teacher berated them for not knowing it, often implying that they would never learn it. While this kind of teacher behavior may occur in some lower-income and minority schools, it is by no means universal. Both Leacock (1969) and Massey, Scott, and Dornbush (1975) found that teachers of lower-class or minority students showed no overt signs of racism, and pupils perceived them as friendly and supportive. But these same teachers had very low academic standards for such students and taught them very little. Similarly, Schindler (1970) observed teachers practicing what he calls a work slowdown, and in an interview one teacher reported:

> In a school like the D_____ [slum school] you're just not expected to complete all that work. It's almost impossible. For instance, in the second grade we're supposed to cover nine spelling words a week. Well, I can do that up

here at the K_____[better school], they can take nine new words a week. But the best class I ever had at the D_____ was only able to achieve six words a week and they had to work pretty hard to get that. So I never finished the year's work in spelling. I couldn't. And I wasn't really expected to [pp. 145–146].

Somehow the system transmitted work expectancies to teachers, who in turn varied the amount taught. Indeed, Schindler observed the emergence of a contract between teacher and students, with both understanding that the teachers would not require too much work if the students did not misbehave or act out.

A similar situation is reported by Wexler (personal communication, April 1976), who is observing classrooms in another large urban school system. He saw a junior-high-school teacher who never gave the students any work, explaining that the students were lucky, and that he was giving them a break. In this case, the students became increasingly irritated because they were not being taught anything, and finally staged a demonstration demanding that they be taught. Given the norm that prevails in some schools, however, that students are "getting away with something" if they can succeed in wasting an entire class, such lazy "teaching" may not always result in a protest. Indeed, Schindler (1970) observed that "most classes supported a teacher-organized and teacher-defined work slowdown [p. 146]." This has serious implications for the differential amount of material presented to students, and for the amount of learning that occurs.

Conclusion

The definitions and measures of the educational outcomes deemed important appear to affect those outcomes to some degree, by defining what constitutes success. Constructing tests to exclude items that everyone answers correctly (no matter how important those items are); regarding only mean scores rather than measures of dispersion as important; and considering only "objectively testable" results as noteworthy, all influence the educational results that are observed and debated. While remaining sensitive to these issues, I choose to live with them for the purpose of analyzing whether educational structures and interactions affect conventional educational outcomes.

A number of school characteristics (see Figure 9.1) are found to have important cognitive and noncognitive consequences: the amount of available resources, the source of money, the degree of control, the type of school governance, the extent of bureaucratization, the totality of schools, their selectivity, integration, tracking, rates of failure, climates

FIGURE 9.1. Educational outcomes

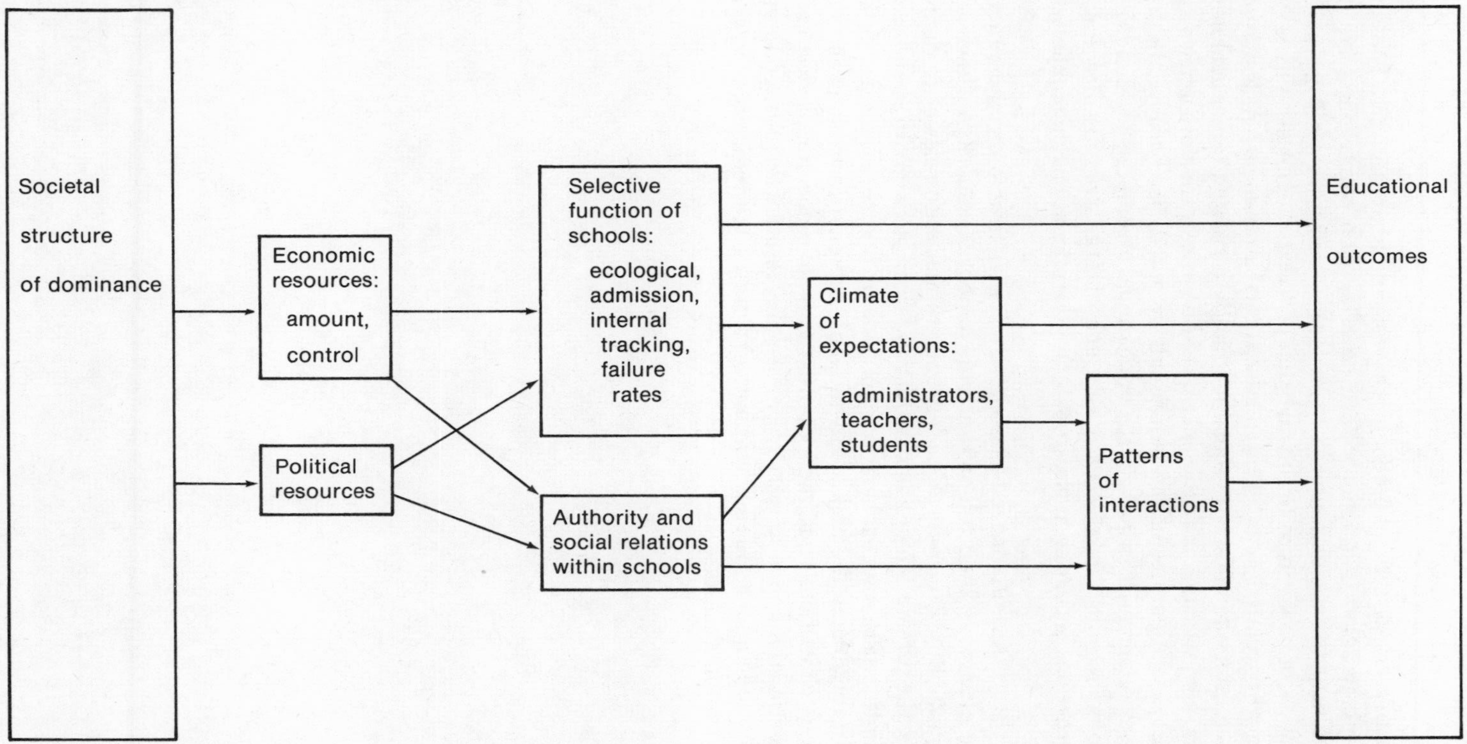

of expectations, type of teacher behavior, and peer attitudes. Those who have concluded that schools have no effects on pupils may have been examining the wrong features.

We can now return to the question posed at the outset. Why is social inequality related to differential educational attainment? As the preceding chapters demonstrate, social inequality is related to unequal educational achievement and attainment, not because of the deficiencies in the genes or the culture of the individuals involved, but because the structure of dominance influences the educational assumptions which prevail, shapes the educational structures which emerge, thereby affecting the interactions occurring in classrooms and the educational outcomes which result.

The differentiating educational concepts, structures, and practices most often take their toll on the achievement of minority or lower-class students. But, even where students are similar with respect to race and class, the pressure to divide students and to treat them differently exists. In both cases, the explanations for school failure which are offered invariably blame the child. Individual characteristics of children may of course contribute, but the potential role of educational systems for educational outcomes must always be considered. The part schools play cannot be understood fully without considering how education is related to social inequality.

10

Life Outcomes

THE RELATIONSHIP BETWEEN EDUCATION and social inequality has been visualized in several different ways. There are actually three different relationships involved (see Figure 10.1, Part A), one between social origins and education, (1) in Figure 10.1A, another between educational attainment and life outcomes, (2) in Figure 10.1A, and finally, the relation between social origin and life outcomes, (3) in Figure 10.1A. The difference in views about the relation between education and inequality hinges upon the relative importance given to different elements in this schema. First, there is what might be termed the "finishing school" or acquisition-of-status view, where social position is very highly related to educational attainment. While educational attainment might determine what one's activities as a member of the upper class might be, membership in that class does not depend upon education. Furthermore, education could never ensure a high social position. Hence there was a strong causal relation between social position and education, but no causal relation between education and high social position (Figure 10.1B). This perspective fits the data reported by Hollingshead (1949).

In contrast, the work of Blau and Duncan (1967) suggests that education is instrumental in securing occupational position and is relatively more important in the process than family background (Figure 10.1C). The importance of the cognitive content of education seems to be implicit in this approach. Because this view has significantly influenced American social thought, I consider below the assumptions upon which it rests.

A third view appears in the work of Jencks et al. (1972), who found very little connection between years of schooling or cognitive skills and income. Father's occupation or education was not especially related to

153

FIGURE 10.1.   Varied views of how education and social inequality are related

Part A: Elements in the model

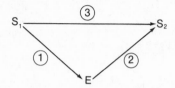

Part B: Education is "polish" (Hollingshead, 1949)

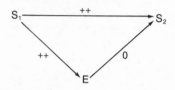

Part C: Education is instrumental (Blau and Duncan, 1967)

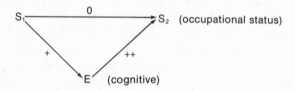

Part D: Education is insignificant (Jencks et al., 1972)

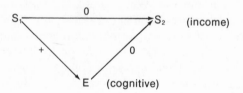

Part E: Education is reproduction and legitimation (Collins, 1971; Bowles and Gintis, 1973)

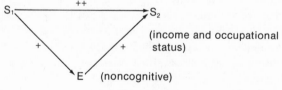

S_1 = class or status of origin
E = education
S_2 = life outcomes—status, class or income

the son's income either (Figure 10.1D). As indicated throughout, Jencks and associates may have ignored or mismeasured many important features and consequences of schools.

Yet another conception has emerged in the work of Collins (1971) and Bowles and Gintis (1976). They share Jencks' view that the cognitive content of education has relatively little causal importance for occupational status or income, but they emphasize the noncognitive features of education, which they see as related to occupational position and income. For them, social position is related to both educational attainment and to life outcomes (Figure 10.1E). Thus they approximate the first view, stressing the importance of social origin, with education being a finishing touch. I find much to support their view, particularly if the possibility that education may also have important instrumental consequences is not overlooked. Therefore, I examine both cognitive and noncognitive (here termed instrumental and experiential) consequences of education for life outcomes, and I consider how these consequences may resign individuals to inequality, as well as contain the potential for change.

Blau and Duncan (1967) have addressed the question of how education is related to life outcomes in terms of the prestige of one's occupational position. While pathbreaking in their own time, Blau and Duncan (1967) conceptualize the relationship between education and life outcomes in rather narrow terms. They begin with the assumption that "the occupational structure is the foundation of the stratification system of contemporary industrial society [p. vii]." But (as discussed in Chapter 3) the range of inequality within the occupational system is much smaller than the disparity between those few who own or control a major portion of the productive wealth in society and those who do not. Thus, by assuming that the occupational hierarchy is the most important basis for inequality in society, Blau and Duncan remove from examination the group of wealth owners and controllers, who, while small in number, are very powerful in effect.

Second, Blau and Duncan emphasize mobility within this occupational structure, thereby implying that it is the major feature of the system. But stability rather than mobility is the predominant characteristic of the American social structure. In the United States, 42 percent of the men with fathers in the top fifth of the occupational hierarchy end up there themselves (Jencks et al., 1972: 179). Moreover, where mobility does occur, it is most likely to take place within a narrow range. These findings do not deny the existence of social mobility in America but do suggest that large numbers of people either do not change their occupational status from one generation to another or change it by only a small amount. Furthermore, by stressing mobility, they seem to suggest that it is the only process involving dynamics. Blau and Duncan (1967) say ". . . processes of social mobility from one generation to the next and from career beginnings to occupational destinations are considered to reflect the dynamics of the occupational structure [p. 1]." However, the maintenance of a relatively stable system of social and economic inequality, marked by a broad range of inequalities, also involves dynamics that need to be understood.

A preeminent focus on mobility has the additional consequence of placing primary concern upon equality of opportunity (for mobility) rather than upon equality of result. Studying mobility assumes that the mobility occurs within an existing system of stratification. If mobility is possible, then the extent of ultimate inequality somehow appears less problematic. By contrast, my intent here is to understand how structures of inequality, termed the structure of dominance, seek to maintain, reproduce and legitimate themselves. A limited amount of social mobility may be one of the mechanisms that helps to maintain and legitimate the existing structure of dominance. Other mechanisms and processes are interesting as well, in particular the role the educational system plays in maintaining and legitimating existing inequalities.

The Wisconsin model of status attainment adds some intervening social-psychological variables to the Blau-Duncan model (Sewell, Haller, and Portes, 1969; Sewell and Shah, 1968a,b). Strongly related to family background, these attitudinal and aspirational variables are important mediating links between ascribed status, educational attainment, and subsequent occupational attainment. This addition to the status-attainment process is quite consistent with Muller's (1972) verification of the importance of a "family residual effect" in the relationship between family status and son's educational and occupational attainments. While the "family residual" concept is not fully specified, it includes all of the family effect, rather than just the father's education and occupation.

The work of Muller and that of Haller and Portes (1973) and Sewell and Hauser (1975) suggest important interpersonal dimensions in the status-attainment process. By stopping the analysis where they do, however, these models represent the relationship between ascribed status and attained status as caused by the attitudes and aspirations of low- and high-status individuals. Here, however, I attribute causal importance to the stratification system and to the socially created concepts and structures that impinge on low-status persons and determine their opportunities, aspirations, and attainments.

In a recent study, Sewell and Hauser (1975) discovered that father's income affected son's ability, educational attainment, occupational attainment, and income, independently of the father's occupational position and educational level. This process needs to be understood, as does the question of how and why education is related to occupational prestige and to income. The importance of this latter problem is underscored when we realize, as Crowder (1971) and Jencks et al. (1972) have pointed out, that there is a wide distribution of income within each category of educational attainment. That is, high school graduates earn widely disparate incomes, and those with Ph.D.s rarely if ever earn as much as those with M.D.s, Ll.D.s, or M.B.A.s. Indeed, using a sample analogous to Blau and Duncan's, Crowder demonstrates that education has a curvilinear relationship with income. This is but one of a number of strands of evidence suggesting that education may be used as a symbolic weapon in the competition among occupational interest groups seeking economic, political, social, and cultural dominance within an existing market situation (in capitalist countries) and within existing political conditions in socialist states.

Thus, an additional limitation to conventional studies of occupational-status attainment is that they take the market situation as given, and neglect to consider the constraints placed upon occupational-status attainment and income by market conditions. The market situation here is considered to be the result of an even more pervasive system of stratification and dominance. Even studies of income generally ignore market factors (e.g., Jencks et al., 1972; Sewell and Hauser, 1975) or, if they do consider them, take them as givens in the situation and not as part of the problem to be understood. As a result, even the few studies that examine inequality of income are confined to an analysis of distributive inequalities rather than inequalities of production and control.[1]

To understand how and why education is related to economic and social inequalities, it is essential to begin, as we have done here, by analyzing what the structure of dominance in society is, and then seeing how it is related to educational ideas, structures, expectations, interactions, and outcomes. Moreover, we must enlarge the scope of the life outcomes that are analyzed in relation to education, just as we expanded the conventional view of the important educational outcomes, before we consider how they are affected by educational experiences.

Given the extent of economic, occupational, and racial inequality in the United States, a guiding concern of this book has been to understand how people apparently come to accept and live with such inequalities. This concern leads to an exploration of the world views and self-conceptions that people come to form and the part that education—in both its instrumental and experiential roles—comes to play in the formation of such consciousness. For example, while I agree with Blau and Duncan (1967) that "men's careers occupy a dominant place in their lives [p. vii]," the real question is, how do they become so salient? Why do Americans focus so heavily on position in the occupational hierarchy rather than upon relative ownership position?

---

[1] Some recent interesting studies which do examine factors affecting the market situation are Rubinson (1976) and Stolzenberg (1975).

Many explanations have been offered—like rising wages leading to the appearance of relatively equal consumption, social mobility, and ethnic divisions—but no one until recently has suggested that the educational system may play a part in the socialization of consciousness (cf. Behn et al., 1974; Bowles and Gintis, 1976; Gintis, 1971a). As schools shifted their focus (from religious and moral instruction to work readiness) there was increasing emphasis on the instrumental, and specifically the cognitive, aspects of education to provide entry into selected occupations and assure subsequent success. This was due in part to the ideology of the meritocracy which required that a measurable form of ability and effort provide the basis for rewards—both in school and in life.

Just as the occupational structure came to be defined as the appropriate arena for definitions of self-identity and life success, the ultimate American criterion of success became consumption. People came to work for more money with which to buy more, better, and newer goods so as to compete with their friends and neighbors for self-esteem and prestige. How does the definition of success in extrinsic and consumption terms arise? Why does what one earns become more important than what one can do, or how well one can do it, or how much one enjoys doing it? Does the school stress the importance of extrinsic rewards (cf. Illich, 1971; Gintis, 1973)? Does the educational system contribute in any way to the analytic categories or alternatives that are perceived as available to people as they try to understand the world? Do students learn that *how* work is to be done and *what* is to be done are decisions to be arrived at democratically? If not, why not?

In an effort to answer these questions, I analyze educational outcomes in both *instrumental* and *experiential* terms and then consider their consequences for the maintenance or disruption of the existing structure of dominance. While this distinction is somewhat arbitrary, it may have analytic utility. The instrumental outcomes of education include cognitive knowledge (like how the human body works, how the economy and polity work) and skills (how to read, write, do arithmetic, organize a meeting, solve a problem, fix something, and so on). Other instrumental consequences of education include the contacts one makes with peers and authorities, the nature of the affect (relationship) engendered in the situation, and the certificates one receives (like diplomas). The personality traits that Gintis (1971a) suggests are important for success in school and on the job may also be considered as instrumental results of education.

The experiential outcomes of education refer to the ways in which educational structures, styles, and content affect the emergence of a particular identity, self-conception, frame of reference, and set of attitudes and values. What features of the educational process have what effects on what kinds of children? Instrumental and experiential aspects undoubtedly interact, with educational consequences.

Are the knowledge and skill acquired through education related to the technical content of jobs? No one denies the threshold necessity of literacy and numeracy (cf. Bowles and Gintis, 1976; Dreeben, 1971), but what is not explained is the rise in educational requirements for the same jobs (Collins, 1974) or that some jobs were being performed in 1960 by people with less schooling than those who held the same jobs in 1940, and others by people with more (reported by Folger and Nam, 1967, cited in Dreeben, 1971: 96).

The overemphasis on the cognitive results of education is supported further by Berg's (1970) finding that years of schooling are generally unrelated (and sometimes negatively related) to performance ratings, and to Super and Crites' (1962) finding that the economic return to vocational schooling is quite low (cited in Gintis, 1971: 267).

The minimal importance of cognitive achievement for income was noted by Bowles and Gintis (1976) and by Jencks et al. (1972). If the argument that technical job requirements connect schooling and work is supported at all, it appears to be so only at the highest level, intellectually demanding, and technologically changing occupations, specifically the professions (Dreeben, 1971: 97). For many jobs, the cognitive content of education appears to be less important than the certificate.

Why are credentials so valuable to employers? Collins (1974) suggests that educational credentials are used to predict normative conformity more than technical training, a view he finds consistent with employers' comments. A businessman who saw education primarily as an initial screening device says:

> Industry places a high value on the college degree, not because it is convinced that four years of schooling insure that individuals acquire maturity and technical competence, but rather because it provides an initial point of division between those more trained and those less trained; those better motivated and those less motivated; those with more social experience and those with less [Gordon and Howell, 1959: 121, cited in Collins, 1974: 440].

Employers in Collins' study gave similar reasons; they required high-school degrees for manual workers, ". . . as an indication of character (perseverance, self-discipline, drive, etc.) rather than of knowledge." Several employers now require high-school degrees of applicants for janitorial and similar positions, "in order that they may be able to read instructions [Collins, 1974: 440]." Thus, educational certification is used as a screening device for motivational and character traits, as well as for minimal levels of competence.

Bowles and Gintis (1976: 95) see educational credentials as providing an additional resource to employers in their efforts to bolster the legitimacy of organizational hierarchies. In contrast, Collins (1976) argues that despite employers' use of credentials as symbolic devices, education has economic payoffs for those who possess educational credentials, at least in the middle and higher occupational ranges, "because education has enabled them to carve out professional and technical monopolies over lucrative services and vulnerable organizational sectors [p. 251]." While I agree with Collins that educational certification has benefited some groups relative to others, I think he assumes that certain occupations and professions are more independent of the societal context, particularly of the structure of dominance, than they actually are. With the possible exception of medicine, most occupations and professions cannot develop autonomously but have considerable constraints imposed upon them with respect to the nature of the work to be done, where it is to be done, and under what conditions. Certain occupations and professions have gained relatively more autonomy and rewards than other groups, a factor which may divert potential critics from attacking wide discrepancies in wealth ownership. Professionals ensconced in their own lucrative enclaves are relatively insulated from the inequalities of wealth which exist, or if close enough to observe them (as is the case of tax lawyers), are well enough socialized and rewarded not to object. Managers tend to be preoccupied with differential income, status, and work relative to others in the organizational hierarchy. Giving ambitious and energetic individuals the chance to compete with one another effectively insulates them from competition with wealth owners. Thus, while occupational elites have benefited from the expansion of educational requirements, the wealth-owning class has also gained.

Education additionally tends to provide what Collins (1976) calls "the solidarity of an esoteric in-group culture." While Collins analyzes this only in relation to the advantages it provides for organizational privilege and income, it can be seen as operating at other levels as well, as work by Baltzell (1958) and Domhoff (1967) suggests. These writers assert that the solidarity of wealth owners tends to be buttressed partly through shared boarding-school experiences, which effectively isolate participants from many other contacts and experiences and develop an esoteric in-group culture, which may be activated at a later date. These shared experiences are important not only for developing a common culture, but also as a source of future information and action opportunities. For the occupational elite, old school ties can provide critical contacts for learning about job openings or business opportunities. The imaginative work of Granovetter (1974) suggests how informal ties facilitate job hunting. Obviously, many jobs have entry requirements that cannot be circumvented by personal contacts. But given all the people with a particular set of job qualifications, those who hear about the job and have someone to "put in a good word" for them have a better chance of getting it. Moreover, the knowledge of what requirements are needed for certain jobs is also a function of one's contacts, beginning with the family and extending into peer and teacher contacts and information giving. The network result of certain educational experiences rather than others is virtually unexplored in the literature relating education to either occupational attainment or income. While everyone at a given preparatory school or college may not be in a particular network, members of the network may have in common their shared educational experience. Granovetter's (1974) interesting finding that higher-salaried jobs and job seekers are more likely to be matched by a network of personal contacts than are lower-paid jobs suggests that interpersonal networks may become increasingly important as their members rise in the occupational or wealth-owning hierarchy. This may be the case because as Levitas (1974) has noted, family and class solidarity increases the higher one goes in the class system.

To summarize, the instrumental consequences of education for work appear to be as follows: Cognitive knowledge and skills have not been found to be related to job performance (although to be sure, with present educational requirements for entrance to many jobs, the range in cognitive knowledge and skills is probably much smaller than it needs to be to adequately test the assertion that the cognitive content of education is totally unrelated to the content of jobs.)[2] It defies common sense to suggest that knowledge and skill are unrelated to any aspects of job performance. And yet, the role that knowledge and skill play in education and in life warrants considerable thought and examination and remains an open question. Clearly, we need to know much more about what background and skills are related to job performances and life satisfactions.

Credentials or certificates are related to employers' requirements and preferences, but we have only impressionistic data about the reasons for this. Some employers appear to use credentials as screening devices for social or motivational attributes. Others look to them to ensure minimal levels of cognitive competence. Bowles and Gintis (1976) suggest that educational requirements strengthen the perceived legitimacy of organizational hierarchies, and in a related vein Collins (1976) suggests that educational requirements benefit certain occupational groups by restricting entrance and providing in-group cultural solidarity. The conception of cultural solidarity is amplified by Granovetter's (1974) conception of social networks and how they operate to aid one in getting

[2]The natural case study reported in the book and later film entitled *The Great Impostor* demonstrates that a high-school dropout was able to perform the jobs of surgeon, prison warden, teacher, and priest not only without being discovered but with distinction (see Crichton, 1959). The rarity of such examples, however, makes it impossible to ascertain how much of Frederick Demara's success was due to exceptional personal qualities and how much is generalizable, and how easily an individual may learn the tasks associated with various occupations. While it is clear that the competent performance of some work, say, surgery, requires some training or experience, it is equally apparent that occupations that restrict work exclusively to those with such credentials may be over-exaggerating the complex and esoteric character of the work involved. For example, experienced nurses may have many of a doctor's skills even though they lack the formal educational background.

a job or advancing occupationally, economically, or socially. All these instrumental resources that may result from education undoubtedly help to explain how the structure of dominance reproduces and legitimates itself.

These processes can be even better understood by an analysis of the experiential consequences of education. Education contributes to the reproduction of structures of dominance in two major experiential ways: through the isolating and insulating of experiences; and the correspondence between the experiential nature of education and the requirements of work. Education occurs in relatively segregated and isolated groups, divided along wealth-owning, occupational, and racial lines (and along sex lines, at least until quite recently). Under such conditions, members of all groups fail to experience each other, or do so only in very restricted ways. They may barely know of the existence of the other groups and certainly know little about the content and nature of their existence. Once groups with different pasts or different futures are identified and separated, they are exposed to quite different experiences that prepare them most appropriately for their respective futures.

The correspondence between educational experience and occupational requirements has been well articulated by Behn et al. (1974), Bowles and Gintis (1976), and Carnoy (1974). Basically, these writers suggest that the class-related differences in the social and authority relations in schools prepare people for their respective positions in the occupational hierarchy. Authority relations produce, label, and reward specific personality traits, generate or discourage alienation from work and authority, and develop certain frames of reference (Ashton, 1973), attitudes, values, and what Bowles and Gintis (1976) call "stratified consciousness."

In what ways do social and authority relations in schools mirror the societal structure of dominance? We have at least impressionistic descriptions of the experiential variations at all levels of education, from nursery school to college. Kanter (1972) observed a nursery school for children from professional families and noticed the congruence between the predominance of bureaucratic organizations in society and the experiential structuring of education, even at this early level. The nursery program, she found, was structured so that it limited uncertainty, coercion, accountability, unpleasantness, and peer conflict. She concluded that this structure oriented children to the organizational reality of the nursery, routinized play, discouraged responsibility, and encouraged children to seek ascendancy over others. Kanter paralleled the nursery structure and experience to the demands of bureaucracy in the larger society.

While I know of no comparable phenomenological study of a program designed for low-income and minority children, we have already discussed (in Chapter 5) the assumptions about the child's and the family's inadequacies on which many such programs appear to be predicated. Bereiter (1967) describes his program in detail, suggesting that the program is designed to "teach children more of what is most valuable and teach it better [p. iv]." The program seeks to inculcate "correct" (dominant) American English into the children, many of whom "come in with practically no spoken language [Bereiter, 1967: 132]." While undoubtedly not deliberate, the message conveyed by the social and authority relations in the program is that the children and their families are worthless, that only experts can teach them anything of value, that they must do what they are told without thinking, and that doing so results in success and rewards as defined by the system.

In public elementary and secondary schools, Bowles and Gintis (1976) write, the "structure of social relations in education not only inures the student to the discipline of the work place, but develops the types of personal demeanor, modes of self-presentation, self-image, and social-class identifications which are the crucial ingredients of job adequacy [p. 131]." Private boarding schools also appear to be designed to inculcate specific social and economic characteristics, particularly those necessary for future leadership.

The exercise of authority associated with highly bureaucratic inner-city schools may be similar to the authority relations those students will encounter in the work world. There is considerable external discipline, which students have no part in formulating; there are many rules, often rigidly enforced; students need passes to go into the hall or to the bathroom; and the teacher's authority is reflected as much in control or haranguing behavior as in teaching. Teachers themselves are often interrupted by a public address system they cannot control or by bureaucratic requirements for behavioral conformity by teachers. Decisions about a child's ability or class assignment or program of study are made impersonally, on the basis of test scores and records, with little opportunity for children, parents, or teachers to shape the result. Information about alternatives is limited, if not withheld, and the number of alternatives is restricted within a particular school. It would not be surprising if, as Behn et al. (1974) suggest, ". . . in such an environment the students learn to take orders and respond to authority. . . .[They see this socialization pattern as corresponding] to the requirements of industry for unskilled workers who need primarily to defer to authority, respond passively to orders, accept alienation from work, and become one of the faceless multitudes at the bottom of the work hierarchy [p. 57]."

Bowles and Gintis draw upon their own research as well as that of Smith (1967, 1970), Edwards (in press), and Meyer (1972) to document the relationship between education, work, and personality characteristics. Thus Gintis (1971a), building on the work of Merton (1940) and

Weber (1958), identifies four traits that are important for adequate job functioning in a bureaucracy: subordinacy, discipline, supremacy of cognitive over affective modes of response, and motivation according to external reward. Edwards (in press, cited in Bowles and Gintis, 1976: 135–6) empirically demonstrates that some of these traits are related to supervisors' ratings of worker performance. Moreover, the salience to supervisors of different personality traits varied for workers at different levels of the production hierarchy, with "rules orientation" most important at the lowest level, "dependability" most relevant at the intermediate level, and the "internalization of norms" most valued at the highest level (Edwards, in press, cited in Bowles and Gintis, 1976: 135). The work of Smith (1967) and Meyer (1972), both cited in Bowles and Gintis (1976), suggests that traits which are rewarded by supervisors are also encouraged and rewarded by teachers.

Grading systems are a major mechanism for distributing teacher rewards. The fact as well as the basis of grading is important, insofar as it emphasizes extrinsic rather than intrinsic rewards. The practice of grading puts students in the position of competing with their peers for evaluations determined by outside authorities—their teachers or sometimes state examiners. Hence what is evaluated as well as by whom are external to the student, conveying the message that they themselves cannot and should not determine or assess their work.

While grades are generally not a good predictor of economic success or job performance (see Hoyt, 1965), Bowles and Gintis (1976) expect that they might be a better predictor if individuals with similar educational experiences are compared in similar jobs. They find one study, by Brenner (1968), that examines one hundred graduates of Los Angeles City schools who went to work for the Lockheed California Company. Brenner obtained the employees' supervisors' evaluations of three aspects of their job performance, an "ability rating," "conduct rating," and "productivity rating," which were analyzed in relation to high-school grade-point averages, absentee rates, and teachers' evaluations of student work habits and cooperation. Brenner found that grades predict job adequacy only through the noncognitive components of teacher evaluations, suggesting that teachers evaluate students and bosses evaluate employees in similar ways. Many people would consider this degree of congruence between school and work an indication that the schools are effectively preparing adolescents for adulthood. Indeed, without knowing more about what goes into these teacher evaluations it would be hard to refute the claim that good work habits, regular attendance, and cooperation might also be evaluated highly by fellow workers in a totally democratic work situation. Thus these data can support a democratic as well as an authoritarian interpretation.

There is, however, evidence suggesting that grades are awarded on a different basis in various types of schools. The personality trait "achievement via conformity" (on Gough's 1967 scale)[3] was more importantly related to grades in an inner-city school than in a suburban school (Alker and Wohl, 1972).

The differential basis of awarding grades in different types of schools may help to explain why the high-school grades of minority students are weaker predictors of college grades than are the grades of suburban students (Thomas and Stanley, 1969, cited in Alker and Wohl, 1972).

Despite the suggestive findings that grades reward different behaviors and performances in students in different types of schools, it is important to stress, as Bowles and Gintis (1976) do, that grading practices are only one aspect of education that differentially socializes students for life position.

The passive, or recipient, perception of students reflected in grading practices may pervade the curriculum as well. Some teachers assume that pupils are empty vessels to be filled by the teacher rather than regarded as active participants in the learning process.

A similar view of the student as an inert mass underlies the practice of tracking. For grouping all the similar-sized vessels together is reasonable only when abilities are assumed to be relatively fixed. If, on the other hand, "ability" is an elastic quality that grows with use, then tracking is a restrictive and inappropriate practice. Moreover, tracking has powerful experiential consequences. As already noted, young people in different tracks relate differently to each other and face different adjustment problems. Because allocation to different tracks is legitimated by alleged differences in innate ability, teachers and other students perceive the students in low tracks as inferior. Besides being perceived and treated as stupid, youngsters assigned to lower tracks are effectively denied "the opportunity to develop their cognitive and manipulative skills beyond a minimal level" (Ashton, 1973: 108). Thus they are unable to develop the skills and earn the certificates necessary for entering occupations other than those of semi-skilled work. Ashton (1973) claims that:

> . . . while the pupils that form the lower streams may reject the dominant values transmitted within the school—of academic achievement and hard work—and stress antiacademic values and 'messing about,' they do accept the definition of themselves as inferior in some respects [p. 108].

The differentiated structure of schools, then, has both cognitive and experiential consequences for students. Ashton (1973) notes, "In this way, by acquiring an image of themselves through their interaction with

---

3 Gough's 1967 scale is cited in Alker and Wohl, 1972.

others as academically incapable, the pupils learn to see those occupations that require some form of educational qualification for entry as beyond their reach [p. 109]." Thus schools operate to reduce the occupational aspirations of youth. If they feel they have had a chance to get the necessary education but did poorly or did not like school, then they can "decide" on lower-paying, lower-opportunity occupations without feeling that the system is totally unjust.

If they do not lower their occupational aspirations as a result of experiencing such educational structures, more deliberate "cooling out" mechanisms are undoubtedly brought to bear, as Clark (1960) trenchantly depicts. Studying junior colleges in California, Clark notes three types of students there: the terminal, transfer, and "latent terminal" student, who aspires to transfer but probably cannot, in the eyes of college officials. As Karabel (1972) notes, ". . . the crux of the dilemma is how to gently convince the latent terminal student that a transfer program is inappropriate for him without seeming to deny him the equal educational opportunity that Americans value so highly [p. 537]." The mechanisms of "persuasion" outlined by Clark (1960) include: (1) preentrance testing, often leading to required enrollment in remedial classes; (2) a counseling interview before registration each semester, in which a student is told the chances for success in particular courses; (3) a special required course called "Orientation to College," designed to help students evaluate their own interests, abilities, and aptitudes in light of the training required for their desired occupation; (4) grades in courses; and (5) probation. Probation serves to "kill off the lingering hopes of the most stubborn latent terminal students," according to Clark. "Cooling out" is furthered by efforts to provide alternative forms of achievement; a series of steps designed to gradually disengage the student; providing denial on the basis of test scores, grades, and the student's cumulative record, thus placing the spotlight on the student's failure rather than on the structural features of schools; and "agents of consolation" in the form of counselors who are experienced in helping students adjust to the idea of lower-status occupations. Clark stresses that this "cooling out" process must be concealed. Thus the rhetoric of the junior college stresses the transfer and terminal programs rather than the role it plays in transforming transfer aspirants into terminal students. Although similar cooling-out practices probably occur in elementary or secondary schools and in four-year colleges, these have not, to my knowledge, been analyzed by anyone except Rosenbaum (1976). These mechanisms suggest how schooling "probably plays a crucial, if negative, role in redirecting many students' interests [Jencks et al., 1972: 184]." Further, more than occupational aspirations are shaped. One's whole view of adult possibilities and options within those parameters are influenced by the differentiating, competitive, extrinsically rewarded experience of school. With whom one compares oneself is affected by physical and social proximity or distance. How one sees oneself is molded by the images reflected by institutional authorities and peers. Fate control, efficacy, and the knowledge and skills to back up these feelings are factors that schools can enhance or depress.

Schools in upper-middle-class suburbs are more likely to adopt open classrooms, permitting greater student participation and direction of activities, less direct supervision and behavioral control, more electives, fewer rules and more negotiation over those that do exist, and in general greater stress on individual development and internalized standards of control. As Behn et al. (1974) suggest:

> Such an environment tends to inculcate those traits that are functional in making decisions about the work organization itself and about the conditions that affect the workers at lower echelons. The experiences provided by the "flexible" nature of school rules and negotiation for special privileges represent preparation for those who will make the rules and engage in conflict resolution with the persons at high levels of decision making. The independence that is reflected in choosing among the range of alternative educational experiences provides good training for selecting among alternative management strategies. The freedom to choose schooling hours and activities is also functional in preparing upper-middle-class students for the relative freedom that they will have in setting their work schedules in contrast with wage and hour arrangements or fixed schedules of lower-level salaried workers. These youngsters are being socialized to be the "bosses," while those in the inner-city school are being prepared to be the workers or the intermittently employed. The former will learn to give the orders and the latter to follow them [p. 58].

This not so subtle preparation for the executive hierarchy also includes, at least in upper-middle-class suburban schools, an emphasis on individual competition (cf. Cohen's, 1973, account of life at the Harvard Business School). It seems, however, that private boarding schools stress somewhat different qualities. Here the emphasis appears to be upon excellence, but in terms of an individual's own performance, rather than relative to others. Mastery of curricular material and of self-impulses is stressed as befitting the economic and social elite (cf. Winter, Alpert, McClelland, 1970). Success is not something that one must go out and earn through one's own efforts. Rather, one merely needs the intellectual and cultural background to gracefully assume a waiting social position. The protected and exclusive environment, contact with one's social equals (along with a few worthy, carefully selected individuals who have been chosen for sponsorship into elite occupational positions), close personal relationships with instructors, many of whom have themselves attended prep schools—all these features contribute to a sense of belonging to an elite group. Good teaching is stressed to ensure competence to the extent possible.

The variations in social and authority relations among elementary and secondary schools of different kinds are carried over into higher education as well. The expansion of higher education has been accompanied by increased stratification (Karabel, 1972) and the already noted "cooling out" of occupational aspirations (acutely analyzed by Clark, 1960). Moreover, Binstock (1970) has studied the patterns of social relations in two- and four-year colleges and universities and found that they correspond very closely to the social background and likely future positions of students who attend them. She did a content analysis of the rules, regulations, and norms set forth in the college handbooks of 52 different schools, classifying the schools according to the degree of academic structure, the nature of regulations governing personal and social conduct, and the amount of control students had over their cultural and extracurricular activities. Binstock (1970) concludes:

> The major variations of college experiences are linked to basic psychological differences in work perception and aspiration among the major social class (occupational) groups who are its major consumers. Each social class is different in its beliefs as to which technical and interpersonal skills, character traits, and work values are most valuable for economic survival (stability) or to gain economic advantage (mobility). Each class (with subvariations based on religion and level of urbanness) has its own economic consciousness, based on its own work experiences and its own ideas (correct or not) of the expectations appropriate to positions on the economic ladder above their own. . . . Colleges compete over the various social class markets by specializing their offerings. Each different type of undergraduate college survives by providing circumscribed sets of "soft" and "hard" skill training that generally corresponds both to the expectations of a particular social class group of customers and to specific needs for sets of "soft" and "hard" skills at particular layers of the industrial system [pp. 3–4, cited in Bowles and Gintis, 1976: 134].

Binstock found that institutions enrolling mainly working-class students and geared to filling lower-level jobs stress followership, behavioral control, and external compliance, while more elite schools, which are more likely to prepare students for higher-level jobs, seek to develop leadership and motivational control. Binstock (1970) suggests that while college aims are in constant flux:

> . . . the college industry remains a ranked hierarchy of goals and practices, responding to social class pressures, with graded access to the technical equipment, organizational skills, emotional perspectives and class (work) values needed for each stratified level of the industrial system [pp. 3–4, cited in Bowles and Gintis, 1976: 134].

Kamens (1976) has gone further and suggested that different types of colleges help to create and legitimate certain membership categories in society, and that they do this by means of different organizational arrangements and status allocation myths.

Schools produce varied levels of skills and differential perceptions of the world in children who are destined for different positions in the structure of dominance. These varied outcomes not only help to reproduce the structure of dominance in society but also help to legitimate the ensuing inequalities.

The foregoing makes the educational system appear to be working very effectively to perpetuate inequalities. In view of the tendencies toward the reproduction of inequality described above, do possible or actual challenges exist? There are at least three potential countervailing forces: (1) rising expectations, (2) increasing skepticism about the existence and the desirability of meritocracy, and (3) a potential crisis of legitimacy.

As educational opportunities have expanded, people have developed higher aspirations about the kinds of jobs and life styles they expect to have. Some economists (e.g., Freeman, 1976) see this as producing a crisis of "over educated" Americans. But the criteria for "over education" is that of the labor market, what it requires, rather than that of the society as a whole and what it needs or what individuals singly or collectively desire. Moreover, the extent and direction of growth in the labor market is decided by a relatively small number of owners of productive resources and their managers, and is influenced by how well they can "read" future markets, or can control those markets. If they misread them, they cut back on areas that were previously growing, and fire the surplus individuals involved. Thus, the parameters of the labor market are set by relatively few, and influence over the shape those parameters take is out of the hands of most participants in the situation. If there is any disjunction between aspirations and the existing labor market, the problem is seen as being an individual's problem: too many people are overeducated and have aspirations that are too high for the existing job structure. Seldom has the structure of jobs itself been challenged. This may be changing. Rising expectations may come to challenge the shape of the labor market and how that shape is determined.

A second major assumption may also be coming under challenge. There is growing evidence that we do not live in a meritocracy, that it may be impossible to ever do so, and that it may be undesirable even if it were possible.

The biggest source of inequality is differential wealth, rather than occupational status or income, and it is indefensible on meritocratic grounds. About half of the very wealthy inherit their money through no individual effort whatsoever, and the other half make their money by happening to invest in a venture that turns out favorably (see Chapter 3).

Considerable evidence has been presented throughout this book illustrating that meritocratic principles of educational selection are frequently not in operation. Race and social class are often more important for track placement than are the alleged criteria of merit such as IQ test scores.

When allegedly meritocratic criteria are used, they are often unreliable (Rosenbaum, 1976). Additionally, the criteria used for educational allocation and hence future occupational opportunities frequently lack validity as predictors of future performance. Indeed, the problems of invalidity and unreliability, combined with the power differential that more favored groups can bring to the process of defining and evaluating merit, make it appear increasingly impossible to achieve a meritocratic selection process.

Finally, several trenchant critics have questioned the desirability of meritocracy, even if it could be achieved. Both Young (1959) and Wrong (1959) have suggested that if stratification were based completely upon merit it would be even more intolerable than the present system. People in higher positions, who could believe they "deserved" to be there, would be more intolerant of those below them than people in a system where many good and able people were found at lower levels. Also, the lower levels would be denied effective leadership, since their most talented members would be skimmed off and raised to high positions. Anxiety and dissatisfaction might be even higher in such a system, because those at lower levels would feel totally responsible for their miserable lot, and have no face-saving excuses available to them. Given the large range of inequality in current society, it would be undesirable to have a totally meritocratic system. In light of these limitations to the meritocratic ideal, such authors as Young (1959) and Wrong (1959) have concluded that rather than aiming for a more complete meritocracy, a better goal would be the reduction of inequality. They both focus upon inequalities of income and occupational status, rather than upon large differences of wealth.

These rising expectations and doubts about the possibility or desirability of meritocracy contain the potential for a crisis of legitimacy. How can gross inequalities, especially of wealth, but to a lesser extent of income as well, possibly be justified? The instrumental-meritocratic ideology is neither adequate nor accurate.

To conclude, a great deal of what schools do seems to have the effect of reproducing and legitimating the social relations of inequality. This result does not seem to be caused by the direct intervention of those in more dominant positions, except under crisis or formative conditions. Instead, prevailing educational assumptions, structures, interactions, and outcomes appear to be largely responsible. The at least tacit approval of dominant groups can be inferred by what they allow to exist without intervention and by where they send their own children to school.

Increasingly, however, the schools as an agent in the reproduction of subordinancy are not working very well, especially in large cities. There are frequent incidents of violence, rebellion, and withdrawal by students. There is a crisis of confidence in the legitimacy of the school's authority and in the authority of the larger social order. The way to rectify this is by reducing the inequalities in the larger society, by eliminating or minimizing selective practices in schools, by having selection occur as late in one's career as possible, and where selection does occur, by having it be based upon criteria that are rationally justifiable, that is, criteria that are both reliable and are valid predictors of important future behaviors or competencies.

Appendix 1

Do Teachers' Expectations Affect Teachers' Behaviors?

Name And Date Of Study	Was Study Of Natural (N) Or Induced (I) Expectations?	Were Teachers' Expectations Measured?	Were Teachers' Behaviors Affected?
Adams & Cohen, 1974	N	Yes	M
Alpert, 1974	N		M
Blakey, 1970	I		+
Brophy & Good, 1970	N	Yes	+
Claiborn, 1969	I		0
Cornbleth et al., 1974	N	Yes	+
Dalton, 1969	N	Yes	+
Gabbert, 1973	N?		0
Given, 1974	N	Yes	+
Grieger, 1970	I		0
Havlin, 1969	I		0
Jeter, 1972	N		+
José & Cody, 1971	I	Yes	0
Kester, 1969	I		+
Kranz, 1970	N		+
Martinez, 1973	N		M
Meichenbaum et al., 1969	I		M
Parsons, 1973	N		M
Peng, 1974	N		+
Pitt, 1956	I	Yes	+
Rist, 1970	N		+
Rothbart et al., 1971	I		M

Name And Date Of Study	Was Study Of Natural (N) Or Induced (I) Expectations?	Were Teachers' Expectations Measured?	Were Teachers' Behaviors Affected?
Rubovitz & Maehr, 1971	I		+
Rubovitz & Maehr, 1973	I		M
M. Silberman, 1969	N	Yes	+
Stefanini, 1973	I		M
Wilkins, 1973	I		0
B. Willis, 1969	N	Yes	+

Key

+ = change consistent with expectation

0 = no significant changes, differences or effects obtained

M = mixed results, i.e., positive changes on some measures or with sub-groups in study, but not all

blank = item was not measured

Appendix 2

Do Teachers' Expectations Affect Students?

Name and Date of Study	Was Study Of Natural (N) Or Induced (I) Expectations?	Were Teachers' Expectations Measured?	Were Teachers' Behaviors Affected?	Possible Effects on Students		
				Cognitive	Behavior	Affect, Self-Concept
Anderson, 1971	I	Yes		+		
Anderson and Rosenthal, 1968	I		+	0	+	
Asbury, 1970	I			M		
Baker, 1973	I			+		
Becker, 1973	I		+	+		
Beez, 1970	I		+	+		
Blakey, 1970	I		+	+		
Broome, 1970	N	Yes		0		
Brown, 1970	I		+	0		
Buford, 1973	N	Yes		+		
Carter, D., 1970	I			+/M		
Carter, R., 1969	I		+	+/M		

175

NAME and DATE OF STUDY	WAS STUDY OF NATURAL (N) OR INDUCED (I) EXPECTATIONS?	WERE TEACHERS' EXPECTATIONS MEASURED?	WERE TEACHERS' BEHAVIORS AFFECTED?	POSSIBLE EFFECTS on STUDENTS		
				COGNITIVE	BEHAVIOR	AFFECT. SELF-CONCEPT
Claiborn, 1969	I		0	0		
Conn et al., 1968	I			+/M		
Davidson & Lang, 1960	N	Yes		+	+	+
Doyle et al., 1971	N	Yes		+		
Dusek & O'Connell, 1973	N	Yes		+		
Dusek & O'Connell, 1973	I			0		
Entwisle et al., 1972	I			M		
Epstein, 1970	I			0		
Evans & Rosenthal, 1969	I			+		
Fielder, Cohen & Feeney, 1971	I			0		
Fine, 1972	I			M		
Finn et al., 1975	N	Yes		M		
Fleming & Anttonen, 1971	I			0		
Flowers, 1966	I		+	+/M		
Gansneder, 1970	N	Yes		0		M
Goldsmith & Fry, 1970	I	Yes		0		
Gosciewski, 1970	I		+	0		0

Name and Date Of Study	Was Study Of Natural (N) Or Induced (I) Expectations?	Were Teachers' Expectations Measured?	Were Teachers' Behaviors Affected?	Possible Effects on Students		
				Cognitive	Behavior	Affect. Self-Concept
Grieger, 1970	I		0	0		
Haskett, 1968	I		+	+		+
Havlin, 1969	I		0		0	
Heintz, 1968	N?	Yes				0
Jew, 1970	I			0	+	0
José , 1969	I	Yes	0	0	0	
Keshock, 1970	I			0		+
Kester, 1969	I		+	0		0
Knill, 1969	I			M		
Krupczak, 1972	N	Yes		+		
Laskaris, 1971	I			+		
Meichenbaum, Bowers & Ross, 1969	I		+	+	+	
Mendels & Flanders, 1973	I			M		
Mulligan, 1972	I			0		
Palardy, 1969	N	Yes		+		
Pellegrini & Hicks, 1972	I			0		
Peng, 1974	N	Yes	+	+		
Persely, 1973	I			+		
Pitt, 1956	I		+	M		
Rist, 1970	N			+	+	+
Rosenthal & Jacobson, 1968	I			M		
Schain, 1972	I		0	0		
Schrank, 1968, 1970	I			+		

NAME and DATE Of STUDY	WAS STUDY Of NATURAL (N) OR INDUCED (I) EXPECTATIONS?	WERE TEACHERS' EXPECTATIONS MEASURED?	WERE TEACHERS' BEHAVIORS AFFECTED?	POSSIBLE EFFECTS on STUDENTS		
				COGNITIVE	BEHAVIOR	AFFECT. SELF-CONCEPT
Seaver, 1973	N			+		
Sheehy, 1974	N	Yes				+
M. Silberman, 1969	N	Yes	+			+
Sorotzkin, Fleming & Anttonen, 1974	I			0/M		
Spielberg, 1973	I	Yes	0	0		
Sutherland & Goldsch- mid, 1974	N		+	+		
Trujillo, 1969	I				0	
Wilkins, 1973	I	Yes		0		
Williams, 1975	N	Yes	+	+		

KEY

+ = change consistent with expectation

0 = no significant changes, differences or effects obtained

M = positive changes on some measures or with some sub-groups in study, but not all, i.e., mixed results

blank = item was not measured

+/M, 0/M are counted as + or 0 in tabulations reported in text.

References

ADAMS, GERALD R., and COHEN, ALLAN S.
1974   Children's physical and interpersonal characteristics that effect (sic) student-teacher interactions. *Journal of Experimental Education, 43*: 1–5.

ADAMS, GERALD R., and LAVOIE, JOSEPH
1974   The effect of student's sex, conduct, and facial attractiveness on teacher expectancy. *Education, 95*: 76–83.

ADAMS, OSCAR FAY.
1903   *Some Famous American Schools.* Boston: D. Estes and Co.

ADKISON, MARION ROBERT
1968   A comparative study of pupil attitudes under conditions of ability and heterogeneous grouping. Doctoral dissertation, Claremont Graduate School. *Dissertation Abstracts International, 28*: 3869A.

ALBAN, BILLIE
1976   Informal conversation, April.

ALEXANDER, KARL, and ECKLAND, BRUCE K.
1975   Contextual effects in the high school attainment process. *American Sociological Review, 40*: 402–416.

ALKER, H.A., and WOHL, J.
1972   Personality and achievement in a suburban and an inner city school. *Journal of Social Issues, 28*: 101–113.

ALPERT, JUDITH LANDON
1975a   Teacher behavior and pupil performance: Reconsideration of the mediation of Pygmalion effects. *Journal of Educational Research, 69*: 53–57.

1975b   Do teachers adapt methods and materials to ability groups in reading? *California Journal of Educational Research, 26*: 120–123.

179

1974   Teacher behavior across ability groups: A consideration of the mediation of Pygmalion effects. *Journal of Educational Psychology,* 66: 348–353.

ALTHUSSER, LOUIS
1971   Ideology and ideological state apparatuses. In *Lenin and Philosophy and Other Essays.* Trans. Ben Brewster. New York: Monthly Review Press. Pp. 127–188.

ANASTASI, A.
1967   Psychology, psychologists, and psychological testing. *American Psychologist,* 22: 297–306.

ANASTASIOW, N. J.
1964   Frame reference of teacher's judgment. The psychophysical model applied to education. *Psychology in Schools, 1*: 382–5.

ANDERSON, B.D.
1973   School bureaucratization and alienation from high school. *Sociology of Education, 46*: 315–334.

1971   Socio-economic status of students and school bureaucratization. *Educational Administration Quarterly, 7*: 12–24.

ANDERSON, BARRY D., and TISSIER, RONALD
1973   Social class, school bureaucratization and educational aspirations. *Educational Administration Quarterly, 9*: 34–49.

ANDERSON, C.A.
1974   Successes and frustrations in the sociology study of education. *Social Science Quarterly, 55*: 282–296.

ANDERSON, C.A. and FOSTER, P. J.
1964   Discrimination and inequality in education. *Sociology of Education, 38*: 1–18.

ANDERSON, DONALD F., and ROSENTHAL, ROBERT
1968   Some effects of interpersonal expectancy and social interaction on institutionalized retarded children. *Proceedings of the 76th Annual Convention of the American Psychological Association, 3*: 479–480.

ANDERSON, PAULINE
1959   *A Selected Bibliography of Literature on the Independent School.* Milton, Mass.: Independent Schools Education Board.

ANDERSON, PEGGY SMITH
1971   Teacher expectation and pupil self-conceptions. Doctoral dissertation, University of California. *Dissertation Abstracts International,* 32: 1619A.

ANGOFF, W. H.
1971   Scales, norms and equivalent scores. In R. L. Thorndike (Ed.), *Educational Measurement.* Washington, D.C.: American Council on Education. Pp. 508–600.

ANSELONE, GEORGE
in
progress   Tracking in college. Doctoral dissertation, New York University.

APTHEKER, HERBERT
1968   Power in America. In G. William Domhoff and Hoyt B. Ballard
         (eds.), *C. Wright Mills and the Power Elite.* Boston: Beacon. Pp.
         133–164.

ARMOR, DAVID J.
1969   *The American School Counselor.* New York: Russell Sage Founda-
         tion.

ARNEZ, NANCY L.
1966   The effect of teacher attitudes upon the culturally different. *School
         and Society,* 94: 149–152.

ASBURY, DAMON FLOYD
1970   The effects of teacher expectancy, subject expectancy, and subject
         sex on the learning performance of elementary school children.
         Doctoral dissertation, The Ohio State University. *Dissertation
         Abstracts International, 31:* 4537A.

ASHTON, D. N.
1973   The transition from school to work: Notes on the development of
         different frames of reference among young male workers.
         Sociological Review, 21: 101–125.

AVERCH, HARVEY A.; CARROLL, STEPHEN J.; DONALDSON, THEODORE S.; KIESL-
ING, HERBERT J.; and PINCUS, JOHN
1972   *How Effective Is Schooling? A Critical Review and Synthesis of
         Research Findings.* Santa Monica, Ca.: The Rand Corporation.

BACCHUS, M. K.
1969   Education, social change, and cultural pluralism. *Sociology of Educa-
         tion, 42:* 368–385.

BACHER, JESSE HIRAM
1964   The effect of special class placement on the self-concept, social
         adjustment, and reading growth of slow learners. Doctoral disserta-
         tion, New York University. *Dissertation Abstracts, 25:* 7071A.

BAIRD, LEONARD L.
1976   Schools of elite: Study of the social environments of selective inde-
         pendent schools. Paper presented at the American Educational
         Research Association annual meeting, April, San Francisco.

BAJEMA, C. J.
1968   A note on the interrelations among intellectual ability, educational
         attainment, and occupational achievement: A follow-up study of a
         male Kalamazoo public school population. *Sociology of Education,
         41:*317–319.

BAKER, J. PHILLIP, and CHRIST, JANET L.
1971   Teacher expectancies: A review of the literature. In J. D. Elashoff
         and R. E. Snow (eds.), *Pygmalion Reconsidered.* Worthington, Ohio:
         Charles A. Jones. Pp. 48–64.

BAKER, SALLY HILLSMAN
1974   Job Discrimination—Schools as the Solution or Part of the Problem?

To appear in Pamela Roby (ed.), *Women in the Work Place: Yesterday and Today* (in press).

BAKER, STEPHEN H.
1973   Teacher effectiveness and social class as factors in teacher expectancy effects on pupils scholastic achievement. Doctoral dissertation, Clark University. *Dissertation Abstracts International, 34:* 2376A.

BALTZELL, E. DIGBY
1958   *Philadelphia Gentlemen.* New York: Free Press.
1964   *The Protestant Establishment: Aristocracy and Caste in America.* New York: Random House.

BAMFORD, T. W.
1967   *The Rise of the Public Schools.* London: Nelson.

BANFIELD, EDWARD
1960   *The Unheavenly City.* Boston: Little, Brown.

BARAN, PAUL, and SWEEZY, PAUL M.
1966   *Monopoly Capital.* New York: Monthly Review.

BARATZ, JOAN, and BARATZ, STEPHEN.
1970   Early childhood intervention: the social scientific basis of institutionalized racism. *Harvard Educational Review, 39:* 29–50.

BARNARD, JAMES W.; ZIMBARDO, PHILIP G.; and SARASON, SEYMOUR B.
1968   Teachers' ratings of student personality traits as they relate to IQ and social desirability. *Journal of Educational Psychology, 59:* 128–132.

BAUDELOT, CHRISTIAN and ESTABLET, ROGER
1974   *L'école Capitaliste en France.* Paris: Maspero.

BECKER, H. S.
1952   Social-class variations in the teacher-pupil relationship. *Journal of Educational Sociology, 25:* 451–465.

BECKER, JAMES L.
1973   The effects of simulated feedback on teacher performance under four combinations of expectancy and capacity. Doctoral dissertation, Temple University. *Dissertation Abstracts International, 34:* 4854A.

BEEZ, WALTER V.
1970   Influence of biased psychological reports on teacher behavior and pupil performance. In Mathew B. Miles and W. W. Charters, Jr. (eds.) *Learning in Social Settings.* Boston: Allyn and Bacon. Pp. 320–334.

BEHN, WILLIAM H.; CARNOY, MARTIN; CARTER, MICHAEL A.; CRAIN, JOYCE C.; and LEVIN, HENRY M.
1974   School is bad; work is worse. *School Review, 83:* 49–68.

BELL, DANIEL
1972   Meritocracy and equality. *The Public Interest, 29:* 29–68.
1960   *The End of Ideology.* Glencoe, Ill.: The Free Press.

BENITEZ, J.
1974   Educational institutionalization: The effect of elite recruitment and training on diffuse socialization outcomes. Doctoral dissertation, Stanford University. *Dissertation Abstracts International, 35:* 1347A.

BENJAMIN, MARGE
  1972   *Three out of Ten: The Nonpublic Schools of New York City.* New York: New York Department of City Planning.

BEREITER, CARL
  1967   Acceleration of intellectual development in early childhood. Urbana, Ill.: Illinois University. ED 014332.*

BEREITER, CARL, and ENGELMANN, SIEGFRID
  1966   *Teaching Disadvantaged Children in Preschool.* Englewood Cliffs, N.J.: Prentice-Hall.

BERG, IVAR E.
  1970   *Education and Jobs: The Great Training Robbery.* New York: Praeger.

BERGER, PETER L., and LUCKMANN, THOMAS
  1967   *The Social Construction of Reality.* New York: Doubleday.

BERLE, ADOLF A., JR., and MEANS, GARDINER C.
  1932   *The Modern Corporation and Private Property.* New York: Macmillan.

BERNIER, NORMAND R., and WILLIAMS, JACK E.
  1973   *Beyond Beliefs: Ideological Foundations of American Education.* Englewood Cliffs, N.J.: Prentice-Hall.

BERNSTEIN, BASIL
  1971   On the classification and framing of educational knowledge. In Michael F. D. Young (ed.), *Knowledge and Control.* London: Collier-Macmillan. Pp. 47–69.

  1961   Social class and linguistic development. In A. H. Halsey, Jean Floud, and C. Arnold Anderson (eds.), *Education, Economy and Society.* New York: Free Press. Pp. 288–314.

BERREMAN, GERALD D.
  1972   Race, caste, and other invidious distinctions in social stratification. *Race, 13:* 385–414.

BERUBE, M. R.
  1971   Achievement and community control. In Patricia C. Sexton (ed.), *School Policy and Issues in a Changing Society.* Boston: Allyn and Bacon. Pp. 224–233.

BIDWELL, CHARLES E.
  1965   The school as a formal organization. In James G. March (ed.), *Handbook of Organizations.* Chicago: Rand McNally. Pp. 972–1022.

BIDWELL, CHARLES E., and KASARDA, JOHN D.
  1975   School district organization and student achievement. *American Sociological Review, 40:* 55–70.

*The ED number refers to the Educational Resources Information Center (ERIC) document number. These documents may be ordered in hardcover or microfiche copy from ERIC Document reproduction Service, P.O. Box 190, Arlington, Va. 22210, Computer Microfilm International. They are also available in libraries having ERIC document collections.

BILLETT, R. O.
1932   *The Administration and Supervision of Homogeneous Grouping.* Columbus, Ohio: Ohio State University Press.

BILLINGSLEY, ANDREW
1973   Black families and white social science. In Joyce Ladner (ed.), *The Death of White Sociology.* New York: Vintage. Pp. 431–450.
1968   *Black Families in White America.* Englewood Cliffs, N.J.: Prentice-Hall.

BINSTOCK, JEANNE
1970   Survival in the American College Industry. Doctoral dissertation, Brandeis University.

BIRREN, J. E., and HESS, R.
1968   Influences of biological, psychological and social deprivations on learning and performance. In *Perspectives on Human Deprivation.* Washington, D.C.: U.S. Government Printing Office.

BLAKEY, MILLARD L.
1970   The relationship between teacher prophecy and teacher verbal behavior and their effect upon adult student achievement. Doctoral dissertation, Florida State University. *Dissertation Abstracts International, 31:* 4615A. ED 051125.

BLAU, PETER, and DUNCAN, OTIS D.
1967   *The American Occupational Structure.* New York: Wiley.

BLOOM, BENJAMIN S.
1971   Mastery Learning. In *Mastery Learning: Theory and Practice.* New York: Holt, Rinehart, and Winston. Pp. 47–63.

BLOOM, BENJAMIN S.; DAVIS, ALLISON; and HESS, ROBERT.
1965   *Compensatory Education for Cultural Deprivation.* New York: Holt, Rinehart, and Winston.

BLUM, A. F.
1971   The corpus of knowledge as a normative order. In Michael F. D. Young (ed.), *Knowledge and Control.* London: Collier-Macmillan. Pp. 117–132.

BLUMER, HERBERT
1969   *Symbolic Interactionism.* Englewood Cliffs, N.J.: Prentice-Hall.
1966   Sociological implications of the thought of George Herbert Mead. *American Journal of Sociology, 71:* 535–544.

BOOCOCK, SARANE S.
1973   The school as a social environment for learning: Social organization and micro-social process in education. *Sociology of Education, 46:*15–50.
1972   *An Introduction to the Sociology of Learning.* Boston: Houghton Mifflin.

BORDIEU, PIERRE
1971   Systems of education and systems of thought. In Michael F.D. Young

(ed.), *Knowledge and Control*. London: Collier-Macmillan. Pp. 189–207.

BORG, WALTER R.
1966   *Ability Grouping in the Public Schools* (2nd ed.). Madison, Wis.: Dembar Educational Research Services.

1964   *An Evaluation of Ability Grouping* (U. S. D. H. E. W. Cooperative Research Project No. 577). Logan: Utah State University.

BORMUTH, J. R.
1970   *On the Theory of Achievement Test Items*. Chicago: University of Chicago.

BOUDON, RAYMOND
1973   *Education, Opportunity, and Social Inequality*. New York: Wiley.

BOWLES, SAMUEL
1972   Getting nowhere: Programmed class stagnation. *Society*, 9: 42–49.

1968   Toward equality of educational opportunity? *Harvard Educational Review*, 38: 89–99.

BOWLES, SAMUEL, and GINTIS, HERBERT
1976   *Schooling in Capitalist America*. New York: Basic Books.

1973   I.Q. in the U.S. class structure. *Social Policy*, 3: 65–96.

BOYLE, R. P.
1966   The effect of the high school on students' aspirations. *American Journal of Sociology*, 71: 628–639.

BRENNER, MARSHALL H.
1968   The use of high school data to predict work performance. *Journal of Applied Psychology*, 52: 29–30.

BRETON, RAYMOND; MCDONALD, JOHN; and RICHER, STEPHEN
1972   *Social and Academic Factors in the Career Decisions of Canadian Youth*. Ottawa: Queen's Printer.

BRIDGEMAN, BRENT, and SHIPMAN, VIRGINIA
1975   *Predictive Value of Measures of Self-Esteem and Achievement Motivation in Four- to Nine-Year-Old Low-Income Children* (ETS-Head Start Longitudinal Study). Princeton, N.J.: Educational Testing Service.

BRIM, ORVILLE G., JR., and WHEELER, STANTON
1966   *Socialization After Childhood: Two Essays*. New York: Wiley.

BRONFENBRENNER, URIE
1972   Is 80% of intelligence genetically determined? In Urie Bronfenbrenner (ed.), *Influences on Human Development*. Hinsdale, Ill.: Dryden. Pp. 118–127.

1970   *Two Worlds of Childhood: U.S. and U.S.S.R.* New York: Basic Books, Russell Sage Foundation.

BROOKOVER, WILBUR B.; GIGLIOTTI, RICHARD J.; HENDERSON, RONALD D.; and SCHNEIDER, JEFFREY M.
1973   Elementary school social climates and school achievement. Paper

presented at the 1973 American Sociological Association meeting. ED 086306.

BROOKOVER, W. B.; LEU, D. J.; and KARIGER, R. H.
1965   Tracking. Unpublished Manuscript (mimeo), Western Michigan University.

BROOKOVER, WILBUR B.; PATERSON, A.; and THOMAS, S.
1962   *Self-concepts of Ability and School Achievement.* East Lansing: Office of Research and Publications, Michigan State University.

BROOKOVER, WILBUR B., and SCHNEIDER, JEFFREY M.
1975   Academic environments and elementary school achievement. *Journal of Research and Development in Education, 9*: 82–91.

BROOME, BILLY J.
1970   An investigation of the effects of teachers' expectations on the achievement in reading of first-grade boys. Doctoral dissertation, Louisiana State University and Agricultural and Mechanical College. *Dissertation Abstracts International, 31*: 4538A–4539A.

BROPHY, JERE E., and GOOD, THOMAS L.
1974   *Teacher–Student Relationships: Causes and Consequences.* New York: Holt, Rinehart, and Winston.

1970   Teachers' communication of differential expectations for children's classroom performance: Some behavioral data. *Journal of Educational Psychology, 60*: 365–374.

BROWN, BYRON W., and SAKS, DANIEL H.
1975   The production and distribution of cognitive skills within schools. *Journal of Political Economy, 83*: 571–594.

BROWN, RICHARD

1973   *Knowledge, Education and Cultural Change: Papers in the Sociology of Education.* London: Tavistock Publications.

BROWN, WILLIAM E.
1969   The influence of student information on the formulation of teacher expectancy. Doctoral dissertation, Indiana University. *Dissertation Abstracts International, 30*: 4822A.

BRUNER, JEROME S.
1960   *The Process of Education.* New York: Vintage.

BUFORD, BETTY I.
1973   Teacher expectancy of the culturally different student subgroups in Texas in relation to student achievement. Doctoral dissertation, Texas A & M University. *Dissertation Abstracts International, 34*: 1158A–1159A.

BURKS, B. S.
1928   The relative influence of nature and nurture upon mental development: A comparative study of foster parent–foster child resemblance and true parent–true child resemblance. In Guy M. Whipple (ed.), *Twenty-seventh Yearbook: Nature and Nurture, Part I, Their*

Influence on Intelligence. Bloomington, Ind.: National Society for the Study of Education. Pp. 219–316.

BURNHAM, JAMES
1941   *The Managerial Revolution.* New York: John Day.

BURT, CYRIL
1972   Inheritance of general intelligence. *American Psychologist, 27*: 175–190.

1966   The genetic determination of difference in intelligence: A study of monozygotic twins reared together and apart. *British Journal of Psychology, 57*: 137–153.

1958   The inheritance of mental ability. *American Psychologist, 13*: 1–15.

1943   Ability and income. *British Journal of Psychology, 13:* 83–98.

BURT, CYRIL, and HOWARD, MARGARET
1956   The multifactorial theory of inheritance and its application to intelligence. *British Journal of Statistical Psychology, 9*: 95–131.

BUTTS, R. FREEMAN, and CREMIN, LAWRENCE A.
1953   *A History of Education in American Culture.* New York: Henry Holt.

BYERS, LORETTA
1961   Ability grouping—Help or hindrance to social and emotional growth. *School Review, 69*: 449–459.

BYRNE, D. S.; WILLIAMSON, W.; and FLETCHER, B. G.
1973   Models of educational attainment: A theoretical and methodological critique. *Urban Education, 8*: 41–74.

CALLAHAN, RAYMOND
1962   *Education and the Cult of Efficiency.* Chicago: University of Chicago Press.

CARNOY, MARTIN
1974   *Education as Cultural Imperialism.* New York: McKay.

CARNOY, MARTIN (ed.)
1972/   *Schooling in a Corporate Society.* New York: McKay.
1975

CARNOY, MARTIN, and LEVIN, HENRY M. (eds.)
1976   *The Limits of Educational Reform.* New York: McKay.

CARROLL, JOHN
1964   *Language and Thought.* Englewood Cliffs, N.J.: Prentice-Hall.

1963   A model of school learning. *Teachers College Record, 64*: 723–733.

CARTER, DALE L.
1970   The effect of teacher expectations on the self-esteem and academic performance of seventh grade students. Doctoral dissertation, University of Tennessee. *Dissertation Abstracts International, 31*: 4539A.

CARTER, RONALD M.
1969   Locus of control and teacher expectancy as related to achievement

of young school children. Doctoral dissertation, Indiana University. *Dissertation Abstracts International, 30:* 467A.

CARVER, RONALD P.
1975   The Coleman report: Using inappropriately designed achievement tests. *American Educational Research Journal, 12:* 77–86.

CHAIKIN, ALAN L.; SIGLER, EDWARD; and DERLEGA, VALERIAN
1974   Nonverbal mediators of teacher expectancy effects. *Journal of Personality and Social Psychology, 30:* 144–149.

CHANDLER, B. J., and ERICKSON, F. D.
1968   *Sounds of Society: A Demonstration Program in Group Inquiry.* Washington, D.C.: U.S. Government Printing Office.

CHAPMAN, PAUL
1972   Intelligence testing movement: Reorganizing the schools for the meritocracy. Unpublished manuscript, Stanford University.

CHARTERS, W. W., JR.
1974   Social class analysis and the control of public education. In E. Useem and M. Useem (eds.), *The Education Establishment.* Englewood Cliffs, N.J.: Prentice-Hall. Pp. 98–113.

CHISWICK, BARRY, and MINCER, JACOB
1972   Time series changes in personal income inequality in the U.S. *Journal of Political Economy, 80* (No. 3, Part 2): S34–S66.

CICOUREL, AARON V., and KITSUSE, JOHN I.
1963   *The Educational Decision-Makers.* Indianapolis: Bobbs Merrill.

CLAIBORN, W. L.
1969   Expectancy effects in the classroom: a failure to replicate. *Journal of Educational Psychology, 60:* 377–383.

CLARK, BURTON R.
1960   The "cooling-out" function in higher education. *American Journal of Sociology, 65:* 569–576.

CLARK, KENNETH E.
1965   *Dark Ghetto.* New York: Harper and Row.

CLIFFORD, M., and WALSTER, E.
1973   The effect of physical attractiveness on teacher expectation. *Sociology of Education, 45:* 248–258.

COHEN, ALBERT
1965   The sociology of the deviant act: Deviance theory and beyond. *American Sociological Review, 30:* 5–14.

COHEN, DAN
1975   Doctoral dissertation outline, New York University.

COHEN, DAVID K.
1970   Politics and research: Evaluation of social action programs in education. *Review of Educational Research, 40:* 213–238.

COHEN, ELIZABETH G.
1972   Sociology and the classroom: Setting the conditions for teacher-stu-

dent interaction. *Review of Educational Research, 42*: 441–452.

COHEN, MICHAEL
1975   Reference group theory, school climates, and the status attainment process: The impact of school contexts on educational aspirations and attainments. Paper presented at the August American Sociological Association annual meeting, San Francisco.

COHEN, PETER
1973   *The Gospel According to the Harvard Business School.* Baltimore: Penguin.

COHEN, SOL
1968   The industrial education movement, 1906–17. *American Quarterly, 20*: 95–110.

COLE, ROBERT DANFORTH
1928   *Private Secondary Education for Boys in the United States.* Philadelphia: Westbrook.

COLEMAN, JAMES S.
1975   Methods and results in the IEA studies of effects of school on learning. *Review of Educational Research, 45*: 335–386.

1968   The concept of equality of educational opportunity. *Harvard Educational Review, 38*: 7–22.

1961   *The Adolescent Society.* New York: Free Press.

COLEMAN, JAMES S.; CAMPBELL, ERNEST Q.; HOBSON, CAROL J.; McPARTLAND, JAMES; MOOD, ALEXANDER M.; WEINFELD, FREDERIC D.; and YORK, ROBERT L.
1966   *Equality of Educational Opportunity.* Washington, D.C.: U.S. Government Printing Office.

COLES, ROBERT
1968   Violence in ghetto children. In S. Chess and A. Thomas (eds.), *Annual Progress in Child Psychiatry and Child Development.* New York: Brunner/Mazel.

COLLINS, RANDALL
1976   Schooling in Capitalist America by Samuel Bowles and Herbert Gintis (book review). *Harvard Educational Review, 46*: 246–251.

1975   *Conflict Sociology.* New York: Academic Press.

1974   Where are educational requirements for employment highest? *Sociology of Education, 47*: 419–442.

1971   Functional and conflict theories of educational stratification. *American Sociological Review, 36*: 1002–1019.

CONANT, JAMES B.
1961   *Slums and Suburbs.* New York: McGraw-Hill.

CONN, LANE K.; EDWARDS, CARL N.; ROSENTHAL, ROBERT; and CROWNE, DOUGLAS
1968   Perception of emotion and response to teachers' expectancy by elementary school children. *Psychological Reports, 22*: 27–34.

COOLEY, CHARLES
1902/   *Human Nature and the Social Order,* Ch. V. New York: Charles
1922   Scribner's Sons.

COOPER, H. M.; BARON, R. M.; and LOWER, C. A.
1975   Importance of race and social class information in formation of
         expectancies about academic performance. *Journal of Educational
         Psychology,* 67: 312–319.

COOPER, JOEL
1971   Self-fulfilling prophecy in the classroom: An attempt to discover the
         processes by which expectations are communicated. ED 063453.

CORNBLETH, CATHERINE; DAVIS, O. L., JR.; and BUTTON, CHRISTINE
1974   Expectations for pupil achievement and teacher–pupil interaction.
         Social Education, 38: 54–58.

CORWIN, RONALD G.
1965   Out of the past: Sociological perspectives on the history of education.
         In *A Sociology of Education: Emerging Patterns of Class, Status,
         and Power in the Public Schools.* New York: Meredith. Pp. 69–106.

COSER, LEWIS
1956   *The Functions of Social Conflict.* New York: Free Press.

COSIN, B. R., et al. (eds.)
1971   *School and Society.* Cambridge, Mass.: MIT Press.
1972   *Education: Structure and Society.* Harmondsworth, England:
         Penguin.

COTTLE, THOMAS J.
1974   What tracking did to Ollie Taylor. *Social Policy,* 5: 21–24.

COUNTS, GEORGE S.
1932   *Dare the Schools Build a New Social Order?* New York: John Day.
1927   *The Social Composition of Boards of Education.* Chicago: University
         of Chicago Press.
1922   *The Selective Character of American Secondary Education.* Chicago:
         University of Chicago Press.

COWLES, M.
1963   A comparative study of certain social and emotional adjustments of
         homogeneous and heterogeneously grouped sixth grade children.
         Doctoral dissertation. University of Alabama, *Dissertation Abstracts
         International,* 23: 4256–4257.

CREMIN, LAWRENCE
1965   *The Genius of American Education.* New York: Teachers College
         Press.
1961   *The Transformation of the School: Progressivism in American
         Education, 1876–1957.* New York: Vintage.

CRICHTON, ROBERT
1959   *The Great Imposter.* New York: Random House.

CRONBACH, LEE J.
1975   Five decades of public controversy over testing. *American Psychologist, 30*: 1–14.

1970   *Essentials of Psychological Testing* (3rd ed.). New York: Harper and Row.

CROWDER, DAVID N.
1971   A critique of Duncan's stratification research. ED 094128

CUBBERLEY, ELLWOOD P.
1916   *Public School Administration: A Statement of the Fundamental Principles Underlying the Organization and Administration of Public Education.* Boston: Houghton Mifflin.

1909   *Changing Conceptions of Education.* Boston: Houghton Mifflin.

CURTI, MERLE
1935   *The Social Ideas of American Educators.* New York: Scribner's. (Reprinted by Littlefield, Adams, 1968.)

DAHL, ROBERT A.
1961   *Who Governs?* New Haven: Yale University Press.

DAHRENDORF, RALF
1959   *Class and Class Conflict in Industrial Society.* Stanford: Stanford University Press.

DALTON, WILLIAM B.
1973   Exploring the expectancy effects phenomenon: A study of the perpetuation of teachers' expectancies of pupils. Doctoral dissertation, George Peabody College for Teachers. *Dissertation Abstracts International, 34*: 3459B.

DANIELS, J. C.
1961   The effects of streaming in the primary school: Part I: What teachers believe. Part II: A comparison of streamed and unstreamed schools. *British Journal of Educational Psychology, 31*: 69–78; 119–127.

DAVIDSON, HELEN H. AND LANG, GERHARD
1960   Children's perception of their teachers' feelings toward them related to self-perception, school achievement, and behavior. *Journal of Experimental Education, 29*: 107–118.

DAVIES, IOAN
1971   The management of knowledge: A critique of the use of typologies in the sociology of education. In Michael F. D. Young (ed.), *Knowledge and Control.* London: Collier-Macmillan. Pp. 267–288.

DAVIS, JAMES
1966   The campus as a frog pond: An application of the theory of relative deprivation to career decisions of college men. *American Journal of Sociology, 27*: 17–31.

DAWE, A.
1970   The two sociologies. *British Journal of Sociology, 21*: 207–218.

DEITZ, S. M. , and PURKEY,W. W.
1969   Teacher expectation of performance based on race of student. *Psychological Reports, 24*: 694.

DENZIN, N. K.
1972   The genesis of self in early childhood. *Sociological Quarterly, 13*: 291–314.

DEUTSCH, MARTIN
1963   The disadvantaged child and the learning process. In A. H. Passow (ed.), *Education in Depressed Areas.* New York: Teachers College Press. Pp. 163–179.

DEUTSCH, MARTIN; BLOOM, RICHARD D; BROWN, BERT R.; DEUTSCH, CYNTHIA P.; GOLDSTEIN, LEO S.; JOHN, VERA P.; KATZ, PHYLLIS A.; LEVINSON, ALMA; PEISACH, ESTELLE C.; and WHITEMAN, MARTIN
1967   *The Disadvantaged Child.* New York: Basic Books.

DEUTSCH, MARTIN; KATZ, IRWIN; and JENSEN, ARTHUR
1968   *Social Class, Race and Psychological Development.* New York: Holt, Rinehart and Winston.

DIBBLE, VERNON
1962   Occupations and ideologies. *American Journal of Sociology, 68*: 229–241.

DILLARD, JOEY L.
1972   *Black English.* New York: Random House.

DOMHOFF, G. WILLIAM
1970   *The Higher Circles.* New York: Vintage.

1967   *Who Rules America?* Englewood Cliffs, N. J.: Prentice-Hall.

DOUGLAS, J. W. B.
1968   *All Our Future.* London: MacGibbon.

1964   *The Home and the School.* London: MacGibbon.

DOYLE, WAYNE J.; HANCOCK, GREG; and KIFER, EDWARD
1971   Teachers' perceptions: Do they make a difference? Paper presented at American Educational Research Association annual meeting, New York. ED 048109.

DREEBEN, ROBERT
1971   American schooling: Patterns and processes of stability and change. In Bernard Barber and Alex Inkeles (eds.), *Stability and Social Change.* Boston: Little, Brown. Pp. 82–119.

1968   *On What is Learned in School.* Reading, Mass.: Addison-Wesley.

DREWS, ELIZABETH M.
1963   *Student Abilities, Grouping Patterns and Classroom Interaction.* Washington, D. C.: Cooperative Research Program, Office of Education, DHEW. ED 002679.

DUNCAN, OTIS D.; FEATHERMAN, DAVID L.; and DUNCAN, BEVERLY
1972   *Socioeconomic Background and Achievement.* New York: Seminar Press.

DUNN, L. M.
1968   Special education for the mildly retarded. Is much of it justifiable? *Exceptional Children, 35*: 5–22.

DURKHEIM, EMILE
1956   *Education and Sociology.* Glencoe, Ill.: Free Press.
1951   *Suicide.* Glencoe, Ill.: Free Press.

DUSEK, JEROME B., and O'CONNELL, EDWARD J.
1973   Teacher expectancy effects on the achievement test performance of elementary school children. *Journal of Educational Psychology, 65*: 371–377.

DYER, H. S.
1968   School factors and equal educational opportunity. *Harvard Educational Review, 38*: 38–56.

DYSON, ERNEST
1965   A study of the relationships between acceptance of self, academic self-concept and two types of grouping procedures used with seventh grade pupils. Doctoral dissertation, Temple University. *Dissertation Abstracts, 26*: 1475–1476.

EASH, M. J.
1961   Grouping: What have we learned? *Educational Leadership, 18*: 429–434.

ECKLAND, BRUCE
1964   Social class and college graduates: Some misconceptions corrected. *American Journal of Sociology, 70*: 36–50.

EDWARDS, NEWTON, and RICHEY, HERMAN G.
1947   *The School in the American Social Order.* Boston: Houghton Mifflin.

EDWARDS, RICHARD C.
in press Personal traits and "success" in schooling and work. *Educational and Psychological Measurement,* cited in Bowles and Gintis, 1976.

EELLS, KENNETH; DAVIS, ALLISON; HAVIGHURST, ROBERT J.; HERRICK, VIRGIL E.; and TYLER, RALPH W.
1951   *Intelligence and Cultural Differences.* Chicago: University of Chicago Press.

EGGLESTON, JOHN (ed.)
1974   *Contemporary Research in the Sociology of Education.* London: Methuen.

EKSTROM, RUTH B.
1961   Experimental studies of homogeneous grouping: A critical review. *School Review, 69*: 216–226. ED 001882.

ELASHOFF, J. D., and SNOW, R. E.
1971   *Pygmalion Reconsidered.* Worthington, Ohio: Charles Jones.

ELDER, GLEN H.
1965   Life opportunity and personality: Some consequences of stratified secondary education in Great Britain. *Sociology of Education, 38*: 173–202.

ELIOT, CHARLES W.
1909   Educational reform and the social order. *School Review, 17*: 217–219.

ELTON, C. F., and SHEVEL, L. R.
1969   *Who Is Talented? An Analysis of Achievement.* (Research Report No. 31). Iowa City, Iowa: American College Testing Program.

ENTWISLE, DORIS R.; CORNELL, EVART; and EPSTEIN, JOYCE
1972   Effect of a principal's expectations on test performance of elementary school children. *Psychological Reports, 31*: 551–556.

EPSTEIN, BERNARD
1970   Determination of the effect of teacher expectancy on student achievement. Doctoral dissertation, University of Missouri, Columbia. *Dissertation Abstracts International, 31*: 5032A.

ESLAND, GEOFFREY M.
1971   Teaching and learning as the organization of knowledge. In Michael F. D. Young (ed.), *Knowledge and Control.* London: Collier-Macmillan. Pp. 70–115.

ESPOSITO, D.
1973   Homogeneous and heterogeneous ability grouping: Principal findings and implications for evaluating and designing more effective educational environments. *Review of Educational Research, 43*: 163–179.

ETZIONI, A.
1971   Essay reviews: Crisis in the Classroom by Charles A. Silberman (book review). *Harvard Educational Review, 41*: 87–98.

EVANS, JUDITH T., and ROSENTHAL, ROBERT
1969   Interpersonal self-fulfilling prophecies: Further extrapolations from the laboratory to the classroom. Unpublished manuscript, Harvard University. ED 034276.

EVETTS, JULIA
1973   *The Sociology of Educational Ideas.* Boston: Routledge and Kegan Paul.

EXLINE, R.
1971   The glances of power and preference. In J. K. Cole (ed.), *Nebraska Symposium on Motivation: 1971.* Lincoln: University of Nebraska Press. Pp. 163–206.

EYSENCK, H. J.
1971   *The I.Q. Argument.* Freeport, N.Y.: Library Press.

FARLEY, REYNOLDS
1975   Residential segregation and its implications for school integration. *Law and Contemporary Problems, 34*: 164–193.

FARRELL, J. P.
1973   Factors influencing academic performance among Chilean primary

students. Paper presented at the American Educational Research Association annual meeting, New Orleans; April.

FEINBERG, WALTER
1975   Educational equality under two conflicting models of educational development. *Theory and Society, 2*: 183–210.

FICK, WAYNE
1962   The effectiveness of ability grouping in seventh grade core classes. Doctoral dissertation, University of Kansas. *Dissertation Abstracts, 23*: 2753–2754.

FIEDLER, W. R.; COHEN, R. D.; and FEENEY, S.
1971   An attempt to replicate the teacher expectancy effect. *Psychological Reports, 29*: 1223–1228.

FINDLEY, WARREN G. , and BRYAN, MIRIAM M.
1970a   *Ability Grouping: 1970—I. Common Practices in the Use of Tests for Grouping Students in Public Schools.* Athens, Georgia: The Center for Educational Improvement, University of Georgia. ED 048381.

1970b   *Ability Grouping: 1970—II. The Impact of Ability Grouping on School Achievement, Affective Development, Ethnic Separation and Socioeconomic Separation.* Athens, Georgia: The Center for Educational Improvement, University of Georgia. ED 048382.

1970c   *Ability Grouping: 1970—III. The Problems and Utilities involved in the Use of Tests for Grouping Children with Limited Backgrounds.* Athens, Georgia: The Center for Educational Improvement, University of Georgia. ED 048383.

1970d   *Ability Grouping: 1970—IV. Conclusions and Recommendations.* Athens, Georgia: The Center for Educational Improvement, University of Georgia. ED 048384.

FINE, LEONARD
1972   The effects of positive teacher expectancy on the reading achievement and IQ gains of pupils in grade two. Doctoral dissertation, Temple University. *Dissertation Abstracts Internatonal, 33*: 1510A–1511A.

FINN, JEREMY D.
1972   Expectations and the educational environment. *Review of Educational Research, 42*: 387–410.

FINN, JEREMY D.; GAIER, EUGENE L.; PENG, SAMUEL S.; and BANKS, RONALD E.
1975   Teacher expectations and pupil achievement. *Urban Education, 10*: 175–197.

FISHER, BERENICE M.
1972   Education in the big picture. *Sociology of Education, 45*: 233–257.

FLANAGAN, J. C.
1960   *Tests of General Ability: Technical Report.* Chicago: Science Research Associates.

FLEMING, ELYSE S., and ANTTONEN, RALPH G.
1971   Teacher expectancy or "My Fair Lady." *American Educational Research Journal,* 8: 241–252.

FLOWERS, C. E.
1966   Effects of an arbitrary accelerated group placement on the tested academic achievement of educationally disadvantaged students. Doctoral dissertation, Columbia University. *Dissertation Abstracts,* 27: 991A.

FOLGER, JOHN D., and NAM, CHARLES B.
1967   *Education of the American Population.* Washington, D. C.: U.S. Bureau of the Census, U.S. Government Printing Office.

FREEMAN, RICHARD B.
1976   *The Over-Educated American.* New York: Academic Press.

FREIBERG, JEROME
1970   The effects of ability grouping on interactions in the classroom. ED 053194.

FRIEND, RONALD M. , and NEAL, JOHN M.
1972   Children's perceptions of success and failure: An attributional analysis of the effects of race and social class. *Developmental Psychology,* 7: 124–128.

FUCHS, ESTELLE
1973   How teachers learn to help children fail. In Nell Keddie (ed.), *The Myth of Cultural Deprivation.* Harmondsworth, England: Penguin. Pp. 75–85.

GABBERT, BURT B.
1973   The influence of pupil socioeconomic status on teacher behavior. Doctoral dissertation, University of Texas. *Dissertation Abstracts International,* 34: 2385A.

GAEBELEIN, FRANK E.; HARRISON, EARL G., Jr.; and SWING, WILLIAM L. (eds.)
1962   *Education for Decision.* New York: Seabury.

GAGE, N. L.
1972   I. Q. heritability, race differences, and educational research. *Phi Delta Kappan,* 53: 308–312.

GALBRAITH, JOHN KENNETH
1967   *The New Industrial State.* Boston: Houghton Mifflin.

GALTUNG, JOHAN and NISHIMA, FUMIKO
n.d.   Learning from the Chinese. Mimeo copy, University of Oslo.

GANSNEDER, BRUCE M.
1970   The relationship between teachers' attitudes toward pupils and pupils' attitudes and achievement. ED 037788.

GAY, G.
1975   Teachers' achievement expectations of and classroom interaction with ethnically different students. *Contemporary Education,* 46: 166–172.

1974   *Differential Dyadic Interactions of Black and White Teachers with*

Black and White Pupils in Recently Desegregated Social Studies Classrooms: A Function of Teacher and Pupil Ethnicity. (U.S. Office of Education Project No. 2F113). ED 091489.

GEARING, F. O. , and TINDALL, B. A.
1973   Anthropological studies of the educational process. *Annual Review of Anthropology, 2:* 95–105.

GEER, B.
1968   Teaching. In David L. Sills (ed.), *International Encyclopedia of the Social Sciences.* New York: Crowell, Collier, and Macmillan. Pp. 560–565.

GERTLER, DIANE B., and BARKER, LINDA A.
1973   *Statistics of Nonpublic Elementary and Secondary Schools, 1970–71.* National Center for Educational Statistics. Washington, D.C.: U.S. Government Printing Office.

GETZELS, JACOB W., and JACKSON, PHILIP W.
1962   *Creativity and Intelligence.* New York: Wiley.

GHISELLI, E. E.
1966   *The Validity of Occupational Aptitude Tests.* New York: Wiley.

GIDDENS, ANTHONY
1975   *The Class Structure of the Advanced Societies.* New York: Harper Torchbooks.

GIGLIOTTI, R. J., and BROOKOVER, W. B.
1975   Learning environment—Comparison of high and low achieving elementary schools. *Urban Education, 10:* 245–261.

GINTIS, HERBERT
1973   A radical critique of Ivan Illich's *Deschooling Society* (book review). Harvard Educational Review, *42:* 70–96.

1971a   Education, technology, and the characteristics of worker productivity. *American Economic Review, 61:* 266–279.

1971b   The politics of education. *Monthly Review, 23:* 40–61.

GITTELL, MARILYN, and HOLLANDER, T. EDWARD
1968   *Six Urban School Districts: A Comparative Study of Institutional Response.* New York: Praeger.

GIVEN, BARBARA K.
1974   Teacher expectancy and pupil performance: Their relationship to verbal and non-verbal communications by teachers of learning disabled children. Doctoral dissertation, Catholic University. *Dissertation Abstracts International, 35:* 1529A.

GLASER, BARNEY, and STRAUSS, ANSELM
1967   *The Discovery of Grounded Theory.* Chicago: Aldine.

GOFFMAN, ERVING
1961   *Asylums.* Garden City, N.Y.: Anchor.

GOLDBERG, ARTHUR S.
1974a   *Mysteries of the Meritocracy.* Madison: Institute for Research on Poverty, University of Wisconsin.

1974b   *Professor Jensen, Meet Miss Burks.* Madison: Institute for Research on Poverty, University of Wisconsin.

GOLDBERG, MIRIAM L.; PASSOW, A. HARRY; and JUSTMAN, JOSEPH
1966   *The Effects of Ability Grouping.* New York: Teachers College Press.

GOLDEN, MARK, and BIRNS, BEVERLY
1972   Social class, intelligence and cognitive style in infancy. *Child Development, 42:* 2114–2116.

GOLDENBERG, IRENE
1971   Social class differences in teacher attitudes toward children. *Child Development, 42:* 1637–1640.

GOLDSMITH, JOSEPHINE, and FRY, EDWARD
1971   The effect of a high expectancy prediction on reading achievement and IQ of students in grade 10. Paper presented at the February American Educational Research Association meeting, New York.

GOLDSTEIN, BERNARD
1967   *Low Income Youth in Urban Areas: A Critical Review of the Literature.* New York: Holt, Rinehart, and Winston.

GOOD, T. L., and DEMBO, M. H.
1973   Teacher expectations: Self-report data. *School Review, 81:* 247–254.

GOODE, WILLIAM J.
1967   The protection of the inept. *American Sociological Review, 32:* 5–19.

GOODLAD, JOHN I.
1960   Classroom organization. In Chester W. Harris (ed.), *Encyclopedia of Educational Research* (3rd ed.). New York: Macmillan. Pp. 221–225.

GORBUTT, D.
1972   The new sociology of education. *Education for Teaching, 89:* 3–11.

GORDON, ROBERT A., and HOWELL, JAMES E.
1959   *Employer Policies in a Changing Labor Market.* Berkeley: Institute of Industrial Relations, University of California.

GOSCIEWSKI, F. W.
1970   The effect of expectancy reinforcement on arithmetic-achievement, self-concept and peer-group status of elementary children. Doctoral disseration, Kent State University. *Dissertation Abstracts International, 31:* 2179A.

GOSLIN, DAVID A.
1967   *Teachers and Testing.* New York: Russell Sage Foundation.

1965   *The School in Contemporary Society.* Glenview, Ill.: Scott, Foresman.

GOSLIN, DAVID A.; EPSTEIN, ROBERTA R.; and HALLOCK, BARBARA
1965   *The Use of Standardized Tests in Elementary Schools, Technical Report No. 2 on the Social Consequences of Testing.* New York: Russell Sage Foundation.

GOSLIN, DAVID A., and GLASS, DAVID C.
1967   The social effects of standardized testing in American elementary and secondary schools. *Sociology of Education, 40*: 115–131.

GOTTLIEB, D.
1964   Teaching and students: The views of Negro and white teachers. *Sociology of Education, 37*: 345–353.

GOULD, STEPHEN JAY
1974   Racist arguments and I. Q. *Natural History, 83*: 24–29.

GOULDNER, HELEN P. and GOULDNER, ALVIN
1963   Modern Sociology. New York: Harcourt, Brace and World.

GRACEY, HARRY L.
1972   Learning the student role: Kindergarten as academic boot camp. In Dennis H. Wrong and Harry L. Gracey (eds.), *Readings in Introductory Sociology* (2nd ed.). New York: Macmillan. Pp. 243–254.

GRAHAM, PATRICIA A.
1974   *Community and Class in American Education, 1865–1918.* New York: Wiley.

GRAMSCI, ANTONIO
1971   *Selections from the Prison Notebooks.* New York: International Publishers.

GRANOVETTER, MARK
1974   *Getting a Job.* Cambridge, Mass.: Harvard University Press.

GRANT, W. VANCE and LIND, C. GEORGE
1976   *Digest of Education Statistics, 1975 Edition.* Washington, D.C.: U.S. Government Printing Office.

GREENE, MAXINE
1971   Curriculum and consciousness. *Teachers College Record, 73*: 253–269.

GREENSTEIN, F.
1965   *Children and Politics.* New Haven: Yale University Press.

GRIEGER, R. M.
1970   The effects of teacher expectancy on the intelligence of students and the behavior of teachers. Doctoral dissertation, Ohio State University. *Dissertation Abstracts International, 31*: 3338A.

GRIFFIN, A.
1969   Effects of secondary school organization on the development of intellectual attainments in England and attitudes to school. *British Journal of Educational Psychology, 39*: 191.

GROSS, MORRIS
1969   Learning readiness in two Jewish groups: A study in "cultural deprivation." An occasional paper. ED 026126.

GUILFORD, J. P.
1968   Intelligence has three facets. *Science, 160* (May 10): 615–620.

GUMBERT, E. H. , and SPRING, J. H.
1975   The Superschool and the Superstate: American Education in the Twentieth Century, 1918–1970. New York: Wiley.

GUSKIN, ALAN E., and GUSKIN, SAMUEL L.
1970   A Social Psychology of Education. Reading, Mass.: Addison-Wesley.

GUSKIN, JUDITH T.
1971   The social perception of language variation: Black and white teachers' attitudes toward speakers from different racial and social class background. Doctoral dissertation, University of Michigan. Dissertation Abstracts International, 31: 3954A.

GUTHERIE, JAMES W.; KLEINDORFER, GEORGE; LEVIN, HENRY M.; and STOUT, ROBERT T.
1971   Schools and Inequality. Cambridge, Mass.: MIT Press.

GUTTENTAG, MARCIA
1973   Children in Harlem's community-controlled schools. In Edwin Flaxman (ed.), Educating the Disadvantaged 1971–72. New York: AMS Press. Pp. 240–255.

HABERMAS, JÜRGEN
1970   Toward a Rational Society. Boston: Beacon.

HAGGARD, E. A.
1957   Socialization, personality and achievement in gifted children. School Review, 65: 318–414.

HALL, EDWARD T.
1966   The Hidden Dimension. Garden City, N.Y.: Doubleday.

HALLER, A., and PORTES, A.
1973   Status attainment processes. Sociology of Education, 46: 51–91.

HALPERN, F.
1970   Self-perception of black children in the civil rights movement. American Journal of Orthopsychiatry, 40: 520–526.

HALSEY, A. H.; FLOUD, JEAN; and ANDERSON, C. ARNOLD (eds.)
1961   Education, Economy, and Society. New York: Free Press.

HAMILTON, C. V.
1971   Black power and participation. In Patricia Cayo Sexton (ed.), School Policy and Issues in a Changing Society. Boston: Allyn and Bacon. Pp. 233–249.

HAMLISH, E., and GAIER, E. L.
1954   Teacher–student personality similarities and marks. School Review, 62: 265–273.

HAMMACK, DAVID C.
1969   The centralization of New York City's public school system, 1896: A social analysis of a decision. Unpublished Master's dissertation, Columbia University.

HANDLER, E.
1972   Organizational factors and educational outcome: A comparison of

two types of preschool programs. *Education and Urban Society, 4*: 441–458.

HANKINSON, OSCAR H.
1970   Expectations for and behavior of pupils in culturally different schools. Doctoral dissertation, University of Wisconsin. *Dissertation Abstracts International, 31*: 1538A.

HANSEN, D. A.; GOLD, D.; and LABOVITZ, E.
1972   Socio-economic inequities in college entry: A critical specification. *American Educational Research Journal, 9*: 573–590.

HARGREAVES, DAVID H.
1967   *Social Relations in a Secondary School.* London: Routledge and Kegan Paul.

HARLEM YOUTH OPPORTUNITIES UNLIMITED.
1964   *Youth in the Ghetto.* New York: Harlem Youth Opportunities Unlimited, Inc.

HARRIS, TERESA C.
1972   The relationship between student teachers' conceptual systems and their formation of expectations of student ability. Doctoral dissertation, University of Texas. *Dissertation Abstracts International, 33*: 4937A.

HARVEY, DALE G., and SLATIN, GERALD T.
1975   The relationship between child's SES and teacher expectations: A test of the middle-class bias hypothesis. *Social Forces, 54*: 140–159.

HASKETT, MARY S.
1968   An investigation of the relationship between teacher expectancy and pupil achievement in the special education class. Doctoral dissertation, University of Wisconsin. *Dissertation Abstracts, 29*: 4348A–4349A.

HASTINGS, HIRAM I., JR.
1970   A study of the relationship between teacher–pupil verbal interaction and pupil achievement in elementary school science. Doctoral dissertation, University of Oregon. *Dissertation Abstracts International, 31*: 5033A. ED 079035.

HAUG, M. R., and SUSSMAN, M. B.
1971   The indiscriminate state of social class measurement. *Social Forces, 49*: 549–563.

HAUSER, ROBERT M.
1972   Disaggregating a social-psychological model of educational attainment. *Social Science Research, 1*: 159–188.

1971   *Socioeconomic Background and Educational Performance* (Arnold M. Rose Monograph Series, American Sociological Association). Washington, D.C.

1970   Educational stratification in the United States. *Sociological Inquiry, 40*: 102–109.

1969   Schools and the stratification process. *American Journal of Sociology, 74*: 587–611.

HAUSER, R. M. ; SEWELL, W. H.; and ALWIN, D. F.
1974   High school effects on achievement. Paper presented at American Sociological Association annual meeting, Montreal.

HAVLIN, NORMA J.
1969   The relationship between teacher expectancy and the behavior of first and second grade students identified as behavior problems. Doctoral dissertation, Southern Illinois University. *Dissertation Abstracts International, 30*: 4276A.

HAWKES, THOMAS H., and FURST, NORMA F.
1971   Race, socioeconomic situation, achievement: IQ and teacher ratings of student behavior as factors relating to anxiety in upper elementary school children. *Sociology of Education, 44*: 333–350.

HAWKRIDGE, DAVID G.; CHALUPSKY, ALBERT B.; ROBERTS, A. OSCAR
1968   *A Study of Selected Exemplary Programs for the Education of Disadvantaged Children, Part II.* Palo Alto, Ca.: American Institutes for Research. ED 023777.

HEATHERS, GLEN
1969   Grouping. In Robert L. Ebel (ed.), *Encyclopedia of Educational Research* (4th ed.). New York: Macmillan. Pp. 559–570.

1967   *Organizing Schools Through the Dual Progress Plan.* Danville, Ill.: Interstate.

HEBER, RICK
1972   An experiment in the prevention of cultural–familial mental retardation. *Environment, Intelligence and Scholastic Achievement: A Compilation of Testimony to the Senate Committee on Equal Educational Opportunity.* Washington, D.C.: U.S. Government Printing Office. Pp. 478–493.

HEDEGARD, JAMES M.
1968   Student–instructor interaction and its effects on student achievement and attitudes. Doctoral dissertation. University of Michigan, *Dissertation Abstracts, 29*: 1161B.

HEILBRONER, ROBERT, L.
1961   *The Future as History.* New York: Grove.

HENDERER, JAMES M.
1971   Teacher voice tone and student academic achievement. Doctoral dissertation, University of Massachusetts. *Dissertation Abstracts International, 32*: 2397B.

HENRY, JULES
1972   *On Education.* New York: Vintage.

HEINTZ, PAUL
1968   The relationship between teacher expectation of academic achievement and current school achievement of educable mentally retarded

pupils in special classes. Doctoral dissertation, Columbia University. *Dissertation Abstracts International, 31:* 1687A.

HERRNSTEIN, RICHARD J.
1973   *IQ in the Meritocracy.* Boston: Atlantic–Little, Brown.

HESS, R., and SHIPMAN, V.
1972   Parents as teachers: How lower class and middle class mothers teach. In C. S. Lavatelli and F. Stendler (eds.), *Readings in Child Behavior and Development.* New York: Harcourt, Brace, Jovanovich. Pp. 437–446.

1965   Early experience and the socialization of cognitive modes in children. *Child Development, 36:* 869–886.

HESS, R.; SHIPMAN, V.; BROPHY, J.; and BEAR, R.
1968   *The Cognitive Environments of Urban Preschool Children.* Chicago: The Graduate School of Education, University of Chicago.

HESS, ROBERT D., and TORNEY, JUDITH V.
1967   *The Development of Political Attitudes in Children.* Chicago: Aldine.

HEYNEMAN, STEPHEN P.
1976   Influences on academic achievement: A comparison of results from Uganda and more industrialized societies. *Sociology of Education, 49:* 200–211.

HEYNS, BARBARA
1974   Social selection and stratification within schools. *American Journal of Sociology, 79:* 1434–1451.

1971   Curriculum assignment and tracking policies in forty-eight urban public high schools. Doctoral dissertation, University of Chicago.

HIDDE, J., and ROSENSHINE, B.
1973   Teacher expectancy and student achievement: A research review. Paper presented at the American Educational Research Association February meeting, New Orleans.

HIERONYMUS, A. N.
1951   A study of social class motivation: Relationships between anxiety for education and certain socio-economic and intellectual variables. *Journal of Educational Psychology, 42:* 193–205.

HILDAHL, S. H.
1972   The allocation function of education in the United States. *International Journal of Comparative Sociology, 13:* 141–149.

HILL, ROBERT
1971   *The Strengths of Black Families.* New York: Emerson Hall.

HILL, SYLVIA I. B.
1971   Race, class and ethnic biases in research on school performance of low-income youth. Doctoral dissertation, University of Oregon.

HIMMELWEIT, H., and SWIFT, B.
1969   A model for the understanding of school as a socializing agent. In

Paul H. Mussen (ed.), *New Directions in Developmental Psychology.* New York: Holt, Rinehart, and Winston. Pp. 154–181.

HOBSON V. HANSEN
1967   *Congressional Record,* June 21, 1967: 16721–16766.

HOEHN, A.
1954   A study of social status differentiation in the classroom behavior of nineteen third grade teachers. *Journal of Social Psychology, 39:* 269–292.

HOEPFNER, RALPH (ed.)
1970   *CSE Elementary School Test Evaluation.* Los Angeles: Center for the Study of Evaluation, UCLA Graduate School of Education.

HOLLAND, J. L., and RICHARDS, J. M. , Jr.
1965   *Academic and Nonacademic Accomplishment: Correlated or Uncorrelated?* (Research Report no. 2.) Iowa City: American College Testing Program.

HOLLINGSHEAD, AUGUST B.
1949   *Elmtown's Youth.* New York: Wiley.

HOLMEN, MILTON G., and DOCTER, RICHARD
1972   *Educational and Psychological Testing: A Study of the Industry and Its Practices.* New York: Russell Sage Foundation.

HOLTZMAN, W. H.
1971   The changing world of mental measurement. *American Psychologist, 26:* 546–553.

HONZIK, M. P.
1957   Developmental studies of parent–child resemblance in intelligence. *Child Development, 28:* 215–228.

HOPPER, EARL (ed.)
1971   *Readings in the Theory of Educational Systems.* London: Hutchinson.

HOYT, DONALD P.
1965   The relationship between college grades and adult achievement: A review of the literature (Research Report No. 7.) Iowa City: American College Testing Program.

HUBER, JOAN
1973   Symbolic interaction as a pragmatic perspective: The bias of emergent theory. *American Sociological Review, 38:* 274–284.

HUBER, JOAN and FORM, WILLIAM H.
1973   *Income and Ideology: An Analysis of the American Political Formula.* New York: Free Press.

HUFF, SHEILA
1974   Credentialing by tests or by degrees: Title VII of the Civil Rights Act and Griggs v. Duke Power Company. *Harvard Educational Review, 44:* 246–269.

HUNT, D. E. , and HARDT, R. H.
  1969   The effect of Upward Bound programs on the attitudes, motivation,
           and academic achievement of Negro students. *Journal of Social
           Issues, 25*: 117–129.

HUNT, J. McV.
  1972   Heredity, environment and class or ethnic differences. In *Invita-
           tional Conference on Testing Problems*. Princeton, N. J. : Educa-
           tional Testing Service. Pp. 3–36.

  1964   The psychological basis for using pre-school enrichment as an anti-
           dote for cultural deprivation. *Merrill–Palmer Quarterly, 10*:
           209–248.

  1961   *Intelligence and Experience*. New York: Ronald.

HUNTER, FLOYD
  1965   *The Big Rich and the Little Rich*. Garden City, N. Y. : Doubleday.

HUSEN, TORSTEN
  1972   *Social Background and Educational Career*. Paris: Center for
           Educational Research and Innovation, Organization for Economic
           Co-operation and Development.

HUSEN, TORSTEN (ed.)
  1967   *International Study of Achievement in Mathematics* (Vols. 1 and 2).
           New York: Wiley.

HUSEN, T., and SVENSSON, N. E.
  1960   Pedagogic milieu and development of intellectual skills. *School
           Review, 68*: 36–51.

ILLICH, IVAN D.
  1971   *Deschooling Society*. New York: Harper and Row.

IRWIN, D. C.
  1960   Infant speech: Effect of systematic reading of stories. *Journal of
           Speech and Hearing Research, 3*: 187–190.

JACKSON, BRIAN, and MARSDEN, DENIS
  1962   *Education and the Working Class*. London: Routledge and Kegan
           Paul.

JACKSON, GREGG, and COSCA, CECILIA
  1974   The inequality of educational opportunity in the Southwest: An
           observational study of ethnically mixed classrooms. *American
           Educational Research Journal, 11*: 219–229.

JACKSON, PHILIP W.
  1968   *Life in Classrooms*. New York: Holt, Rinehart, and Winston.

JACKSON, P. W., and LAHADERNE, H. M.
  1968   Inequalities of teacher–pupil contacts. *Psychology in the Schools, 4*:
           204–211.

JAFFE, A. J. , and ADAMS, W.
  1970   *Academic and socio–economic factors related to entrance and*

retention at two- and four-year colleges in the late 1960's. New York: Bureau of Applied Social Research, Columbia University.

JENCKS, CHRISTOPHER
1968   Social stratification and higher education. *Harvard Educational Review, 38:* 277–316.

JENCKS, CHRISTOPHER; SMITH, MARSHALL; ACLAND, HENRY; BANE, MARY JO; COHEN, DAVID; GINTIS, HERBERT; HEYNS, BARBARA; and MICHELSON, STEPHAN
1972   *Inequality.* New York: Basic Books.

JENSEN, ARTHUR R.
1973   *Educability and Group Differences.* New York: Harper and Row.

1972   *Genetics and Education.* New York: Harper and Row.

1969   How much can we boost I. Q. and scholastic achievement? *Harvard Educational Review, 39:* 1–123.

JENSEN, M. , and ROSENFELD, L. B.
1974   Influence of mode of presentation, ethnicity, and social class on teacher evaluations of students. *Journal of Educational Psychology, 66:* 540–547.

JETER, J. T.
1974   Can teacher expectations function as self-fulfilling prophecies? *Contemporary Education, 46:* 161–165.

1973   Teacher expectancies and teacher classroom behavior. *Educational Leadership, 30:* 677–681.

JEW, WING
1970   Effects of teacher and pupil expectancy upon school achievement. Doctoral dissertation, University of the Pacific. *Dissertation Abstracts International, 31:* 2109A.

JOHNSON, EUGENE B.
1970   Pygmalion in the testing setting: Nonverbal communication as a mediator of expectancy fulfillment. Doctoral dissertation, University of Michigan, *Dissertation Abstracts International, 31:* 6716A.

JOHNSON, PALMER O.
1932   Educational research and statistics: The benefactions of philanthropic foundations and who receive them. *School and Society, 35:* 264–268.

JONES, JAMES D.; ERICKSON, EDSEL L.; and CROWELL, RONALD
1972   Increasing the gap between whites and blacks: Tracking as a contributory source. *Education and Urban Society, 4:* 339–349.

JOSÉ, JEAN, and CODY, JOHN J.
1971   Teacher–pupil interaction as it relates to changes in teacher expectancy of academic ability and achievement. *American Educational Research Journal, 8:* 39–50.

JOSÉ, NORMA JEAN
1969   Teacher–pupil interaction as it relates to attempted changes in

teacher expectancy of academic ability and achievements. Doctoral dissertation, Southern Illinois University, *Dissertation Abstracts International, 30*: 4277A.

JUEL-NIELSEN, N.
1965   Individual and environment: A psychiatric-psychological investigation of monozygotic twins reared apart. *Acta Psychiatrica et Neurologica Scandinavica* (monograph supplement 183).

JUSTON, N.
1972   Mexican–American achievement hindered by culture conflict. *Sociology and Social Research, 56*: 471–479.

KAESTLE, CARL
1973   *The Evolution of an Urban School System: New York City: 1750–1850.* Cambridge, Mass.: Harvard University Press.

KAGAN, J.
1968   His struggle for identity. *Saturday Review*, December 7. Pp. 80–82, 87–88.

KALTON, G.
1966   *The Public Schools: A Factual Survey.* London: Longmans.

KAMENS, DAVID
1976   Legitimating myths and educational organization: The relationship between organizational ideology and formal structure. Paper presented at the Eastern Sociological Association annual meeting, Boston.

1974   Colleges and elite formation: The case of prestigious American colleges. *Sociology of Education, 47*: 354–378.

KAMIN, LEON J.
1974   *The Science and Politics of I.Q.* Potomac, Md.: Erlbaum.

KANDEL, DENISE, and LESSER, GERALD S.
1969   Parental and peer influences on educational plans of adolescents. *American Sociological Review, 34*: 212–223.

KANTER, R. M.
1972   The organization child: Experience management in a nursery school. *Sociology of Education, 45*: 186–212.

KARABEL, J.
1972   Community college and social stratification. *Harvard Educational Review, 42*: 521–563.

KARIER, CLARENCE J.
1973   Testing for order and control in the corporate liberal state. In Clarence J. Karier, Paul Violas, and Joel Spring (eds.), *Roots of Crisis: American Education in the Twentieth Century.* Chicago: Rand McNally. Pp. 108–137.

KARIER, CLARENCE J.; VIOLAS, PAUL; and SPRING, JOEL (eds.)
1973   *Roots of Crisis: American Education in the Twentieth Century.* Chicago: Rand McNally.

KARIGER, ROGER B.
1962   The relationship of lane grouping to the socioeconomic status of the parents of seventh-grade pupils in three junior high schools. Doctoral dissertation, Michigan State University. *Dissertation Abstracts, 23*: 4586.

KATZ, FRED E.
1964   The school as a complex organization. *Harvard Educational Review, 34*: 425–455.

KATZ, I.
1968   Factors influencing Negro performance in the desegregated school. In M. Deutsch, I. Katz, and A. Jensen (eds.), *Social Class, Race, and Psychological Development.* New York: Holt, Rinehart, and Winston. Pp. 254–298.

1964   Review of evidence relating to effects of desegregation on the intellectual performance of Negroes. *American Psychologist, 19*: 381–399.

KATZ, MICHAEL B.
1975   *Class, Bureaucracy and Schools* (expanded ed.). New York: Praeger.
1971   *Class, Bureaucracy and Schools.* New York: Praeger.
1968   *The Irony of Early School Reform: Educational Innovation in Mid-Nineteenth Century Massachusetts.* Boston: Beacon.

KEDDIE, NELL (ed.)
1973   *The Myth of Cultural Deprivation.* Harmondsworth, England: Penguin.
1971   Classroom knowledge. In Michael F.D. Young (ed.), *Knowledge and Control.* London: Collier-Macmillan. Pp. 133–160.

KEELEY, DONALD L.
1973   Some effects of the label juvenile delinquent on teacher expectations of student behavior. Doctoral dissertation, University of Georgia. *Dissertation Abstracts International, 34*: 4746A.

KELLER, SUZANNE
1963a   *Beyond the Ruling Class.* New York: Random House.
1963b   The social world of the urban child: Some early findings. *American Journal of Orthopsychiatry, 33*: 823–834.

KELLY, D.
1975   Tracking and its impact upon self-esteem: A neglected dimension. *Education, 96*: 2–9.

KELLY, D. H., and PINK, W. T.
1973   Social origins, school status, and the learning experience: A theoretical and empirical examination of two competing viewpoints. *Pacific Sociological Review, 16*: 121–134.

KEHLE, THOMAS J.
1972   Effect of the student's physical attractiveness, sex, race, intelligence, and socioeconomic status on teachers' expectations for the student's

personality and academic performance. Doctoral dissertation, University of Kentucky. *Dissertation Abstracts International, 34*: 1131A.

KELSALL, R.K.; POOLE, ANNE; and KUHN, ANNETTE
1972   *Graduates: The Sociology of an Elite.* London: Methuen.

KERCKHOFF, ALAN C.
1975   Patterns of educational attainment in Great Britain. *American Journal of Sociology, 80*: 1428–1437.

KERR, NORMAN D.
1973   The school board as an agency of legitimation. In Sam Sieber and David Wilder (eds.), *The School in Society.* New York: Free Press. Pp. 380–400.

KESHOCK, JOHN D.
1970   An investigation of the effects of the expectancy phenomenon upon the intelligence, achievement and motivation of inner-city elementary school children. Doctoral dissertation. *Dissertation Abstracts International, 32*: 243A.

KESTER, SCOTT W.
1969   The communication of teacher expectations and their effects on the achievement and attitudes of secondary school pupils. Doctoral dissertation, University of Oklahoma. *Dissertation Abstracts International, 30*: 1434A.

KESTER, SCOTT, and LETCHWORTH, GEORGE
1972   Communication of teacher expectations and their effects on achievement and attitudes of secondary school students. *Journal of Educational Research, 66*: 51–55.

KIESLING, HERBERT J.
1971   *A study of successful compensatory education projects in California.* Santa Monica: The Rand Corporation.

KINNIE, ERNEST J., and STERNLOF, RICHARD E.
1971   The influence of nonintellective factors on the I.Q. scores of middle and lower class children. *Child Development, 42*: 1989–1995.

KIRP, DAVID L.
1974   Student classification, public policy and the courts. *Harvard Educational Review, 44*: 7–52.

KLEIN, S.P.
1971   The uses and limitations of standardized tests in meeting the demands for accountability. *UCLA Evaluation Comment, Center for the Study of Evaluation, 2 (No. 4).*

KNILL, FRANKLIN P.
1969   The manipulation of teacher expectancies: Its effect on intellectual performance, self-concept, interpersonal relationships, and the institutional behavior of students. Doctoral dissertation, University of Cincinnatti. *Dissertation Abstracts International, 30*: 5239B–5240B.

KOHN, PAUL M.
1973   Relationships between expectations of teachers and performance of students. *Journal of School Health, 43*: 498–503.

KOZOL, JONATHAN
1967   *Death at an Early Age.* Boston: Houghton Mifflin.

KRANZ, PATRICIA L.; WEBER, WILFORD A.; and FISHELL, KENNETH N.
1970   The relationship between teacher perception of pupils and teacher behavior toward those pupils. Paper presented at American Educational Research Association annual meeting, Minneapolis. ED 038346.

KRATHWOHL, DAVID R.; BLOOM, BENJAMIN S.; and HAISIE, BERTRAM B.
1964   *Taxonomy of Educational Objectives. Handbook I: Cognitive Domain; Handbook II: Affective Domain.* New York: McKay.

KRAUSS, IRVING
1964   Sources of educational aspirations among working-class youth. *American Sociological Review, 20*: 867–879.

KRETCH, D.; ROSENZWEIG, M.; and BENNET, E.L.
1962   Relations between brain chemistry and problem solving among rats raised in enriched and impoverished environments. *Journal of Comparative Physiological Psychology, 55*: 801–807.

KRUG, EDWARD
1964   *The Shaping of the American High School.* New York: Harper and Row.

KRUPCZAK, WILLIAM P.
1972   Relationships among student self-concept of academic ability, teacher perception of student academic ability and student achievement. Doctoral dissertation, University of Miami. *Dissertation Abstracts International, 33*: 3388A–3389A.

KUNKEL, PETER, and KENNARD, SARA S.
1971   *Spout Spring: A Black Community.* New York: Holt, Rinehart, and Winston.

LABOV, W.; COHEN, P.; ROBINS, C.; and LEWIS, J.
1968   *A Study of the Nonstandard English of Negro and Puerto Rican Speakers in New York City.* Final Report, U.S. Office of Education, Cooperative Research Project No. 3288.

LABOV, WILLIAM
1973   The logic of nonstandard English. In Nell Keddie (ed.), *The Myth of Cultural Deprivation.* Harmondsworth, England: Penguin. Pp. 21–66.
1972   *Language in the Inner City.* Philadelphia: University of Pennsylvania Press.

LACEY, COLIN
1970   *Hightown Grammar.* Manchester, England: University of Manchester Press.

1966   Some sociological concomitants of academic streaming in grammar school. *British Journal of Sociology, 17*: 245–262.

LAMPMAN, ROBERT
1962   *The Share of the Top-Wealth–Holders in National Wealth, 1922–56.* Princeton: Princeton University Press.

LARKIN, R.W.
1972   Class, race, sex and preadolescent attitudes. *California Journal of Educational Research, 23*: 213–223.

LARRY P. et al. v. WILSON RILES et al.
1972   343 *Federal Supplement*, U.S. District Court, Northern District, Calif. 1306–1315. St. Paul, Minn.: West Publishing Co.

LASKARIS, JANE B.
1971   Some effects of the experimental manipulation of teacher expectations on the measured academic growth of fifth-grade children. Doctoral dissertation, University of Delaware. *Dissertation Abstracts International, 32*: 6209A.

LAVIN, DAVID E.
1965   *The Prediction of Academic Performance.* New York: Russell Sage Foundation.

LaVOIE, J. C., and ADAMS, G. R.
1974   Teacher expectancy and its relation to physical and interpersonal characteristics of the child. *Alberta Journal of Educational Research, 20*: 122–132.

LAWLOR, F. X., and LAWLOR, E.
1973   Teacher expectations: A study of their genesis. *Science Education, 57*: 9–14.

LAZERSON, M.
1973   Review essay: Revisionism and American educational history. *Harvard Educational Review, 43*: 269–283.

1971   *Origins of the Urban School: Public Education in Massachusetts 1870–1915.* Cambridge, Mass.: Harvard University Press.

LAZERSON, MARVIN, and GRUBB, NORTON
1974   *American Education and Vocationalism: A Documentary History, 1870–1970.* New York: Teachers College Press.

LEACOCK, ELEANOR BURKE (ed.)
1971a   *The Culture of Poverty: A Critique.* New York: Simon and Schuster.

1971b   Theoretical and methodological problems in the study of schools. In M. L. Wax, S. Diamond, and F. O. Gearing (eds.), *Anthropological Perspectives on Education.* New York: Basic Books. Pp. 169–179.

1969   *Teaching and Learning in City Schools.* New York: Basic Books.

LEFEBVRE, HENRI
1968   Ideology and the sociology of knowledge. In *The Sociology of Marx.* New York: Vintage. Pp. 59–88.

LEGAL IMPLICATIONS OF CULTURAL BIAS IN INTELLIGENCE TESTING OF DISADVAN-
TAGED SCHOOL CHILDREN
  1973   *Georgetown Law Review, 61*: 1027–1066.

LEGAL IMPLICATIONS OF THE USE OF STANDARDIZED TESTS IN EMPLOYMENT AND
EDUCATION
  1968   *Columbia Law Review, 69*: 691–744.

LENNARDS, JOSEPH L.
  1969   The secondary school system in the Netherlands: Some social conse-
            quences of streaming. ED 029365.

LENNON, ROGER T.
  1971   Accountability and performance contracting. Paper given at the
            American Educational Research Association annual meeting, New
            York.

LENSKI, GERHARD
  1966   *Power and Privilege.* New York: McGraw-Hill.

LeSHAN, L. L.
  1952   Time orientation and social class. *Journal of Abnormal and Social
            Psychology, 47*: 589–592.

LESSER, GERALD, and STODOLSKY, SUSAN S.
  1967   Learning patterns in the disadvantaged. *Harvard Educational
            Review, 37*: 546–593.

LESYK, CAROLEE K.; KATZENMEYER, CONRAD G.; and HYNES, MARY ELLEN
  1971   *Student attitudes toward grouping and their effects on self-concept
            and school satisfaction.* Kent, Ohio: Bureau of Educational Research,
            Kent State University, ED 047861.

LEVENSON, STANLEY
  1972   The attitudes and feelings of selected sixth grade children toward
            reading in ability groups. Doctoral dissertation, United States Inter-
            national University. *Dissertation Abstracts International, 33*: 2819A.

LEVIN, HENRY M.
  1972   The case for community control of the schools. In Martin Carnoy (ed.),
            Schooling in a Corporate Society. New York: McKay. Pp. 193–210.

LEVIN, HENRY M.; GUTHRIE, JAMES W.; KLEINDORFER, GEORGE B.; and STOUT,
ROBERT T.
  1971   School achievement and post-school success: A review. *Review of
            Educational Research, 41*: 1–16.

LEVINE, DANIEL U.
  1975   Educating alienated inner-city youth: Lessons from the street
            academies. *The Journal of Negro Education, 44*: 139–148.

LEVITAS, MAURICE
  1974   *Marxist Perspectives in the Sociology of Education.* London:
            Routledge and Kegan Paul.

LEWIS, OSCAR
  1966a   *La Vida: A Puerto Rican Family in the Culture of Poverty—San Juan
            and New York.* New York: Random House.
  1966b   The culture of poverty. *Scientific American, 215* (October): 19–25.

LEWONTIN, R.C.
1970   Race and intelligence. *Bulletin of the Atomic Scientists, 26*: 2–8.

LICHTMAN, RICHARD
1970/   Symbolic interactionism and social reality: Some Marxist queries.
1971   *Berkeley Journal of Sociology, 15*: 75–94.
1975   Marx's theory of ideology. *Socialist Revolution, 23*: 45–76.

LIEBOW, ELLIOT
1967   *Tally's Corner.* Boston: Little, Brown.

LIPSET, S. M.
1972   Social mobility and equal opportunity. *The Public Interest, 29*: 90–108.

LITWAK, EUGENE, and MEYER, HENRY J.
1973   The school and the family: Linking organizations and external primary groups. In Sam Sieber and David Wilder (eds.), *The School in Society.* New York: Free Press. Pp. 425–435.

LOEHLIN, JOHN C.; LINDZEY, GARDNER; and SPUHLER, J. N.
1975   *Race Differences in Intelligence.* San Francisco: Freeman.

LONG, BARBARA H. , and HENDERSON, EDMUND H.
1974   Certain determinants of academic expectancies among Southern and non-Southern teachers. *American Educational Research Journal, 11*: 137–147.

1971   Teachers' judgments of black and white school beginners. *Sociology of Education, 44*: 358–368.

LONG, S., and LONG, R.
1973a   Teacher-candidates attitudes regarding poverty and the disadvantaged. *Urban Education, 7*: 371–382.

1973b   Sociopolitical ideology as a correlate of teacher candidates' attitudes concerning poverty and disadvantaged. *Urban Education, 8*: 249–270.

LORTIE, DAN
1976   *School–Teacher.* Chicago: University of Chicago Press.

LOVELL, JOHN T.
1960   The Bay High School experiment. *Educational Leadership, 17*: 383–387.

LUCHINS, ABRAHAM S., and LUCHINS, EDITH H.
1948   Children's attitudes toward homogeneous grouping. *Journal of Genetic Psychology, 72*: 3–9.

LUKÁCS, GYÖRGY
1971   *History and Class Consciousness.* Cambridge, Mass.: M.I.T. Press.

LUNDBERG, FERDINAND
1968   *America's Sixty Families.* New York: Citadel.

LUNN, JOAN C.
1970   *Streaming in the Primary School.* London: National Foundation for Educational Research.

214   *References*

MACCOBY, MICHAEL, and MONDIANO, NANCY
1966   On culture and equivalence. In J. S. Bruner, R. R. Oliver, and P. M. Greenfield (eds.), *Studies in Cognitive Growth*. New York: Wiley. Pp. 257–269

MACHOWSKY, HERBERT
1973   The effects of teacher's locus of control, teacher's knowledge of intellectual potential and informational source status on teacher's judgments of children's expected academic ability. Doctoral dissertation, Temple University. *Dissertation Abstracts International, 34*: 1753B.

MACKLER, BERNARD, and GIDDINGS, MORSLEY G.
1965   Cultural deprivation: A study in mythology. *Teachers College Record, 66*: 608–613.

MANDLER, G., and SARASON, S. B.
1952   A study of anxiety and learning. *Journal of Abnormal and Social Psychology, 47*: 166–173.

MANN, MAXINE
1960   What does ability grouping do to self-concept? *Childhood Education, 36*: 356–360.

MARJORIBANKS, K.
1972a   Ethnicity and learning patterns: A replication and an explanation. *Sociology, 6*: 417–431.

1972b   Environment, social class and mental abilities. *Journal of Educational Psychology, 63*: 103–109.

MARTINEZ, DAVID H.
1973   A comparison of the behavior during reading instruction, of teachers of high and low achieving in first grade classes. Doctoral dissertation, University of Oregon, *Dissertation Abstracts International, 34*: 7520A.

MARX, KARL
1963   *Economic and Philosophical Manuscripts* (originally published in 1844). Translated and edited by Thomas B. Bottomore. New York: McGraw-Hill.

1904   *A Contribution to the Critique of Political Economy* (originally published in 1859). Translated by N. I. Stone. Chicago, Ill.: Charles H. Kerr.

1906/   *Capital* (originally published in 1867, 1885, 1894). Translated by
1909   Samuel Moore and Edward Aveling and edited by Frederick Engels. Chicago: Charles H. Kerr.

MARX, KARL, and ENGELS, FREDERICK
1947   *The German Ideology* (originally published in 1844, 1845). Translated and edited by R. Pascal. New York: International.

MASON, EMANUEL J.
1973   Teachers' observations and expectations of boys and girls as

influenced by biased psychological reports and knowledge of the effects of bias. *Journal of Educational Psychology*, 65: 238–243.

MASSEY, GRACE CARROLL; SCOTT, MONA VAUGHN; and DORNBUSCH, SANFORD M.
1975   Racism without racists: Institutional racism in urban schools. *The Black Scholar*, 3: 2-11.

MATZEN, STANLEY P.
1965   The relationship between racial composition and scholastic achievement in elementary classrooms. Doctoral dissertation, Stanford University. *Dissertation Abstracts*, 26: 6475.

MAYESKE, GEORGE W.
1972   On the explanation of racial-ethnic group differences in achievement test scores. In *Environment, Intelligence, and Scholastic Achievement: A Compilation of Testimony to the Select Committee on Equal Educational Opportunity, United States Senate*. Washington, D.C.: U.S. Government Printing Office. Pp. 542–556.

MAYESKE, GEORGE W.; WISLER, CARL E.; BEATON, ALBERT E., Jr.; WEINFELD, FREDERIC D.; COHEN, WALLACE M.; OKADA, TETSUO; PROSHEK, JOHN M., and TABLER, KENNETH A.
1972   *A Study of Our Nation's Schools*. Washington, D.C.: U.S. Government Printing Office.

McCANDLES, ROBERT, and ROBERTS, ALBERT
1972   Teachers' marks, achievement test scores and aptitude relations with respect to social class, race and sex. *Journal of Educational Psychology*, 63: 153–159.

McCANDLESS, BOYD R.
1952   Environment and intelligence. *American Journal of Mental Deficiency*, 56: 674–691.

McCARTHY, JOHN, and YANCEY, WILLIAM L.
1971   Uncle Tom and Mr. Charlie: Metaphysical pathos in the study of racism and personal disorganization. *American Journal of Sociology*, 76: 648–672.

McCLELLAND, DAVID C.
1974   Testing for competence rather than for "intelligence." In Alan Gartner, Colin Greer, and Frank Riessman (eds.), *The New Assault on Equality*. New York: Social Policy. Pp. 163–197.

1958   *Talent and Society*. Princeton, N.J.: Van Nostrand.

McDILL, EWARD L.; MEYERS, EDMUND D.; and RIGSBY, LEO C.
1967   Institutional effects on academic behavior of high school students. *Sociology of Education*, 40: 181–199.

1966   *Sources of educational climates in high schools*. Unpublished manuscript, Department of Social Relations, Johns Hopkins University.

McDILL, EDWARD L., and RIGSBY, LEO C.
1973   *Structure and Process in Secondary Schools: The Academic Impact*

of Educational Climates. Baltimore: Johns Hopkins University Press.

MCLACHLAN, JAMES
1970   *American Boarding Schools: A Historical Study.* New York: Scribner's.

MCPARTLAND, JAMES
1969   The relative influence of school desegregation and of classroom desegregation on the academic achievement of ninth grade Negro students. *Journal of Social Issues, 25:* 93–102.

MCQUEEN, WILLIAM M., JR.
1970   The effect of divergent teacher expectations on the performance of elementary school children on a vocabulary learning task. Doctoral dissertation, University of South Carolina. *Dissertation Abstracts International, 31:* 5206A.

MEAD, GEORGE HERBERT
1934   *Mind, Self, and Society.* Chicago: University of Chicago Press.

MEHL, ROBERT F., JR.
1965   A study of relationships between homogeneous grouping in the school and the social class structure in an up-state New York community. Doctoral dissertation, State University of New York at Albany. *Dissertation Abstracts International, 27:* 4085A.

MEHRABIAN, A.
1971   Nonverbal communication. In J. K. Cole (ed.), *Nebraska Symposium on Motivation: 1971.* Lincoln: University of Nebraska Press.

MEICHENBAUM, DONALD H.; BOWERS, KENNETH S; and ROSS, ROBERT R.
1969   A behavioral analysis of teacher expectancy effect. *Journal of Personality and Social Psychology, 13:* 306–316.

MENDELS, GLEN E., and FLANDERS, JAMES P.
1973   Teachers' expectations and pupil performance. *American Educational Research Journal, 10:* 203–212.

MEPHUM, JOHN
1972   The theory of ideology in Capital. *Radical Philosophy, 6:* 12–19.

MERCER, JANE R.
1972   *Labeling the Mentally Retarded.* Berkeley: University of California Press.

1971   Institutionalized Anglocentrism: Labeling mental retardates in the public schools. In P. Orleans and W. R. Eliss (eds.), *Race, Change and Urban Society. Urban Affairs Annual Review (Vol. 5).* Los Angeles: Sage.

MERTON, ROBERT K.
1973   Plenary address at the American Sociological Association August meeting, New York.

1957   *Social Theory and Social Structure* (revised ed.). Glencoe, Ill.: Free Press.

1940   Bureaucratic structure and personality. *Social Forces, 17:* 560–568.

MEYER, J.
  1970   High school effects on college intentions. *American Journal of Sociology, 76*: 59–70.

MEYER, PETER J.
  1970   Schooling and the reproduction of the social division of labor. Honors thesis, Harvard University.

MICHAEL, JOHN A.
  1961   High school climates and plans for entering college. *Public Opinion Quarterly, 25*: 585–595.

MILLER, CHARLES; MCLAUGHLIN, JOHN A.; HADDON, JOHN; and CHANSKY, NORMAN M.
  1968   Socioeconomic class and teacher bias. *Psychological Reports, 23*: 806.

MILLER, H. L.
  1973   Race v. class in teachers' expectations. *Psychological Reports, 32*: 105–106.

MILLER, HARRY L., and WOOCK, ROGER R.
  1970   *Social Foundations of Urban Education.* Hinsdale, Ill.: Dryden.

MILLER, S. M. and ROBY, PAMELA
  1970   *The Future of Inequality.* New York: Basic Books.

MILLER, W. S., and OTTO, H. J.
  1930   Analysis of experimental studies in homogeneous grouping. *Journal of Educational Research, 21*: 95–102.

MILLS, C. WRIGHT
  1956   *The Power Elite.* London: Oxford University Press.
  1943   The professional ideology of social pathologists. *American Journal of Sociology, 49*: 165–180.

MILNER, MURRAY, JR.
  1972   *The Illusion of Equality.* San Francisco: Jossey-Bass.

MOELLER, G.H., and CHARTERS, W. W., JR.
  1970   Relation of bureaucratization to sense of power among teachers. In Matthew W. Miles and W. W. Charters, Jr. (eds.), *Learning in Social Settings.* Boston: Allyn and Bacon. Pp. 638–655.

MORRISON, A., and MCINTYRE, D.
  1969   *Teachers and Teaching.* Harmondsworth, England: Penguin.

MORTON, D. C., and WATSON, D. R.
  1971   Compensatory education and contemporary liberalism in the U.S.A.: A sociological view. *International Review of Education, 71*: 289–307.

MOSTELLER, FREDERICK, and MOYNIHAN, DANIEL P.
  1972   *On Equality of Education.* New York: Vintage.

MOYNIHAN, DANIEL PATRICK
  1965   *The Negro Family: The Case for National Action.* Washington, D.C.: U.S. Government Printing Office.

MUHLENBERG, WILLIAM AUGUSTUS
1828   *The Application of Christianity to Education: Being the Principles and Plan of Education to be Adopted in the Institute at Flushing, Long Island.* Jamaica, N.Y.: Sleight and George.

MULIGAN, JOSEPH P.
1972   Teacher and student expectations and student achievement in college reading improvement courses. Doctoral dissertation, Rutgers University. *Dissertation Abstracts International, 33:* 3776A.

MULLER, W.
1972   Family background, education and career mobility. *Social Science Information, 11:* 223–255.

MURRAY, ALBERT
1970   *The Omni-Americans: New Perspectives on Black Experience and American Culture.* New York: Dutton.

MURRAY, HOWARD B.
1972   The effects of locus of control and pattern of performance on teachers' evaluation of a student. Doctoral dissertation, University of Minnesota. *Dissertation Abstracts International, 33:* 6181A.

NAPHTALI, ZVIA
1976   Notes towards an investigation. Doctoral dissertation in progress, New York University.

NATIONAL EDUCATION ASSOCIATION
1968   Ability Grouping (Research Summary 1968–S3). Washington D.C.: National Education Association.

1962   Ability Grouping (Research Memo 1962–29). Washington D.C.: National Education Association.

NELSON, JOEL I.
1972   High school context and college plans: The impact of social structure on aspiration. *American Sociological Review, 37:* 143–148.

NEW YORK STOCK EXCHANGE.
1976   *Share Ownership, 1975.* New York: New York Stock Exchange.

NEWCOMB, THEODORE M.
1943   *Personality and Social Change: Attitude Formation in a Student Community.* New York: Dryden.

NEWMAN, H. N.; FREEMAN, F. N.; and HOLZINGER, K. J.
1937   *Twins: A Study of Heredity and Environment.* Chicago: University of Chicago Press.

NIELSON, WALDEMAR A.
1972   *The Big Foundations.* New York: Columbia University Press.

O'CONNELL, E. J.; DUSEK, J. B.; and WHEELER, R. J.
1974   Follow-up study of teacher expectancy effects. *Journal of Educational Psychology, 66:* 325–328.

OGLETREE, EARL
1969   Homogeneous ability grouping British style. *Peabody Journal of Education, 47:* 20–25.

OLAVARRI, MARTIN C.
1967   Some relationships of ability grouping to student self-concept. Doctoral dissertation, Berkeley, University of California. *Dissertation Abstracts, 28*: 2518A.

OLLMAN, BERTELL
1973   Marxism and political science: Prolegomenon to a debate on Marx's method. *Politics and Society, 3*: 491–521.

PAGE, ELLIS B.
1958   Teacher comments and student performance: A seventy-four classroom experiment in school motivation. *Journal of Educational Psychology, 49*: 173–181.

PALARDY, J. MICHAEL
1969   What teachers believe—What children achieve. *Elementary School Journal, 69*: 370–374.

PARKER, RICHARD
1972   *The Myth of the Middle Class.* New York: Harper Torchbooks.

PARKIN, FRANK
1971   *Class, Inequality and Political Order.* New York: Praeger.

PARSONS, DENNIS E.
1973   A study of student teachers' expectations, and their verbal and nonverbal behaviors. Doctoral dissertation, University of Georgia. *Dissertation Abstracts International, 33*: 5012A.

PARSONS, T.
1959   The school class as a social system: Some of its functions in American society. *Harvard Educational Review, 29*: 297–318.

PELLEGRINI, ROBERT J., and HICKS, ROBERT A.
1972   Prophecy effects and tutorial instruction for the disadvantaged child. *American Educational Research Journal, 9*: 413–419.

PENG, SAMUEL S.
1974   Expectations, instructional behavior and pupil achievement. Doctoral dissertation, State University of New York at Buffalo. *Dissertation Abstracts International, 35*: 1508A.

PENNA, FIRME THEREZA
1969   Effects of social reinforcement on self-esteem of Mexican-American children. Doctoral dissertation, Stanford University. *Dissertation Abstracts International, 30*: 3332A.

PERSELL, CAROLINE HODGES
1976   *Quality, Careers and Training in Educational and Social Research.* New York: General Hall.

PERSELY, GEORGE
1973   Teacher expectancy, student expectancy and performance feedback effects on academic performance. ED 090331.

PETERSON, RICHARD LEE
1966   An experimental study of the effects of ability grouping in grades

220   *References*

seven and eight. Doctoral dissertation, University of Minnesota. *Dissertation Abstracts, 28*: 103A.

PETTIGREW, THOMAS F.
1958   Personality and sociocultural factors in intergroup attitudes: A cross-national comparison. *Journal of Conflict Resolution, 2*: 29–42.

PIDGEON, DOUGLAS A.
1970   *Expectation and Pupil Performance.* London, England: National Foundation for Educational Research.

PITT, CLIFFORD C. V.
1956   An experimental study of the effects of teachers' knowledge of pupil IQs on teachers' attitudes and practices and pupils' attitudes and achievement. Doctoral dissertation, Columbia University. *Dissertation Abstracts, 16*: 2387–2388.

PLATT, WILLIAM J.
1974   Policy making and international studies in educational evaluation. *Phi Delta Kappan, 55*: 451–456.

PLOWDEN REPORT
1967   *Children and Their Primary Schools: A Report of the Central Advisory Council for Education (England).* London: Her Majesty's Stationery Office.

POLLARD, D.
1973   Educational achievement and ethnic group membership. *Comparative Education Review, 17*: 362–374.

PORTER, JAMES N.
1974   Race, socialization and mobility in educational and early occupational attainment. *American Sociological Review, 39*: 303–316.

PRICE, PHILIP B.; TAYLOR, CALVIN N.; RICHARDS, JAMES M., JR.; and JACOBSEN, TONY L.
1963   *Performance Measures of Physicians.* Salt Lake City: University of Utah Press. ED 003284.

PUGH, LEE G.
1974   Teacher attitudes and expectations associated with race and social class. Paper presented at the American Educational Research Association April meeting, Chicago. ED 094018.

Racial and Social Isolation in the Schools (preliminary report).
1969   Albany, New York: New York State Education Department.

RAINES, JOHN CURTIS
1975   *Illusions of Success.* Valley Forge, Pa.: Judson.

RAUBINGER, FREDERICK, and HAND, HAROLD C.
1967   It is later than you think. Unpublished manuscript, University of Illinois.

RAVITCH, DIANE
1974   *The Great School Wars: 1805–1972.* New York: Basic Books

RIBICH, THOMAS I.
1968   *Education and Poverty.* Washington, D.C.: Brookings Institution.

RICHER, STEPHEN
1975 School effects: The case for grounded theory. *Sociology of Education, 48*: 383–399.

1974a Programme composition and educational plans. *Sociology of Education, 47*: 337–353.

1974b Middle-class bias of schools: Fact or fancy? *Sociology of Education, 47*: 532–534.

RIESMAN, DAVID; DENNEY, REUEL; and GLAZER, NATHAN
1950 *The Lonely Crowd.* New Haven: Yale University Press.

RIESSMAN, FRANK
1962 *The Culturally Deprived Child.* New York: Harper and Row.

RIST, RAY C.
1976 Becoming a success or failure in school: A theoretical and methodological synthesis. In A. H. Halsey and J. Karabel (eds.), *Power and Ideology in Education.* New York: Oxford.

1973 *The Urban School: A Factory for Failure.* Cambridge: M.I.T. Press.

1972a Social distance and social inequality in a ghetto kindergarten classroom: An examination of the "culture gap" hypothesis. *Urban Education, 7*: 241–260.

1972b The milieu of a ghetto school as a precipitator of educational failure. *Phylon, 33*: 348–360.

1970 Student social class and teacher expectations: The self-fulfilling prophecy in ghetto education. *Harvard Educational Review, 40*: 411–451.

RITTERBAND, PAUL
1973 Race, resources and achievement. *Sociology of Education, 46*: 162–170.

ROBINSON, LEO A.
1973 Teacher cognitive complexity and cognitive demands made upon perceived high and low achieving students. Doctoral dissertation, Indiana University. *Dissertation Abstracts International, 34*: 4044A.

RODMAN, HYMAN
1968 Family and social pathology in the ghetto. *Science, 161*: 756–62.

1965 *Marriage, Family and Society: A Reader.* New York: Random House.

ROEBER, EDWARD D.
1970 The influence of information about students on the expectations of teachers. Doctoral dissertation, University of Michigan. *Dissertation Abstracts International, 32*: 1344A.

ROGERS, DAVID
1968 *110 Livingston Street: Politics and Bureaucracy in the New York City School System.* New York: Random House.

ROSENBAUM, JAMES E.
1976 *Making Inequality.* New York: Wiley-Interscience.

1975 Contest and tournament mobility: Norm, policy and practice in

222   *References*

educational selection. Paper presented at American Sociological Association annual meeting, San Francisco.

1974   The stratification of socialization processes. *American Sociological Review, 40*: 48–54.

ROSENBERG, MORRIS, and SIMMONS, ROBERTA

1971   *Black and White Self-Esteem: The Urban School Child.* Washington, D.C.: American Sociological Association.

ROSENFELD, LAWRENCE B.

1973   An investigation of teachers' stereotyping behavior: The influence of mode of presentation, ethnicity, and social class on teachers' evaluation of students. ED 090172.

ROSENSHINE, BARAK

1971   New directions for research on teaching. In *How Teachers Make a Difference.* Washington, D.C.: U.S. Government Printing Office. Pp. 66–95.

1970a   The stability of teacher effects upon student achievement. *Review of Educational Research, 40*: 647–662.

1970b   Interaction analysis: A tardy comment. *Phi Delta Kappan, 51*: 445–446.

ROSENTHAL, ROBERT

1974   The pygmalion effect: What you expect is what you get. *Psychology Today Library Cassette, 12.* New York: Ziff-Davis.

ROSENTHAL, ROBERT, and JACOBSON, LENORE

1968a   *Pygmalion in the Classroom.* New York: Holt, Rinehart, and Winston.

1968b   Teacher expectations for the disadvantaged. *Scientific American, 218*: 19–23.

ROSTOW, EUGENE

1975   Paper given on world hunger and oil crisis to the Society for Values in Higher Education, New York City, February.

ROTH, DAVID R.

1974   Intelligence testing as a social activity. In Aaron V. Cicourel, Kenneth H. Jennings, Sybillyn H. M. Jennings, Kenneth C. W., Leiter, Robert MacKay, Hugh Mehan, and David R. Roth (eds.), *Language Use and School Performance.* New York: Academic. Pp. 143–217.

ROTHBART, M.; DALFEN, S.; and BARRETT, R.

1971   Effects of teacher expectancy on student–teacher interaction. *Journal of Educational Psychology, 62*: 49–59.

RUBINSON, RICHARD

1976   The world economy and the distribution of income within states: A cross-national study. *American Sociological Review, 41*: 638–659.

RUBOVITS, P., and MAEHR, M.

1973   Pygmalion black and white. *Journal of Personality and Social Psychology, 25*: 210–218.

1971   Pygmalion analyzed: Toward an explanation of the Ro-
        senthal–Jacobson findings. *Journal of Personality and Social Psy-
        chology, 19*: 197–203.

RUNCIMAN, W. G.
1972   Race and social stratification. *Race, 13*: 497–509.

SALAMINI, LEONARDO
1974   Gramsci and Marxist sociology of knowledge: An analysis of hege-
        mony-ideology-knowledge. *Sociological Quarterly, 15*: 359–380.

SAMUDA, RONALD J.
1975   *Psychological Testing of American Minorities.* New York: Dodd,
        Mead.

SAMUELSON, PAUL
1967   *Economics.* New York: McGraw-Hill.

SARASON, S. B., and MANDLER, G.
1952   Some correlates of test anxiety. *Journal of Abnormal and Social Psy-
        chology, 47*: 810–817.

SARTHORY, JOSEPH A.
1968   The effects of ability grouping in the multi-cultural school situation.
        Doctoral dissertation, University of New Mexico. *Dissertation
        Abstracts, 29*: 451A.

SCARR, S.
1968   Environmental bias in twin studies. *Eugenics Quarterly, 15*: 34–40.

SCARR-SALAPATEK, S.
1971   Race, social class and I.Q. *Science, 174*: 1285–1295.

SCARR-SALAPATEK, SANDRA, and WEINBERG, RICHARD A.
1975   When black children grow up in white homes . . . *Psychology
        Today, 9*: 80–82.

SCHAFER, WALTER, and OLEXA, CAROL
1971   *Tracking and Opportunity.* Scranton, Pa.: Chandler.

SCHAFER, WALTER E.; OLEXA, CAROL; and POLK, KENNETH
1973   Programmed for social class: Tracking in American high schools. In
        Norman K. Denzin (ed.), *Children and Their Caretakers.* New
        Brunswick, N.J.: Transaction Books. Pp. 200–226.

SCHAIN, STEPHEN
1972   Learning of low ability children and tutor behavior as a function of
        the self-fulfilling prophecy. Doctoral dissertation, University of
        Illinois. *Dissertation Abstracts International, 34*: 642A.

SCHINDLER, PAUL T.
1970   Learning to fail: Ranking procedures and the self-fulfilling proph-
        ecy in an elementary school. Doctoral dissertation, Northwestern
        University.

SCHRAG, PETER
1967   *Village School Downtown.* Boston: Beacon.

SCHRANK, WILBURN
1970   A further study of the labeling effects of ability grouping. *Journal of Educational Research, 63*: 358–360.

1968   The labeling effect of ability grouping. *Journal of Educational Research, 62*: 51–52.

SCHUDSON, MICHAEL S.
1972   Organizing the "meritocracy": A history of the College Entrance Examination Board. *Harvard Educational Review, 42*: 34–69.

SCHWARTZ, AUDREY J.
1971   The culturally advantaged: A study of Japanese-American pupils. *Sociology and Social Research, 55*: 341–353.

SCOTFORD-ARCHER, MARGARET, and VAUGHAN, MICHALINA
1971   *Social Conflict and Educational Change, 1780–1850.* Cambridge, England: Cambridge University Press.

SEAVER, WILLIAM B., JR.
1973   Effects of naturally induced teacher expectancies. *Journal of Personality and Social Psychology, 28*: 333–342.

1971   Effects of naturally induced teacher expectancies on the academic performance of pupils in primary grades. Doctoral dissertation, Northwestern University.

SEGREGATION OF POOR AND MINORITY CHILDREN INTO CLASSES FOR THE MENTALLY RETARDED BY THE USE OF I.Q. TESTS.
1973   *Michigan Law Review, 71*: 1212–1250.

SENNETT, RICHARD, and COBB, JONATHAN
1972   *The Hidden Injuries of Class.* New York: Random House.

SEWELL, W. H.
1971   Inequality of opportunity for higher education. *American Sociological Review, 36*: 793–809

SEWELL, WILLIAM, and ARMER, J. MICHAEL
1966   Neighborhood context and college plans. *American Sociological Review, 31*: 159–168.

SEWELL, W.H.; HALLER, A. O.; and PORTES, A.
1969   The educational and early occupational attainment process. *American Sociological Review, 34*: 82–92.

SEWELL, WILLIAM H., and HAUSER, ROBERT M.
1975   *Education, Occupation, and Earnings.* New York: Academic.

SEWELL, W. H.; and SHAH, V. P.
1968a   Social class, parental encouragement, and educational aspirations. *American Journal of Sociology, 73*: 559–572.

1968b   Parents' education and children's educational aspirations and achievements. *American Sociological Review, 33*: 191–209.

1967   Socioeconomic status, intelligence, and the attainment of higher education. *Sociology of Education, 40*: 1–23.

SEXTON, PATRICIA C.
1961   *Education and Income.* New York: Viking.

SHEEHY, EILEEN
1974   Children's perceptions of teachers' expectations among selected able and specifically disabled learners in regular and special classrooms. Doctoral dissertation, University of Southern California. *Dissertation Abstracts International,* 35: 3579A.

SHIELDS, J.
1962   *Monozygotic Twins Brought Up Apart and Brought Up Together.* London: Oxford University Press.

SHOCKLEY, WILLIAM
1972   Dysgenics, geneticity, raceology: A challenge to the intellectual responsibility of educators. *Phi Delta Kappan,* 53: 297–307.

SIEBER, SAM D.
n.d.   Organizational resistances to innovative roles in educational organizations. Unpublished manuscript. Columbia University.

SIEBER, SAM D., and WILDER, DAVID E. (eds.)
1973   *The School in Society.* New York: Free Press.

SILBERMAN, CHARLES E.
1970   *Crisis in the Classroom.* New York: Random House.

SILBERMAN, MELVIN L.
1969   Behavioral expression of teachers' attitudes toward elementary students. *Journal of Educational Psychology,* 60: 402–407.

SIU, PING K.
1974   The relationship between motivational patterns and academic achievement in minority group children. ED 063443.

SKEEN, ELOIS M.
1974   A community-controlled school: The effects on student perceptions of locus of control. *Journal of Black Studies,* 5: 210–224.

SKODAK, M., and SKEELS, H. M.
1949   A final follow-up study of one hundred adopted children. *Journal of Genetic Psychology,* 75: 85–125.

SMITH, DANIEL J.
1976   Self-fulfilling prophecies in educational settings: A review and classification of the literature prior to 1975. Master's thesis, New York University, Department of Sociology.

SMITH, GENE M.
1970   Non-intelligence correlates of academic performance. Unpublished manuscript, cited in Bowles and Gintis, 1976.
1967   Personality correlates of academic performance in three dissimilar populations, *Proceedings of the 77th Annual Convention, American Psychological Association,* cited in Bowles and Gintis, 1976.

SMITH, LOUIS M., and GEOFFREY, WILLIAM
1968   *The Complexities of an Urban Classroom.* New York: Holt, Rinehart, and Winston.

SNOW, RICHARD E.
1969   Unfinished Pygmalion. *Contemporary Psychology, 14:* 197–199.

SØRENSEN, AAGE BØTTGER
1970   Organizational differentiation of students and educational oppor-tunity. *Sociology of Education, 43:* 355–376.

SOROTZKIN, F.; FLEMING, E.; and ANTTONEN, R.
1974   Teacher knowledge of standardized test information and its effect on pupil IQ and achievement. *Journal of Experimental Education, 43:* 79–85.

SOWELL, THOMAS
1976   Patterns of black excellence. *The Public Interest, 43:* 26–58.
1972   *Black Education: Myths and Tragedies.* New York: McKay.

SPADY, WILLIAM G.
1974   The authority system of the school and student unrest: A theoretical exploration. In C. Wayne Gordon (ed.), *Uses of Sociology of Education. 73rd Yearbook of the National Society for the Study of Education.* Chicago: University of Chicago Press. Pp. 36–77.
1971   Educational mobility and access: Growth and paradoxes. *American Journal of Sociology, 73:* 273–286.

SPIELBERG, DEANNA B.
1973   Labeling, teacher expectations, pupil intelligence level, and condi-tions of learning. Doctoral dissertation, Boston University. *Dissertation Abstracts International, 34:* 1716A

SPRING, JOEL H.
1976   *The Sorting Machine.* New York: McKay.
1972   *Education and the Rise of the Corporate State.* Boston: Beacon.

SPRINGER, EUSTACE L.
1967   *Independent School Administration.* New York: Harper and Row.

SQUIBB P. G.
1973   The concept of intelligence—A sociological perspective. *The Sociological Review, 21:* 57–75.

SQUIRE, JAMES R.
1966   National study of high school English programs: A school for all seasons. *English Journal, 55:* 282–290.

ST. JOHN, NANCY HOYT
1975   *School Desegregation.* New York: Wiley.

STAINES, J.
1958   The self-picture as a factor in the classroom. *British Journal of Education, 23:* 97-111.

STEFANNI, M. C.
1973   An analysis of classroom verbal interaction to determine the effects

of expectations induced by the introduction of ability group labels. Doctoral dissertation, Boston University. *Dissertation Abstracts International, 34*: 1599A.

STEIN, ANNIE
1975   Talk about Chinese educational system, to New York City Teachers, New York University, October.

1971   Strategies of failure. *Harvard Educational Review, 41*: 158–204.

STEWART, WILLIAM A.
1969   Linguistic and conceptual deprivation—Fact or fancy? Paper presented at the annual meeting of the Society for Research in Child Development, Santa Monica.

STOLZENBERG, ROSS M.
1975   Occupations, labor markets and the process of wage attainment. *American Sociological Review, 40*: 645–665.

SUMMERS, ANITA A., and WOLFE, BARBARA L.
1975   Which school resources help learning? Efficiency and equity in Philadelphia public schools. *Business Review*, February: pp. 4–28. Philadelphia: Federal Reserve Bank.

SUPER, DONALD, and CRITES, JOHN O.
1962   *Appraising Vocational Fitness.* New York: Harper.

SUTHERLAND, ANN, and GOLDSCHMID, MARCEL L.
1974   Negative teacher expectation and IQ change in children with superior intellectual potential. *Child Development, 45*: 852–856.

TAYLOR, C.; SMITH, W.R.; and GHISELIN, B.
1963   The creative and other contributions of one sample of research scientists. In C. W. Taylor and F. Barron (eds.), *Scientific Creativity: Its Recognition and Development.* New York: Wiley.

THOMAS, ALEXANDER; HERTZIG, MARGARET E.; and DRYMAN, IRVING
1973   Examiner effect in I.Q. testing of Puerto Rican working-class children. In Erwin Flaxman (ed.), *Educating the Disadvantaged.* New York: AMS Press. Pp. 361–374.

THOMAS, C. L., and STANLEY, J. C.
1969   Effectiveness of high school grades for predicting college grades of black students: A review and discussion. *Journal of Educational Measurement, 6*: 203–215.

THOMAS, W. I.
1931   The relation of research to the social process. In *Essays on Research in the Social Sciences.* Washington: Brookings Institution. Pp. 175–194.

THORNDIKE, EDWARD L.
1920   Intelligence and its uses. *Harper's, 144*: 227–235.

1912   The measurement of educational products. *School Review, 20*: 289–299.

THORNDIKE, ROBERT L.
1968   Rosenthal, Robert, and Jacobson, Lenore, "Pygmalion in the

Classroom." (book review) *American Educational Research Journal*, 5: 708–711.

THORNDIKE, R. L., and HAGAN, E.
1959   *10,000 Careers.* New York: Wiley.

THUROW, LESTER C.
1976   Tax wealth, not income. *New York Times Magazine*, April 11. pp. 32–33; 102-107.

1972   Education and economic equality. *The Public Interest, 28*: 66–81.

TRIMBERGER, E. K.
1973   Open admissions: A new form of tracking? *The Insurgent Sociologist*, 4: 29–43.

TROW, MARTIN
1966   The second transformation of American secondary education. In Reinhard Bendix and Seymour M. Lipset (eds.), *Class, Status and Power.* New York: Free Press. Pp. 437–449.

TRUJILLO, GREGORY
1969   The effect of teacher and peer expectancies on student social behavior: A study in the self-fulfilling prophecy. Doctoral dissertation, University of New Mexico. *Dissertation Abstracts International, 31*: 1582A.

TUCKMAN, BRUCE W., and BIERMAN, MILTON
1971   Beyond Pygmalion: Galatea in the schools. Paper presented at American Educational Research Association annual meeting, New York. ED 047077.

TULKIN, S.
1972   An analysis of the concept of cultural deprivation. *Developmental Psychology, 6*: 326–339.

TURNER, RALPH H.
1964   *The Social Context of Ambition.* San Francisco: Chandler.

TYACK, DAVID
1974   *The One Best System.* Cambridge: Harvard.

TYO, A. M.
1972   A comparison of the verbal behavior of teachers in interaction with migrant and non-migrant students. ED 075160.

U.S. BUREAU OF THE CENSUS
1975   *Statistical Abstract of the United States* (96th ed.). Washington, D.C.: U.S. Government Printing Office.

1970a   *Current Population Reports* (Series P-60), October.

1970b   *Census of Population: Characteristics of the Population.* Washington, D.C.: Department of Commerce.

U.S. INTERNAL REVENUE SERVICE
1972   *Statistics of Income, Personal Wealth* (Supplemental Report). Washington, D. C.: U.S. Government Printing Office.

VALENTINE, CHARLES A.
1971a   Deficit, difference, and bicultural models of Afro-American

behavior. *Harvard Educational Review, 41*: 137–157.

1971b   The "culture of poverty": Its scientific significance and its implications for action. In Eleanor Leacock (ed.), *The Culture of Poverty: A Critique.* New York: Simon and Schuster. Pp. 193–225.

1968   *Culture and Poverty.* Chicago: University of Chicago Press.

VALENTINE, C. A., and VALENTINE, B. L.
1975   Brain damage and the intellectual defense of inequality. *Current Anthropology, 16*: 117–150.

In press Afro-American social networks and black culture in the Western hemisphere. In A. M. Pescatello (ed.), *Black Experiences in the Americas.* N.p.

WADE, NICHOLAS
1976   IQ and heredity: Suspicion of fraud beclouds classic experiment. *Science 194* (November 26): 916–919.

WAKEFORD, JOHN
1969   *The Cloistered Elite.* New York: Praeger.

WALBERG, H. J., and ANDERSON, G. J.
1972   Properties of the achieving urban class. *Journal of Educational Psychology, 63*: 381–385.

WALLER, DAVID A., and CONNERS, C. KEITH
1966   A follow-up study of intelligence changes in children who participated in Project Head Start. Johns Hopkins University School of Medicine. ED 020786.

WATSON, D. R.
1973   Urban education and cultural competence: Competing theoretical models in social science. *Urban Education, 8*: 20–40.

WAX, M. L., DIAMOND, S. and GEARING, F. O.
1971   *Anthropological Perspectives on Education.* New York: Basic.

WAX, MURRAY L., and WAX, ROSALIE
1971   Cultural deprivation as an educational ideology. In Eleanor B. Leacock (ed.), *The Culture of Poverty: A Critique.* New York: Simon and Schuster. Pp. 127–139.

WEBER, MAX
1947   *The Theory of Social and Economic Organization* (originally published, 1922). Translated and edited by A. M. Henderson and Talcott Parsons. Glencoe, Ill.: Free Press.

1946   *From Max Weber: Essays in Sociology.* Translated and edited by H. H. Gerth and C. Wright Mills. New York: Oxford University Press.

WEBSTER, NOAH
1848   *The Elementary Spelling Book.* New York: G. F. Cooledge and Brother.

WEBSTER, MURRAY
1969   Source of evaluations and expectations for performance. *Sociometry, 32*: 243–258.

WECHSLER, D.
1944   *The Measurement of Adult Intelligence.* Baltimore: Williams and Wilkins.

WEIDMAN, JOHN C.; PHELAN, WILLIAM T.; and SULLIVAN, MARY A.
1972   The influence of educational attainment on self-evaluation of competence. *Sociology of Education, 45*: 303–312.

WEINBERG, C., and SKAGER, R.
1966   Social status and guidance involvement. *Personnel and Guidance Journal, 44*: 586–590.

WEINBERG, IAN
1967   *English Public Schools: The Sociology of Elite Education.* New York: Atherton.

WEINBERG, MEYER
1975   The relationship between school desegregation and academic achievement: A review of the research. *Law and Contemporary Problems, 34*: 240–270.

WESMAN, A. G.
1968   Intelligent testing. *American Psychologist, 23*: 267–274.

WESSMAN, ALDEN E.
1973   Scholastic and psychological effects of a compensatory education program for disadvantaged high school students: Project ABC. In E. Flaxman (ed.), *Educating the Disadvantaged.* New York: AMS Press. Pp. 269–278.

WEST, C. K.
1974   A review of the teacher expectancy effect: The question of preponderant causation. ED 092240.

WEXLER, STEVEN
1976   Personal communication based upon doctoral research at New York University, April.

WHEELER, STANTON
1966   The structure of formally organized socialization settings. In O. G. Brim and S. Wheeler (eds.), *Socialization after Childhood.* New York: Wiley. Pp. 51–116.

WHITE, ROBERT W.
1959   Motivation reconsidered: The concept of competence. *Psychological Review, 66*: 317–318.

WHITTY, GEOFF
1974   Sociology and the problem of radical educational change. In Michael Flude and John Ahier (eds.), *Educability, Schools and Ideology.* New York: Halsted. Pp. 112–137.

WILCOX, JOHN
1963   A search for the multiple effects of grouping upon the growth and behavior of junior high school pupils. Doctoral dissertation, Cornell University. *Dissertation Abstracts, 24*: 205.

WILKINS, WILLIAM E.
1973   The role of teacher expectations in the academic and social

behaviors of students. Doctoral dissertation, Cornell University. *Dissertation Abstracts International, 34*: 7602A. ED 080567.

WILKINSON, R.
1969   *Governing Elites.* London: Oxford University Press.
1964   *Gentlemanly Power.* New York: Oxford University Press.

WILLHELM, SIDNEY M.
1973   Equality: America's racist ideology. In Joyce Ladner (ed.), *The Death of White Sociology.* New York: Vintage.
1971   *Who Needs the Negro?* Garden City, N.Y.: Doubleday Anchor.

WILLIAMS, FREDERICK, and WHITEHEAD, JACK L.
1971   Language in the classroom: Studies of the Pygmalion effect. *English Record, 21*: 108–113.

WILLIAMS, F.; WHITEHEAD, J. L.; and MILLER, L.
1972   Relations between language attitudes and teacher expectancy. *American Educational Research Journal, 9*: 263–277.

WILLIAMS, RAYMOND
1973   Base and superstructure in Marxist cultural theory. *New Left Review, 82*: 3–16.
1961   *The Long Revolution.* London: Chatto and Windus.

WILLIAMS, ROBERT L.
1971   Abuses and misuses in testing black children. *The Counseling Psychologist, 2*: 62–73.

WILLIAMS, TREVOR
1975   Teacher prophecies and inheritance of inequality. Paper presented at American Sociological Association annual meeting, San Francisco.

WILLIAMS, W. M. (ed.)
1974   *Occupational Choice.* London, England: George Allen and Unwin.

WILLIG, C. J.
1963   Social implications of streaming in the junior school. *Educational Research, 5*: 151–154.

WILLIS, BILL J.
1969   The influence of teacher expectation on teachers' classroom interaction with selected children. Doctoral dissertation, George Peabody College. *Dissertation Abstracts International, 30*: 5072A.

WILLIS, SHERRY L.
1972   Formation of teachers' expectations of students' academic achievement. Doctoral dissertation, University of Texas. *Dissertation Abstracts International, 33*: 4960A.

WILSON, ALAN B.
1970   Sociological perspectives on the development of academic competence in urban areas. Paper presented at the series of lectures, "Urban Education—Another Look," Teachers College, Columbia University, New York, March 10. ED 039272.

1968   Social class and equal educational opportunity. *Harvard Educational Review, 38*: 77–84.

1967   Educational consequences of segregation in a California community. In *Racial Isolation in the Public Schools II: A Report of the U.S. Commission on Civil Rights.* Washington, D.C.: U.S. Government Printing Office. Pp. 165–206.

1963   Social stratification and academic achievement. In A. Harry Passow (ed.), *Education in Depressed Areas.* New York: Teachers College Press, Columbia University. Pp. 217–235.

1959   Residential segregation of social classes and aspirations of high school boys. *American Sociological Review, 24:* 836–845.

WINTER, D. G.; ALPERT, R.; and McCLELLAND, D. C.

1970   The classic personal style. In M. B. Miles and W. W. Charters, Jr. (eds.), *Learning in Social Settings.* Boston: Allyn and Bacon. Pp. 58–75.

WISE, ARTHUR E.

1967   *Rich Schools, Poor Schools.* Chicago: University of Chicago press.

WISE, RALPH J.

1972   Teacher and pupil factors related to teacher expectations for children. Doctoral dissertation, Yeshiva University. *Dissertation Abstracts International, 33:* 6191A.

WITHEY, STEPHEN B.

1972   *A Degree and What Else?* New York: McGraw-Hill.

WRIGHTSTONE, J. W.

1968   Ability grouping and the average child. *National Education Association Journal, 57:* 9–11.

WRONG, DENNIS H.

1961   The oversocialized conception of man in modern sociology. *American Sociological Review, 26:* 183–193.

1959   The functional theory of stratification: Some neglected considerations. *American Sociological Review, 24:* 772–782.

YATES, ALFRED (ed.)

1966   *Grouping in Education.* New York: Wiley.

YEE, ALBERT H.

1968   Source and direction of causal influence in teacher–pupil relationships. *Journal of Educational Psychology, 59:* 275–282.

YOUNG, MICHAEL F. D.

1972   On the politics of educational knowledge. *Economy and Society, 1:* 194–215.

YOUNG, MICHAEL F. D. (ed.)

1971   *Knowledge and Control.* London: Collier-Macmillan.

YOUNG, MICHAEL

1959   *The Rise of the Meritocracy, 1870–2033.* Baltimore: Penguin.

YOUNG, VIRGINIA H.

1970   Family and childhood in a Southern Negro community. *American Anthropologist, 72:* 269–288.

ZANNA, M. P.; SHERAS, P. L.; COOPER, J.; and SHAW, C.
1975   Pygmalion and Galatea: Interactive effect of teacher and student expectancies. *Journal of Experimental Social Psychology, 11*: 279–287.

ZANSITIS, PETER, P., JR.
1965   A study of the impact of communicated expected achievement upon actual achievement in college science. Doctoral dissertation, University of Illinois. *Dissertation Abstracts, 26*: 2572.

ZIRKEL, P. A.
1972   Enhancing the self-concept of disadvantaged students. *California Journal of Educational Research, 23*: 125–137.

Name Index

Subject Index